MW01078908

The Bases of Empire

The Bases of Empire

The Global Struggle against U.S. Military Posts

Edited by
CATHERINE LUTZ

NEW YORK UNIVERSITY PRESS

Washington Square, New York

First published in the U.S.A. by
NEW YORK UNIVERSITY PRESS
Washington Square
New York, NY 10003
www.nyupress.org

Copyright © Catherine Lutz 2009

The right of the individual authors to be identified as the authors of this work
has been asserted by them in accordance with the Copyright, Designs and
Patents Act 1988.

Library of Congress Cataloging-in-Publication Data
The bases of empire : the global struggle against U.S. military posts / edited by
Catherine A. Lutz.
    p. cm.
Includes bibliographical references and index.
    ISBN-13: 978-0-8147-5243-2 (hbk. : alk. paper)
    ISBN-10: 0-8147-5243-8 (hbk. : alk. paper)
    ISBN-13: 978-0-8147-5244-9 (pbk. : alk. paper)
    ISBN-10: 0-8147-5244-6 (pbk. : alk. paper)
    1. Military bases, American—Foreign countries. 2. Military bases,
American—Political aspects. 3. Military bases, American—Social aspects.
I. Lutz, Catherine. II. Title: Global struggle against U.S. military posts.

UA26.A2B37 2008
355.7—dc22
                              2008033630

This book is printed on paper suitable for recycling and made from
fully managed and sustained forest sources. Logging, pulping and
manufacturing processes are expected to conform to the environmental
standards of the country of origin. The paper may contain up to 70 percent
post consumer waste.

c 10 9 8 7 6 5 4 3 2 1
p 10 9 8 7 6 5 4 3 2 1

CPI Antony Rowe, Chippenham and Eastbourne

CONTENTS

LIST OF ILLUSTRATIONS

ACKNOWLEDGEMENTS

This book came together with the help of innumerable people. Most crucial has been the inspiration of the many brilliant activist scholars and energetically research-conducting activists I have been able to meet in travels through the Philippines, the Republic of Korea, Okinawa, Guam, and the United States over the last several years, including the authors of the chapters collected here. The motivation to edit this book comes from seeing the tirelessness with which so many people have worked, often for decades, to see that the world learns about the injustices and violence that day to day accompany the quest for empire through military power, even when the guns of war seem silent. Thousands of people have dedicated themselves, sometimes even at risk of their lives, to throw light on the hidden, and the visible but normalized, worlds of U.S. overseas military presence. I have also been fortunate to have the help of a remarkable set of students, but especially Jennifer Soroko, whose important work has examined the impact of the United States' Kwajalein missile range on the people of the Marshall Islands. In addition, Anna Christiansen, Matthew Lawrence, Lindsay Mollineaux, and Colleen Brogan proved astute and unstinting research assistants. Brown University and the Watson Institute for International Studies provided crucial resources for the research and the two conferences on which this book depended for its collective creation.

I also gratefully acknowledge the cartographer Chris Brest, anthropologist David Vine, and Princeton University Press for permission to reprint the global map of U.S. military basing from *Island of Shame: The Secret History of the U.S. Military Base on Diego Garcia* (Princeton: Princeton University Press, 2009).

Finally, I want to thank my children, Jonathan and Lianna, whose ideals as they enter adulthood inspire my hope for the future, and Matt for his lifelong, creative work toward a more just world.

FOREWORD

Cynthia Enloe

Get out your world map – the one that includes all the smallest island countries – and a pad of neon-colored post-it notes. Now you're ready to chart an empire. It used to be, back in the nineteenth and early twentieth centuries, that the world map would already have the imperial colors painted in, the most famous being pink for the colonies that comprised the far-reaching British Empire. If you were sitting in a classroom in, say, 1920 – in Mombasa, Colombo, Kingston, or Rangoon – you would look up at your teacher's map and see a world carpeted in pink. Nowadays, however, it is harder to see the expanses of an empire. You have to do more of the investigating yourself – with the help, thankfully, of Catherine Lutz and her sharp-eyed contributors.

Today the world map is an array of colors. Puerto Rico, Guam, and American Samoa remain colonies of the United States, the Falklands remain a colony of Britain, France still claims dominion over Guadeloupe and Martinique. Still, Kenya, Sri Lanka, Jamaica, and Myanmar, each now legally sovereign, have shed their imperial pink and taken on cartographic colors of their own. But that is only half the story. The chapters you are about to read help tell the rest of it – how imperial designers in the early twenty-first century carry out their plans while so many sovereign flags now fly.

The workings of would-be empire building have become less blatant. As these chapters make wonderfully clear, one of those mechanisms is the establishment of overseas military bases, created with the apparent agreement of officials acting in the name of the current sovereign local state. These bases appear as tiny dots, or not at all, on contemporary maps. But their impact is huge and the map and the broader sociopolitical mapping provided in this book shows us not only where they are, but how they operate.

One of the revelations that these authors offer us is how dynamic this military-base creating process is. Most American military strategists would explain that the U.S. government opens and closes its bases according to its own strategic assessments – what region is deemed crucial to U.S. national security at the moment, what are the ranges of refueling of the U.S. planes and ships, what terrains provide useful training habitats, which allies want to cement their cooperation with the United States by hosting a U.S. base. However, it turns out that those alterations of strategic calculus are not the only reasons for the historical changes. As the writers here show us, it is often the mobilization of local citizens critical of the U.S. bases that causes a given base to close down or to be off-limits for a particular military mission – whether in the Philippines, in Puerto Rico, in Panama, in Okinawa, or in Turkey.

Not all popular movements which bring pressure to bear on their own local officials to close a U.S. base have been successful, just as not all twentieth-century anti-colonial popular movements were successful in the short run. But one of the positive results of these local critics' efforts is that they highlight that there is a U.S. base *there*. Moreover, the cumulative effect of these movements has been to make the empire-building project more difficult overall.

The maps we put together of this basing policy have rarely circulated among the U.S. public, which has little awareness about U.S. military activities beyond the bare bones of the latest war.

Why is that?

It is always useful to dig into a lack of curiosity. A great deal of the unequal and often harmful dynamics of international politics depend on ordinary citizens becoming and staying *un*curious. What assumptions and attitudes prevalent among ordinary Americans allow the high-level decisions and daily operations of U.S. military-basing politics to persist with virtually no U.S. citizen concern? First of the culprits may be the widespread belief among Americans that any U.S. military base is of material value to the people living within its vicinity. After all, people in most U.S. towns that host a military base exert pressure on their

Congressional representatives in order to keep those bases, on the assumption that whatever social or environmental damage the base may cause is outweighed by the good it is doing for the local economy. Of course, it is not clear whether townspeople in Arizona, North Carolina, Massachusetts, and Maine would rally around a base if that base were staffed and controlled by the Japanese or the French military.

A second assumption dampening American citizen curiosity about U.S. military global-basing politics may be that any U.S. base created overseas is at the invitation of that country's own officials. There is virtually no news coverage – no journalists' or editors' curiosity – about the pressures or lures at work when the U.S. government seeks to persuade officials of Romania, Aruba, or Ecuador that providing U.S. military-basing access would be good for their countries. Thus this popular assumption derives from faith, not evidence.

A third common belief nurturing Americans' current incuriosity could be that their military is the most advanced, perhaps even the most "civilized," military in the world, and thus, whatever ripple effects it sends out from one of its overseas bases can only prove beneficial to the fortunate host society. Propping up this belief are the usually unexamined presumptions that U.S. male soldiers are models of responsible masculinity, that the U.S. military as an institution is a model of public disease prevention and of environmental accountability. Persisting in these presumptions requires not listening to the stories of ordinary women and men who have lived around – lived with – U.S. military bases in Okinawa, Diego Garcia, the Philippines, and Spain.

In fact, employing a gender analysis – even an explicitly feminist curiosity – when reading these chapters will enhance the experience. Watch for the assumptions about local women, as well as the actual experiences of local women living with U.S. military bases nearby. Keep an eye out for the assumptions about U.S. male soldiers' leisure time, on-leave entertainments, morale, marriage prospects, and sexuality. And slow down as you read about the mobilization of popular movements which challenge officials' claims that U.S. military bases are in everyone's best interest. Most of these movements are gendered. Women have been held up by movements as symbols of the bases' negative social impacts. But women have also provided crucial leadership and support for many of those movements, sometimes as activists within the anti-bases movement, other times splitting off to create their own autonomous women's anti-bases movements after they experience the sexism inside even an anti-militarist campaign.

A fourth comforting popular belief in the United States might be that insuring that country's national security in an age of an allegedly diffuse "global terror" trumps any other "lesser" concerns. Holding this belief implies a deep-seated militarism. It suggests not only that the believer embraces militarized notions of enemy, of threat, and of security, but that coping with that trinity must be unquestioningly prioritized over all other forms of danger and insecurity.

Together, these four popular beliefs in the United States and the incuriosity about U.S. military bases the quartet feeds pose a daunting challenge for those, including the thoughtful contributors to this book, who want more of us to take a critical look at the causes and consequences of U.S. military global-basing politics. Yet that challenge does not need to be taken on by U.S. citizens acting alone. In fact, it cannot be. It is the women and men living with each overseas military base who will be the best sources of information for anyone who wants to become curious about U.S. bases and move on from there to action.

INTRODUCTION
BASES, EMPIRE, AND GLOBAL RESPONSE

Catherine Lutz

Much about our current world is unparalleled: holes in the ozone layer, the commercial patenting of life forms, degrading poverty on a massive scale, and, more hopefully, the rise of concepts of global citizenship and universal human rights. Less visible but just as unprecedented is the global omnipresence and unparalleled lethality of the U.S. military, and the ambition with which it is being deployed around the world. These bases bristle with an inventory of weapons whose worth is measured in the trillions and whose killing power could wipe out all life on earth several times over. Their presence is meant to signal, and sometimes demonstrate, that the United States is able and willing to attempt to control events in other regions militarily.

Officially, over 190,000 troops and 115,000 civilian employees are massed in 909 military facilities in 46 countries and territories.[1] There, the U.S. military owns or rents 795,000 acres of land, and 26,000 buildings and structures valued at $146 billion. These official numbers are entirely misleading as to the scale of U.S. overseas military basing, however, excluding as they do the massive building and troop presence in Iraq and Afghanistan over the last many years, as well as secret or unacknowledged facilities in Israel, Kuwait, the Philippines and many other places. In only three of the years of the Iraq and Afghanistan wars, $2 billion in military construction money was expended. Just one facility in Iraq, Balad Air Base, houses 30,000 troops and 10,000 contractors, and extends across 16 square miles with an additional 12-square-mile "security perimeter."

1

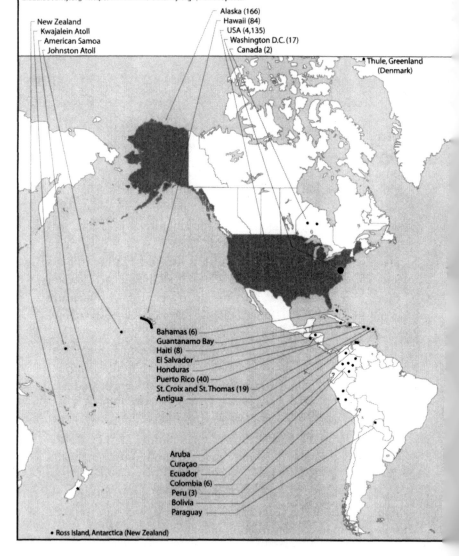

U.S. Military Bases

Because of the base network's size, complexity, and secrecy, base numbers cited are the most accurate available; locations are not always precise. "?" indicates a base under development or negotiation or where a base is suspected but cannot be confirmed.

Sources: Department of Defense, "Base Structure Report, Fiscal Year 2007 Baseline (A Summary of DoD's Real Property Inventory)," 2007; Transnational Institute, "Military Bases Google Earth File," available at http://www.tni.org/detail_page.phtml?act_id=17252; Chalmers Johnson, *The Sorrows of Empire: Militarism, Secrecy, and the End of the Republic* (New York: Metropolitan Books, 2004); Chalmers Johnson, *Nemesis: The Last Days of the American Republic* (New York: Metropolitan Books, 2007); GlobalSecurity.org <http://www.GlobalSecurity.org>; news reports.

New Zealand
Kwajalein Atoll
American Samoa
Johnston Atoll

Alaska (166)
Hawaii (84)
USA (4,135)
Washington D.C. (17)
Canada (2)

Thule, Greenland (Denmark)

Bahamas (6)
Guantanamo Bay
Haiti (8)
El Salvador
Honduras
Puerto Rico (40)
St. Croix and St. Thomas (19)
Antigua

Aruba
Curaçao
Ecuador
Colombia (6)
Peru (3)
Bolivia
Paraguay

• Ross Island, Antarctica (New Zealand)

Map of global U.S. military bases.

Source: Chris Best and David Vine, *Island of Shame: The Secret History of the U.S. Military Base on Diego Garcia* (Princeton: Princeton University Press, 2009)

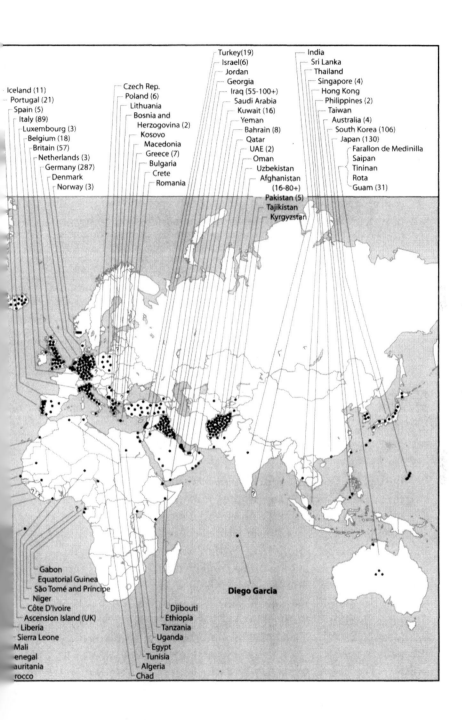

Iceland (11)
Portugal (21)
Spain (5)
Italy (89)
Luxembourg (3)
Belgium (18)
Britain (57)
Netherlands (3)
Germany (287)
Denmark
Norway (3)

Czech Rep.
Poland (6)
Lithuania
Bosnia and
Herzogovina (2)
Kosovo
Macedonia
Greece (7)
Bulgaria
Crete
Romania

Turkey(19)
Israel(6)
Jordan
Georgia
Iraq (55-100+)
Saudi Arabia
Kuwait (16)
Yemen
Bahrain (8)
Qatar
UAE (2)
Oman
Uzbekistan
Afghanistan
(16-80+)
Pakistan (5)
Tajikistan
Kyrgyzstan

India
Sri Lanka
Thailand
Singapore (4)
Hong Kong
Philippines (2)
Taiwan
Australia (4)
South Korea (106)
Japan (130)
Farallon de Medinilla
Saipan
Tininan
Rota
Guam (31)

Gabon
Equatorial Guinea
São Tomé and Príncipe
Niger
Côte D'Ivoire
Ascension Island (UK)
Liberia
Sierra Leone
Mali
enegal
auritania
rocco

Djibouti
Ethiopia
Tanzania
Uganda
Egypt
Tunisia
Algeria
Chad

Diego Garcia

Deployed from those battle zones in Afghanistan and Iraq to the quiet corners of Curaçao, Korea, and Britain, the U.S. military domain consists of sprawling army bases, small listening posts, missile and artillery testing ranges, and berthed aircraft carriers.[2] While the bases are literally barracks and weapons depots and staging areas for war-making and ship repair facilities and golf courses and basketball courts, they are also political claims, spoils of war, arms sales showrooms, toxic industrial sites, laboratories for cultural (mis)communication, and collections of customers for local bars, shops, and prostitution.

The environmental, political, and economic impact of these bases is enormous and, despite Pentagon claims that the bases simply provide security to the regions they are in, most of the world's people feel anything but reassured by this global reach. Some communities pay the highest price: their farm land taken for bases, their children neurologically damaged by military jet fuel in their water supplies, their neighbors imprisoned, tortured, and disappeared by the autocratic regimes that survive on U.S. military and political support given as a form of tacit rent for the bases. Global opposition to U.S. basing has been widespread and growing rapidly, however, and it is the aim of this book to describe both the worldwide network of U.S. military bases and the vigorous campaigns to hold the United States accountable for that damage and to reorient their countries' security policies in other, more human, and truly secure directions.

Military bases are "installations routinely used by military forces" (Blaker 1990:4). They represent a confluence of labor (soldiers, paramilitary workers, and civilians), land, and capital in the form of static facilities, supplies, and equipment. Their number should also include the eleven U.S. aircraft carriers, often used to signal the possibility of U.S. bombing as they are brought to "trouble spots" around the world and which were the primary base of U.S. air power during the invasion of Iraq in 2003. The U.S. Navy refers to each carrier as "four and a half acres of sovereign U.S. territory." These moveable bases and their land-based counterparts are just the most visible part of the larger picture of U.S. military presence overseas. This picture of military access includes (1) U.S. military training of foreign forces, often in conjunction with the provision of U.S. weaponry, (2) joint exercises meant to enhance U.S. soldiers' exposure to a variety of operating environments, from jungle to desert to urban terrain and interoperability across national militaries, and (3) legal arrangements made to gain overflight rights and other forms of ad hoc use of others' territory as well as to preposition military equipment there.

U.S. forces train 100,000 soldiers annually in 180 countries, the presumption being that beefed-up local militaries will help pursue U.S. interests in local conflicts and save the United States money, casualties, and bad publicity when human rights abuses occur.[3] Moreover, working with other militaries is important, strategists say, because "these low-tech militaries may well be U.S. partners or adversaries in future contingencies, [necessitating] becoming familiar with their capabilities and operating style and learning to operate with them" (Cliff and Shapiro 2003:102). The blowback effects are especially well known since September 11 (Johnson 2000). Less well known is that these training programs strengthen the power of military forces in relation to other sectors within those countries, sometimes with fragile democracies, and they may include explicit training in assassination and torture techniques. Fully 38 percent of those countries with U.S. basing were cited in 2002 for their poor human rights record (Lumpe 2002:16).

The U.S. military presence also involves jungle, urban, desert, maritime, and polar training exercises across wide swathes of landscape. These exercises have sometimes been provocative to other nations, and in some cases become the pretext for substantial and permanent positioning of troops; in recent years, for example, the United States has run approximately 20 exercises annually on Philippine soil. This has meant a near continuous presence of U.S. troops in a country whose people ejected U.S. bases in 1992 and continue to vigorously object to their reinsertion, and whose constitution forbids the basing of foreign troops (Docena 2007; see Simbulan, this volume). In addition, these exercises ramp up even more than usual the number and social and environmental impact of daily jet landings and sailors on liberty around U.S. bases (Lindsay-Poland 2003).

Finally, U.S. military and civilian personnel work every day to shape local legal codes to facilitate U.S. access. They have lobbied, for example, to change the Philippine and Japanese constitutions to allow, respectively, foreign troop basing and a more-than-defensive military. "Military diplomacy" with local civil and military elites is conducted not only to influence such legislation but also to shape opinion in what are delicately called "host" countries. U.S. military and civilian officials are joined in their efforts by intelligence agents passing as businessmen or diplomats; in 2005, the U.S. ambassador to the Philippines impoliticly mentioned that the United States has 70 agents operating in Mindanao alone.

Much of the United States' unparalleled weaponry, nuclear and otherwise, is stored at places like Camp Darby in Italy, Kadena Air Force Base in Okinawa, and the Naval Magazine on Guam, as well as in nuclear submarines and on the navy's other floating bases.[4] The weapons, personnel, and fossil fuels involved in this U.S. military presence cost billions of dollars, most coming from U.S. taxpayers but an increasing number of billions from the citizens of the countries involved. Elaborate bilateral negotiations exchange weapons, cash, and trade privileges for overflight and land-use rights. Less explicitly, but no less importantly, rice import levels or immigration rights to the United States or overlooking human rights abuses have been the currency of exchange (Cooley 2008).

Bases are the literal and symbolic anchors, and the most visible centerpieces, of the U.S. military presence overseas. To understand where those bases are and how they are being used is essential for understanding the United States' relationship with the rest of the world, the role of coercion in it, and its political economic complexion. The United States' empire of bases – its massive global impact and the global response to it – are the subject of the chapters in this book. Unlike the pundits and the strategic thinkers who corner the market on discussions of the U.S. military, these authors concentrate on the people around those bases and the impact of living in their shadow. The authors describe as well the social movements which have tried to call the world's attention to the costs those bases impose on them without their consent. In this introduction, I ask why the bases were established in the first place, how they are currently configured around the world and how that configuration is changing, what myths have developed about the functions U.S. overseas bases serve, and, finally, introduce the global movement to push back or expel the bases altogether.

What are Bases for?

Foreign military bases have been established throughout the history of expanding states and warfare. They have proliferated, though, only where a state has imperial ambitions, that is, where it aspires to be an empire, either through direct control of territory or through indirect control over the political economy, laws, and foreign policy of other places. Whether or not it recognizes itself as such, a country can be called an *empire* when its policies aim to assert and maintain dominance over other regions. Those policies succeed when wealth is extracted from peripheral areas and redistributed to the imperial center. An empire of bases, then, is associated with a growing gap between the wealth and welfare of the powerful center and the regions affiliated with it. Alongside and supporting these goals has often been elevated self-regard in the imperial power, or a sense of racial, cultural, or social superiority.

The descriptors *empire* and *imperialism* have been applied to the Romans, Incas, Mongols, Persians, Portuguese, Spanish, Ottomans, Dutch, British, the Soviet Union, and the United States, among others. Despite the striking differences between each of these cases, each used military bases to maintain some forms of rule over regions far from their center. The bases also eroded the sovereignty of allied states on which they were established by treaty; the Roman Empire was accomplished not only by conquest, but also by taking her weaker [but still sovereign] neighbors under her wing and protecting them against her and their stronger neighbors ... The most that Rome asked of them in terms of territory was the cessation, here and there, of a patch of ground for the plantation of a Roman fortress. (Magdoff et al. 2002)

What have military bases accomplished for these empires through history? Bases are usually presented, above all, as having rational, strategic purposes; the empire claims that they provide forward defense for the homeland, supply other nations with security, and facilitate the capture and control of trade and resources. They have been used to protect non-economic actors and their agendas as well – missionaries, political operatives, and aid workers among them. In the sixteenth century, the Portuguese, for example, seized profitable ports along the route to India and used demonstration bombardment, fortification, and naval patrols to institute a semi-monopoly in the spice trade. They militarily coerced safe-passage payments and duties from local traders via key fortified ports. More recently as well, bases have been used to control the political and economic life of the host nation: U.S. bases in Korea, for example, have been key parts of the continuing control that the U.S. military commander exercises over Korean forces in wartime, and Korean foreign policy more generally, extracting important political and military support, for example, for its wars in Vietnam and Iraq. Politically, bases serve to signal and encourage other governments' endorsement of U.S. military and other foreign policy. Moreover, bases have not simply been planned in keeping with strategic and political goals, but are the result of bureaucratic and political economic carry-on imperatives, that is, corporations and the military itself as an organization have profited from bases' continued existence, regardless of their strategic value.

Alongside their military and political economic purposes, bases have symbolic and psychological dimensions. They can be seen as expressions of a nation's will to status and power. Strategic elites have built bases as a visible sign of the nation's standing, much as they have constructed monuments, cities, and battleships. So, too, contemporary U.S. politicians and public have treated the number of their bases as indicators of the nation's hyperstatus and hyperpower. More darkly, overseas military bases can also be seen as symptoms of irrational or untethered fears, even paranoia, as they are built with the goal of taming a world perceived to be out of control. Empires frequently misperceive the world as rife with threats, and themselves as objects of violent hostility from others. Militaries' interest in organizational survival has also contributed to the amplification of this fear and imperial basing structures as the solution as they "sell themselves" to their populace by exaggerating threats, underestimating the costs of basing and war itself, as well as understating the obstacles facing preemption and belligerence (Van Evera 2001).

As the world economy and its technological substructures have changed, so have the roles of foreign bases. By 1500, new sailing technologies allowed much longer-distance voyages, even circumnavigational ones, and so empires could aspire to long networks of coastal naval bases to facilitate the control of sea lanes and trade. They were established at distances that would allow provisioning the ship, taking on fresh fruit that would protect sailors from scurvy, and so on. By the twenty-first century, technological advances have at least theoretically eliminated many of the reasons for foreign bases, including the in-transit refueling of jets and aircraft carriers, the nuclear powering of submarines and battleships, and other advances in sea- and airlift of military personnel and equipment.

States that invest their people's wealth in overseas bases have paid direct as well as opportunity costs, the consequences of which in the long run have usually been collapse of the empire. In *The Rise and Fall of Great Powers*, Kennedy notes that previous empires which established and tenaciously held onto overseas bases inevitably saw their wealth and power decay and that history

demonstrates that military "security" alone is never enough. It may, over the shorter term, deter or defeat rival states ... [b]ut if, by such victories, the nation over-extends itself geographically and strategically; if, even at a less imperial level, it chooses to devote a large proportion of its total income to "protection," leaving less for "productive investment," it is likely to find its economic output slowing down, with dire implications for its long-term capacity to maintain both its citizens' consumption demands and its international position (Kennedy 1987:539).[5]

Nonetheless, U.S. defense officials and scholars have continued to argue that bases lead to "enhanced national security and successful foreign policy" because they provide "a credible capacity to move, employ, and sustain military forces abroad" (Blaker 1990:3), and the ability "to impose the will of the United States and its coalition partners on any adversaries."[6] This belief, along with a number of others to be examined below, helps sustain the web of bases.

A Short History of U.S. Bases

In 1938, the United States had 14 military bases outside its continental borders. Seven years and 35 million World War II deaths later, the United States had an astounding 30,000 installations large and small in approximately 100 countries. While this number was to contract to 2,000 by 1948, the global scale of U.S. military basing would remain primarily the twentieth-century outcome of World War II, and with it, the rise to global hegemony of the United States (Blaker 1990:22).

The United States did not begin, though, with the idea of becoming an empire. Instead, the Founders saw themselves as men who were establishing a form of governance in some opposition to the empires of Europe (Shy 1976). Nonetheless, the early U.S. military became entwined with the frontier project of removing Indians from the land and protecting colonists who settled there. In this sense, every Western fort – and there were 255 of them – was a foreign military base, established on native land during the Indian campaigns and the Mexican–American War (Weigley 1984:267). The overseas U.S. basing structure of the nineteenth century was thin because the vast wealth of land and resources in North America represented a fertile enough field for much economic and military ambition in the United States. Moreover, the colonial expansion of the European states in the nineteenth and early twentieth century effectively closed off much of the world to the U.S. military.

Like other major powers of the late nineteenth century, including Japan and Germany, the necessity for building a large navy was touted by U.S. strategists and politicians. While the growth of its navy is commonly explained by the United States' position between two vast oceans, there were internal factors at work as well: with their gigantic steel tools, navies represented a much more lucrative site for industrial production and profit than armies and marines. The United States spent much effort ensuring that coaling and provisioning stations were available for its navy, initially via capture of what remained of Spanish naval assets in the Pacific, Southeast Asia, and Latin America.

After consolidation of its continental dominance, there were three periods of global ambition in U.S. history beginning in 1898, 1945, and 2001, and each is associated with the acquisition of significant numbers of new overseas military bases. The Spanish–American War resulted in the acquisition of a number of colonies, many of which have remained under U.S. control in the century since. Nonetheless, by 1920, popular support for international expansion in the United States had been diminished by the Russian Revolution, by growing domestic labor militancy, and by a rising nationalism, culminating in the U.S. Senate's rejection of the League of Nations (Smith 2003). So it was that as late as 1938 the U.S. basing system was far smaller than that of its political and economic peers, including many European nations as well as Japan. U.S. soldiers were stationed in just 14 bases, in Puerto Rico, Cuba, Panama, the Virgin Islands, Hawai'i, Midway, Wake, Guam, the Philippines, Shanghai, two in the Aleutians, American Samoa, and Johnston Island (Harkavy 1982), this small number the result in part of a strong anti-statist and anti-militarist strain in U.S. political culture (Sherry 1995). From the perspective of many in the United States through the inter-war period, to build bases would be to risk unwarranted entanglement in others' conflicts.

International bases of this era were primarily those of rival empires, with by far the largest number belonging to the British

Empire. In order of magnitude, the other colonial powers included France, Spain, Portugal, the Netherlands, Italy, Japan, and, only then, the United States. Conversely, countries with large militaries and with militarism on the rise had relatively few overseas bases; Germany and the Soviet Union had almost none. But it was the attempt to acquire such bases that was an important contributing cause of the war (Harkavy 1989:5).

The bulk of the U.S. basing system was established during World War II, beginning with a deal cut with Great Britain for the long-term lease of base facilities in six British colonies in the Caribbean in 1941 in exchange for some fairly decrepit U.S. destroyers. The same year, the United States assumed control of former Danish bases in Greenland and Iceland (Harkavy 1982:68). The rationale for building bases in the Western Hemisphere was in part to discourage or prevent the Germans from doing so; at the same time, the United States did not, before Pearl Harbor, build or expand bases in the Asia Pacific regions, on the assumption that to do so would provoke the Japanese to war. Then, as now, basing decisions bore the imprint of American racial assumption: the Japanese were "insecure," it was said, aware as they were of their inferiority, and to build bases in their backyard, but not the Germans', might inflame them (Blaker 1990:28–29; Dower 1987).

By the end of the war in 1945, the United States had the 30,000 installations spread throughout the world, as already mentioned. The Soviet Union had bases in Eastern Europe, but virtually no others until the 1970s, when they expanded rapidly, especially in Africa and the Indian Ocean area (Harkavy 1982). While Truman was intent on maintaining posts the United States had taken in the war, many were closed by 1949 (Blaker 1990:30). He was ultimately frustrated by pressure from Australia, France, and Britain, as well as from Panama, Denmark, and Iceland, for return of bases in their own territory or colonies, and domestic pressure to demobilize the 12-million-man military (a larger military would have been needed to maintain the vast basing system). The push to retract was also the result of the Soviet Union's ambitions and the contradictions of an American "nationalist globalism" (Smith

2003:xvi–xvii). On the other hand, military planners also knew they could do more with less given the longer flight ranges of aircraft developed by the late 1940s.

More important than the shrinking number of bases, however, was the codification of U.S. military access rights around the world outlined in a comprehensive set of legal documents. These established security alliances with multiple states within Europe (NATO), the Middle East and South Asia (CENTO), and Southeast Asia (SEATO), and they included bilateral documents with Japan, Taiwan, South Korea, Australia, and New Zealand. These documents assumed a common security interest between the United States and other countries and were the charter for U.S. basing in each place. Status of Forces Agreements (SOFAs) were crafted in each country to specify what the military could do; these usually gave U.S. soldiers broad immunity from prosecution for crimes committed and environmental damage created. These agreements and subsequent base operations have usually been shrouded in secrecy (see Simbulan, and Heller and Lammerant, this volume), much less promulgated with public input or democratic processes.

In the United States, the National Security Act of 1947, along with a variety of executive orders, instituted what can be called a second, secret government or the "national security state" that created the National Security Agency, National Security Council, and Central Intelligence Agency and allowed for a presidency that took on new, more imperial powers. From this point on, domestic and especially foreign military activities and bases were to be heavily masked from public oversight (Lens 1987). Begun as part of the Manhattan Project, the black budget is a source of defense funds secret even to Congress, and one that became permanent with the creation of the CIA. Under the Reagan administration, it came to be relied on more and more for a variety of military and intelligence projects and by one estimate was $36 billion in 1989 (Blaker 1990:101; Weiner 1990:4). Many of those unaccountable funds went then and still go now into use overseas, flowing out of U.S. embassies and military bases. There they have helped the United States to work vigorously to undermine and change local laws that stand in the way of its military plans; it has interfered for years in the domestic affairs of nations in which it has or desires military access, including attempts to influence votes on and change anti-nuclear and anti-war provisions in the constitutions of the Pacific nation of Belau and of Japan.

The number of U.S. bases was to rise again during the Korean and Vietnam Wars, reaching back to 1947 levels by the year 1967 (Blaker 1990:33). The presumption was established that bases captured or created during wartime would be permanently retained. Certain ideas about basing and what it accomplished were to be retained from World War II as well, including the belief that "its extensive overseas basing system was a legitimate and necessary instrument of U.S. power, morally justified and a rightful symbol of the U.S. role in the world" (Blaker 1990:28).

Nonetheless, over the second half of the twentieth century United States bases were either evicted or voluntarily withdrawn from dozens of countries.[7] Between 1947 and 1990, the United States was asked to leave France, Yugoslavia, Iran, Ethiopia, Libya, Sudan, Saudi Arabia, Tunisia, Algeria, Vietnam, Indonesia, Peru, Mexico, and Venezuela. Popular and political objection to the bases in Spain, the Philippines, Greece, and Turkey in the 1980s meant that those governments were able to negotiate significantly more compensation from the United States. Portugal threatened to evict the United States from important bases in the Azores unless it ceased its support for independence for its African colonies, a demand with which the United States complied.[8] In the 1990s and later, the United States was sent packing, most significantly, from the Philippines, Panama, Saudi Arabia, Vieques, and Uzbekistan (see McCaffrey, this volume).

Of its own accord and for a variety of reasons, the United States decided to leave countries from Ghana to Ecuador to Fiji. It did so based on the sense that the priorities of containing the Soviet Union and the possibilities allowed by new military technologies made some of the basing it held obsolete. The Pentagon determined, for example, that U.S. domestic bases could serve the functions of those that had been in Latin America, and European bases the functions of those in North Africa. At the same time, U.S. bases were newly built after 1947 in remarkable numbers (241) in the Federal Republic of Germany, as well as in Italy, Britain, and Japan (Blaker 1990:45). The defeated Axis powers continued to host the most significant numbers of U.S. bases: at its height, Japan was peppered with 3,800 U.S. installations.

As battles become bases, so bases become battles; the bases in East Asia acquired in the Spanish–American War and in World War II, such as Guam, Thailand, and the Philippines, became the primary sites from which the United States was able to wage war on Vietnam. Without them, the war would not have been fought as intensely as it was. The number of bombing runs over North and South Vietnam required tons of bombs unloaded at the Naval Station in Guam, stored at the Naval Magazine in the southern area of the island, and then shipped up to be loaded onto B-52s at Anderson Air Force Base every day during years of the war. The morale of ground troops based in Vietnam, as fragile as it was to become through the latter part of the 1960s, depended on R&R (rest and recreation) at bases outside the country which would allow them to leave the war zone and yet be shipped back quickly and inexpensively for further fighting (Baker 2004:76). The war also depended on the heroin that the CIA was able to quickly ship in from its secret bases in Laos to the troops back on the battlefield in Vietnam (Johnson 2004:134). In addition to the bases' role in fighting these large and overt wars, they facilitated the movement of military assets to accomplish the over 200 military interventions the United States waged in the Cold War period (Blum 1995).

As technology becomes bases, bases become technology as well. When France withdrew from NATO's integrated military structure in 1966, the United States had to shift its many logistics and aircraft sites from France to Germany. That plus the Cold War scenarios projected to unfold at the Iron Curtain between the two Germanys fundamentally structured the design of the F-16 then getting under way. The shorter distance that would be required for bombing missions from Germany in comparison with France led designers to trade off range for other more advanced capacities. The closing of the French logistics sites also led the United States on a search for bases elsewhere that would be more protected from Warsaw Pact attack than Germany (Blaker 1990:46–47).

Technological changes in warfare have also had important effects on the configuration of U.S. bases. Long-range missiles and the development of ships that could make much longer runs without resupply tended to radically alter the need for a line of bases to move forces forward into combat zones. So did the development of the capacity for aerial refueling of military jets. The rise of what Kaldor has called "The Baroque Arsenal," which is to say, more and more complex and lethal weaponry requiring fewer and fewer of each to be produced, has also reduced the need for masses of spare parts and other supplies. At the same time, each aircraft was exponentially more expensive, and so more strategic effort went into dispersing, hiding, and moving them and other military assets. An arms airlift from the United States to the British in the Middle East in 1941–42, for example, required a long hopscotch of bases, from Florida to Cuba, Puerto Rico, Barbados, Trinidad, British Guiana, northeast Brazil, Fernando de Noronha, Takoradi (now in Ghana), Lagos, Kano (now in Nigeria), and Khartoum before finally making delivery in Egypt. In the early 1970s, U.S. aircraft could make the same delivery with one stop in the Azores, and today could do so non-stop. While speed of deployment is framed as an important continued reason for forward basing, troops could be deployed anywhere in the world from U.S. bases without having to touch down en route. In fact, U.S. soldiers are being increasingly billeted on U.S. territory for this reason as well as to avoid the political and other costs of foreign deployment.

With the will to gain military control of space, as well as gather intelligence, the United States over time, and especially in the 1990s, established a large number of new military bases to facilitate the strategic use of communications and space technologies. In Columbia and Peru, and in secret and mobile locations elsewhere in Latin America, radar stations, now totaling 17, are primarily used for anti-trafficking operations (Roncken 2004).

On the other hand, the pouring of money into military R&D (the Pentagon spent over $85 billion in 2009 and employed over 90,000 scientists) and corporate profits to be made in the development and deployment of the resulting technologies have been significant factors in the ever larger numbers of technical facilities on foreign soil. These include such things as missile early-warning radar, signals intelligence, space-tracking telescopes and laser sources, satellite control, downwind air sampling monitors, and research facilities for everything from weapons testing to meteorology. Missile defense systems and network-centric warfare increasingly rely on satellite technology with associated requirements for ground facilities. These facilities have increasingly been established in violation of arms-control agreements such as the 1967 Outer Space Treaty meant to limit the militarization of space.

The assumption that the U.S. bases served local interests in a shared ideological and security project dominated into the 1960s: allowing base access showed a commitment to fight communism and gratitude for past U.S. military assistance. But with decolonization and the U.S. war in Vietnam such arguments began to lose their power, and the number of U.S. overseas bases began to decline from an early-1960s peak. Where access was once automatic, many countries now had increased leverage over what the United States had to give in exchange for basing rights, and those rights could be restricted in a variety of important ways, including through environmental and other regulations. The bargaining chips used by the United States were mostly weapons, and increasingly sophisticated weapons, as well as rent payments for the land on which bases were established.[9] These exchanges also often become linked with trade and other kinds of agreements, such as access to oil and other raw materials and investment opportunities (Harkavy 1982:337). They also, particularly when advanced weaponry is the medium of exchange, have had destabilizing effects on what are considered regional arms balances. From the earlier ideological basis for the bases, global post-war recovery and decreasing inequality between the United States and the countries – mostly in the global North – that housed the majority of U.S. bases helped birth a more pragmatic or economic grounding to basing negotiations, albeit often thinly veiled by the language of friendship and common ideological bent. The 1980s saw countries whose populations and governments had strongly opposed U.S. military presence, such as Greece, agree to U.S. bases on their soil only because they were in need of the cash, and Burma, a neutral but very poor state, went into negotiations with the United States over basing troops there (Harkavy 1989:4–5).

The Soviet basing network was never as extensive as that of the United States, but included dozens of large sites, including in Algeria, Angola, Cuba, Ethiopia, India, Libya, Peru, South Yemen, and Vietnam (Harkavy 1982). Both the Soviets and the United States dealt with the heavy costs of their bases by outsourcing military operations to proxy forces, and making extensive use of advisors, training, and weapons transfers: such measures both controlled costs and avoided the direct confrontations that both sides feared. The escalating costs of bases ultimately convinced the USSR to scale back its own. By 1991, the Soviet Union had, as Chalmers Johnson put it, lost the Cold War first, with at least one reason being its imperial overstretch.

The third period of accelerated imperial ambition began in 2000, with the election of George Bush and the ascendancy to power of a group of men who believed in a more aggressive and unilateral use of military power, some of whom stood to profit handsomely from the increased military budget that would require (Scheer 2008). They wanted "a network of 'deployment bases' or 'forward operating bases' to increase the reach of current and future forces" and focused on the need for bases in Iraq: "While the unresolved conflict with Iraq provides the immediate justification, the need for a substantial American force presence in the Gulf transcends the issue of the regime of Saddam Hussein" (Donnelly 2000). This plan for expanded U.S. military presence around the world has been put into action.

Pentagon transformation plans, outlined in detail by Gerson in Chapter 1, design U.S. military bases to operate not defensively vis-à-vis particular threats but as offensive, expeditionary platforms from which military capabilities can be projected quickly, anywhere. Where bases in Korea, for example, were once meant to defend South Korea from attack from the north, they are now, like bases everywhere, meant to project power in any number of directions and serve as stepping stones to battles far from themselves. The Global Defense Posture Review of 2004 announced these changes, focusing not just on reorienting the footprint of U.S. bases away from Cold War locations, but on the imperial ambitions of remaking legal arrangements that support expanded military activities with other allied countries and prepositioning equipment in those countries to be able to "surge" military force quickly, anywhere.

In these transformations, much attention has been paid to gaining access to overseas areas and to avoiding the politically sensitive appearance of establishing permanent basing, as has been the case with the way in which the US administration and presidential candidates have discussed basing in Iraq (see Engelhardt, this volume). As a recent army strategic document notes, "Military personnel can be transported to, and fall in on, prepositioned equipment significantly more quickly than the equivalent unit could be transported to the theater, and prepositioning equipment overseas is generally less politically difficult than stationing U.S. military personnel" (Cliff and Shapiro 2003:101). New names are being used to suggest that a military base is less significant or permanent or externally controlled than a base is typically assumed to be. Terms like "facility," "outpost," or "station" are used to label smaller bases, or bases with a narrower range of functions. The term "base" has been used to refer only to those installations in which the United States exercises full control over the military location rather than the many in which it shares that power with another nation.

The Department of Defense currently distinguishes between three types of military facilities. "Main operating bases" are those with permanent personnel, strong infrastructure, and often including family housing, such as Kadena Air Base in Japan and Ramstein Air Force Base in Germany. "Forward operating sites" are "expandable warm facilit[ies] maintained with a limited U.S. military support presence and possibly prepositioned equipment," such as Incirlik Air Base in Turkey and Soto Cano

Air Base in Honduras (U.S. Defense Department 2004:10). Finally, "cooperative security locations" are sites with few or no permanent U.S. personnel, which are maintained by contractors or the host nation for occasional use by the U.S. military, and often referred to as "lily pads." These are cropping up around the world, especially throughout Africa, as in Dakar, Senegal, where facilities and use rights have been newly established.

Central to these plans are attempts to divert local attention from the U.S. presence. This strategy, in other words, is in part a response to the effectiveness of past protests of U.S. military presence and activities. Speaking for the state, security writer Robert Kaplan distills these ideas in discussing U.S. presence in the Pacific:

> Often the key role in managing a CSL [cooperative security location] is played by a private contractor ... usually a retired American noncom [who] rents his facilities at the base from the host country military, and then charges a fee to the U.S. Air Force pilots transiting the base. Officially he is in business for himself, which the host country likes because it can then claim it is not really working with the American military ... a relationship with the U.S. armed forces [that] is indirect rather than direct eases tensions.[10]

What are Common Myths about U.S. Military Stationing Overseas?

Why and how are the bases tolerated and sustained in a world of nation-states where sovereignty and nationalism are still such important phenomena and when abuses of local people and environments so regularly occur? How are they accepted by the U.S. public, whose own Declaration of Independence focused on the British offense of "Quartering large bodies of armed troops among us" and "protecting them, by a mock Trial, from punishment for any Murders which they should commit on the Inhabitants of these States?" One of the most important explanations is that the bases are naturalized or normalized, meaning that they are thought of as unremarkable, inevitable, and legitimate. Bases are normalized through a commonly circulating rhetoric that suggests their presence is natural and even gift-like rather than the outcomes of policy choices made in keeping with the aim of pursuing a certain imperial vision of U.S. self-interest. Militarism is an ideology that supports such policies by suggesting that the world is naturally a dangerous place which requires the control brought by armies (Johnson 2004). Bases, then, are presented as simple safety devices against objective risks. Metaphorically, the military is spoken of as "arm" of the state, as having "posture," "reach," "stance," and perhaps most tellingly, a "footprint." These body images naturalize and suggest unity to what is in fact a very heterogeneous and socially constructed entity. Everyone involved, however – the true believers, the cynical opportunists, the managers and the nationalists – is participating in a complicated system of beliefs about the bases and American power.

By framing situations as requiring U.S. military access (the world is dangerous, terrorism must be dealt with by means of the most powerful military tools available, etc.), U.S. commentators suggest that the current military realignment and new base building in Korea, Guam, and elsewhere are inevitable. By focusing on existing bases as "facts on the ground" that new base planning must adapt to or augment, those commentators suggest there is no alternative, ignoring the many that critics have suggested. In these ways, discussion of alternatives to the projection of U.S. military power around the world is preempted.

What is the cultural language of U.S. basing? Asked why the United States has a vast network of military bases around the world, Pentagon officials argue, first, via utilitarianism and realism, that the bases "project power" and so get things done for the United States, and, second, on humanitarian grounds, that the bases "project care" and provide things for other countries.

The utilitarian arguments come in three common forms:

Bases provide security for the United States by deterring attack from hostile countries and preventing or remedying either unrest or military challenges.

- "American armed forces stationed abroad ... should be considered as the first line of American defenses, providing reconnaissance and security against the prospect of larger crises and conducting stability operations to prevent their outbreak" (Donnelly et al. 2000:15).
- "Potential security challenges in Asia [include collapse of the Indonesian state, creating refugee flows and regional unrest]. Under such circumstances, the U.S. ... could be compelled to intervene to restore order" (Davis and Shapiro 2003:94).

The strategic language used to justify bases in the wake of 9/11 has become increasingly emphatic in portraying foreign military access as key to the projection of power, and portraying the bases as requiring no more rationale than uncertainty and contingency in the world. This naturalizes the bases even further than in the past, when specific strategic goals or localized violent adversaries were used to justify them.

- "The present era requires an Army that can move a powerful military force to distant, perhaps unprepared, theaters quickly" (Davis and Shapiro 2003:4).
- "To contend with uncertainty and to meet the many security challenges we face, the United States will require bases and stations within and beyond Western Europe and Northeast Asia, as well as temporary access arrangements for the long-distance deployment of U.S. forces."[11]

Bases serve the national economic interests of the United States, ensuring access to markets and commodities needed to maintain the American standard of living, primarily by maintaining influence over the domestic and foreign policy of the countries in which they are found.

- "The threat may take many postures, not just military. Our access to energy sources remains an imperative, as does open trade, access to the routes of commerce, and unfettered international exchange. Economic and cyber warfare is a distinct possibility. Human rights violations, natural disaster, epidemics, and the breakdown of national and international order are all plausible contingencies that may require the United States to act across the range of its capabilities. In virtually every case, our base structure will be an essential part of these capabilities" (Overseas Basing Commission 2005:8).

- "The United States' foreign military presence remains a compelling symbol and bellwether of U.S. attitudes and approaches to foreign and defense policy ... As the military analyst Andrew Bacevich of Boston University has observed, 'the political purpose [of U.S. troops abroad] is [now] not so much to enhance stability, but to use U.S. forces as an instrument of political change'" (Campbell and Ward 2003:100).

This type of argument says that the bases are the necessary platforms for a constant set of military and other efforts to change the countries and regions in which they are located in the U.S. economic and strategic interest. Because it suggests that U.S. bases work to manipulate events overseas and primarily in the interest of control and access to resources and profit, it has not been articulated publicly by government and military officials as much as has the first, deterrence argument. Nonetheless, it remains a rationale with strong support in elite circles, and in some conservative mainstream discussion.

Bases are symbolic markers of U.S. power and credibility.

- "The presence of American forces in critical regions around the world is the visible expression of the extent of America's status as a superpower ... Security guarantees that depend solely upon power projected from the continental United States will inevitably become discounted" (Donnelly et al. 2000).
- "The basing posture of the United States, particularly its overseas basing, is the skeleton of national security upon

which flesh and muscle will be molded to enable us to protect our national interests and the interests of our allies, not just today, but for decades to come" (Overseas Basing Commission 2005).

This type of argument says that bases need no other rationale than their presence and visibility. It also suggests, by implication, that more bases are better than fewer since a multitude of locations is just that much more visible.

A second set of arguments for overseas bases sees them as positive expressions of American character, and particularly its humanitarian ethos. Prone to see their nation as a generous one, Americans typically far overestimate the amount of their government's foreign aid and misunderstand its motives. The military has worked hard to present itself as helping or rescuing others through such things as hurricane or tsunami relief or military operations presented as liberating or democratizing others. Bases participate in this same set of assumptions. In them, U.S. overseas bases are donations to the world in two respects, first, as demanding obligations to assist the countries in which they are located:

Bases are gifts to other nations, both as defense sites and as wealth generators. They represent American altruism and sacrifice.

- "The new U.S. global posture strategy ... reflects the American commitment to a global insurance policy for an emerging security landscape" (Henry 2006:48).
- "Guam's 160,000 residents stand to benefit economically from the island's increased military presence. Each additional submarine would bring roughly 150 sailors to Guam and $9 million in salaries for them and their support personnel" (Erickson and Mikolay 2006:87).
- "The United States bears the brunt of the most arduous security duties ... [Its allies who do not contribute to joint military endeavors] cannot relate either to the hard responsibilities that come with military intervention or to the expense

in blood and treasure that the American people experience on a continuous basis" (Bloomfield 2006:63).

- "U.S. preeminence presents an opportunity, and even perhaps a duty, to use American power to make the world a better and safer place" (Davis and Shapiro 2003:9).

These last examples point to what can be called the "gift economy of bases." This takes many shapes. In the several decades following World War II and the Korean War, many in the military saw the lands they acquired during the war as just returns on their service. So, a guide to U.S. Army posts published for soldiers in 1963 says of its installations in Okinawa, "Every square mile now occupied by U.S. servicemen on Okinawa cost more than 100 American lives" (Scanlan 1963:347). Local civilians as well have sometimes seen the bases in this way, as when older residents of Guam and South Korea express gratitude for the U.S. military's ejection of the Japanese or the North Koreans in World War II and the Korean War. A younger generation in these places has begun to debate this, suggesting the debt was paid off long ago, but less frequently is the idea questioned that a gift was given in the first place.

Bases serve universal purposes by protecting the free trade that benefits many or even all nations, and by serving as a wedge for the expansion of freedom.

- "By guaranteeing the security of East Asian sea lanes – a public good that China is not yet able to provide – America facilitates the flow of energy and trade in a region that depends on both to maintain its impressive economic growth" (Erickson and Mikolay 2006:77).
- "Oman plays a critical role in helping to assure the free passage of shipping through one of the world's most important sea lanes ... Under [a joint] agreement, the United States gained access to three of Oman's air bases and several of its ports."[12]
- "In the 1960's, America's naval policy in the Indian Ocean had many ingredients. The foremost was to deter Russia

from interrupting the flow of oil from the Persian Gulf countries to America and Europe."[13]

Neither of these two kinds of myths of altruism deal with the problem that many of those bases were taken during wartime and kept, or "given" to the United States by another of the war's victors. In most of these cases, documents were drawn up in the aftermath to legitimate the conquest. So Anderson Air Force Base in Guam is located on land taken from the Spanish in 1898 and retaken from the Japanese in 1944; so the United States ultimately took land from the people of Guam who owned and farmed it, currently fully one-third of the island's 212 square miles (Aguon 2006). Recognizing that a legal fig leaf was needed in an era of surging decolonization, the United States made the people of Guam U.S. citizens (though limited in their ability to vote in national elections) (Department of Chamorro Affairs 2002). Even with the most recent example of base establishment by conquest, in Iraq, U.S. military strategists repeat the notion that the United States does not behave like previous empires when it acquires military access: "conquest is more or less irrelevant, precluded by emerging international norms or "laws" [sic] – though it seems unlikely that the U.S. military will be abandoning the bases it has seized or created in Afghanistan and Iraq any time soon" (Harkavy 2006).

Critical observers of U.S. foreign policy, Chalmers Johnson foremost among them, have thoroughly dissected and dismantled several of the arguments that have been made for maintaining a global military basing system (Johnson 2004). They have shown that the system has often failed in its own terms, that is, has not provided more safety for the United States or its allies, and U.S. apologists fail to characterize what the bases actually do: while said to provide defense and security, the U.S. presence has often created more attacks rather than fewer, as in Saudi Arabia or in Iraq. They have made the communities around the base a key target of Soviet or other nations' missiles, and local people recognize this. So on the island of Belau in the Pacific, site of sharp resistance to U.S. attempts to install a submarine base and jungle training center, people describe their experience of military basing in World War II: "When soldiers come, war comes." Likewise, on Guam, a common joke has it that few people but nuclear targeters in the Kremlin knew where their island is. Finally, U.S. military actions have often produced violence in the form of blowback rather than squelched it, undermining their own stated realist objectives (Johnson 2000).

Evidence for the second, national economic interest rationale can be found in the history of base negotiations and the establishment of U.S. bases in countries with key strategic resources, for example, along the routes of numerous oil and gas pipelines in Central Asia and the Middle East from 2001 on, and the renewed interest in basing in Africa, from which fully one quarter of U.S. oil imports are expected by 2015.[14] The profits from the bases' presence have gone first of all, however, to the corporations who build and service the bases. Halliburton Corporation's former engineering and construction subsidiary, Kellogg, Brown, and Root (KBR), is the largest private contractor working for the Pentagon in Iraq. In July 2006, the Department of Defense announced that it would no longer rely solely on KBR as the caretaker of U.S. troops abroad; however, the contract for this work has earned Halliburton $15 billion between 2001 and 2006 (see Engelhardt, this volume).[15]

The altruism or "foreign aid" argument must contend with the nature of U.S. strategic thinking about bases, which often centers on planning and equipping the bases for expeditionary warfare rather than local or defensive warfare. To take just two examples, U.S. bases in the Philippines were used to wage war on Vietnam, and U.S. bases in Germany to transport material to fight the war in Iraq. The costs for local economies and polities of hosting military bases can be substantial. They include immediate debits such as pollution, noise, and crime which cannot be offset by soldiers' local spending or employment of locals, and a number of other economic costs, to be detailed below. Moreover, U.S. bases used in this way are perhaps more likely to make countries the target of attacks for having allied themselves with the United States than they are to protect it.

Gaining and maintaining access for U.S. bases has often involved close collaboration with despotic governments. This has been the case especially in the Middle East and Asia. The United States worked closely with Ferdinand Marcos to maintain the Philippines bases, with Korean dictators until 1993, and Singapore's infamous Lee Kuan Yew, to give just a few examples. These governments have been gifted with substantial amounts of military equipment in exchange for U.S. access to bases. In 2002, Uzbekistan received $120 million worth of military hardware and surveillance equipment in addition to $82 million for its security services, in exchange for U.S. use of the Karshi-Khanabad airbase. Such U.S. equipment has much more often been used against citizens of the nation which receives it than in defense of its borders. For example, in 2005 Uzbek security forces attacked thousands of demonstrators who were protesting the conviction of 23 businessmen who were accused of being Muslim extremists, killing between 400 and 1,000 protestors (Cooley 2008).

Each of these arguments from rationalism and altruism ignores some of the most powerful incentives for continued foreign

Richard Nixon with Ferdinand Marcos, during a visit to the Philippines.
(University of California, Los Angeles, Charles E. Young Research Library, Department of Special Collections).

military basing. These include the "carry-on imperative" that exists in military and other bureaucracies, desires for control, and intense fears, not even so much of attack by others as of a world potentially disordered (Theweleit 1987). This is not to say that the arguments raised *against* the bases somehow draw from a simply rational and altruistic well: they, too, draw from a panoply of deeply held convictions and engage powerful cultural myths and culturally constructed feelings in each place they are created. But the empires of the Enlightenment world have claimed reason as their own (Robinson, Gallagher, and Denny 1961).

The reasons given for stationing U.S. forces overseas, though, cannot simply be called wrong. While the weight of evidence just briefly reviewed suggests that they are, the pursuit of the immense project of circling the globe with soldiers and equipment is fueled as much by mythic structures as by reason and rationality. It then becomes difficult to distinguish one from the other. While such myths may be invalidated by rational argumentation, their explanatory power often remains powerfully intact.

Support for foreign military bases hinges first on the idea that war is often necessary and ultimately inevitable. It is widely believed that humans are naturally violent and that war can be a glorious and good venture. Racism adds the notion that the modern and not coincidentally white nations have the responsibility, intelligence, religious ethic, and right to control more primitive (and more chaotically violent) others through violence if necessary. These racial ideas made it possible for people in the United States and Europe to support colonial exterminationist wars in the nineteenth century, but to find wars between industrialized or civilized states increasingly unthinkable during the late nineteenth century (despite what went on to happen in the twentieth). They also underpin the assumption that Gusterson (1999) has labeled "nuclear orientalism," which holds that only the United States and European powers can truly be trusted with nuclear weapons. Such beliefs provide important foundation stones for support of the U.S. basing system.[16]

The World Responds

How has the world responded to these bases?[17] How have local communities reacted to the idea that the bases benefit their nation? How have they accounted their costs? Social movements have proliferated around the world in response to the empire of U.S. bases. Many have been concerned as well with the approximately 150 foreign military bases of other countries, primarily European, Russian, and Chinese, and with their own militaries' bases, often used against elements within the nation itself. The vastly larger number and lethality of the U.S. military bases and their weaponry, however, has made those bases their focus.

In defining the problem they face, some groups have focused on the base itself, its sheer presence as matter out of place in a world of national borders, that is, they have seen the problem as one of affronts to sovereignty and national pride. Others focus on the purposes the bases serve, which is to stand ready to and sometimes wage war, and see the bases as implicating them in the violence projected from them. These objections to war are variously on grounds that are ethical (it is immoral to kill, or modern war necessarily kills civilians and so is unacceptable, or offensive wars are unacceptable), socioeconomic (war drains resources from other, more important social needs and investments), or realist–strategic (current U.S. war-making policy is counterproductive to its and its allies' national security). Most also focus on the noxious effects of the bases' daily operations, a high impact matter given that bases are often the tools of mass industrial warfare, which is a highly toxic, labor-intensive, and violent operation that employs an inordinate number of young males. For years, the movements have logged and described past and current confiscation of land, the health effects from military jet noise and air and water pollution, soldiers' crimes, especially rapes, other assaults, murders, and car crashes, and the impunity they have usually enjoyed, the inequality of the nation-to-nation relationship often undergirded by racism and other forms of disrespect, the culture of militarism that infiltrates local societies and its consequences, including higher rates of enlistment, death and injury to local youth, the cost to local treasuries in payments to the United States for support of the bases, and the use of the bases for prisoner extradition and torture.[18]

The sense that U.S. bases represent a massive injustice to the community and the nation is an extremely common one in the countries where U.S. bases are most ubiquitous and of longest standing. These are places where people have been able to observe military practice and inter-state relations with the United States closely and over a long period of time. In Okinawa, most polls show that 70 to 80 percent of the island's people want the bases, or at least the marines, to leave: they want base land back and they want an end to aviation crash risks, higher rates of prostitution and drug trafficking, and sexual assault and other crimes by U.S. soldiers (see Akibayashi and Takazato, this volume; Cheng 2003; Sturdevant and Stoltzfus 1993). One family built a large peace museum right up against the edge of the fence to Futenma Air Base there, with a stairway to the roof which allows busloads of schoolchildren and other visitors to view the sprawling base after looking at art depicting the horrors of war.

In Korea, the great majority of the population feels that a reduction in U.S. presence would *increase* national security.[19] Many feel that U.S. bases, while providing nuclear and other deterrence against North Korean attack, have prevented reunification. As well, the U.S. military is seen as disrespectful of Koreans. In recent years, several violent deaths at the hands of U.S. soldiers brought out vast candlelight vigils and other protests across the country. And the original inhabitants of Diego Garcia, evicted from their homes between 1967 and 1973 by the British on behalf of the United States, have organized a concerted campaign for the right to return, bringing legal suit against the British government (see Vine and Jeffery, this volume). There is also resistance to the U.S. expansion plans into new areas. In 2007, a number of African nations balked at U.S. attempts at military basing access (Hallinan 2007). In Eastern Europe, despite well-funded campaigns to convince Poles and Czechs of the value of U.S. bases and much sentiment in favor of taking the bases in pursuit of a more Western European identity and of promised economic benefits, vigorous protests including hunger strikes have emerged (see Heller and Lammerant, this volume).[20]

Very different degrees of resistance to the presence and practices of the U.S. military exist around the world. This results partly from differences in the U.S. presence in each place. Marine bases create more criminal behavior than air force bases, which produce more toxins per square foot than army bases, and navy bases produce more episodic and so visible social impacts as ships dock and spill what are sometimes thousands of men and women into a community, many looking for sex and alcohol. Small bases obviously create less impact than large ones, and urban bases sit on more valuable land than rural ones. More recently built bases also claim more attention than long-standing ones, which may disappear into a normalized background. In some countries, the bases create discontent in the communities immediately surrounding the bases but not elsewhere where the costs are less visible.

In many places, the bases provide jobs for local workers and revenues to some local businesses and this mutes dissent (Inoue 2004). For many families, the coming of a U.S. base means income from sales to soldiers or jobs on post. To the very real fear of job or income loss should a base close, however, are added more general community fears of loss prompted by the public relations arms of the military and local chambers of commerce, which often suggest that the economic benefits of military bases are much more significant and positive than they in fact are. The alternative uses, economic benefits, property taxes, and historically sustainable livelihoods that had or might come from the land when not used by the military are not calculated.[21] The social problems which accompany bases, including violence against women, auto crashes, and environmental and health damage, have to be handled by local communities without compensation from the United States, driving up local taxes. The U.S. dollars brought in, particularly through high living allowances given to U.S. military families stationed overseas, drive land and product prices up for local families. Guam, for example, is currently experiencing a land price explosion as a U.S. base build-up begins, putting homes out of reach for many island residents.

Moreover, the economic impact figures publicized to help build local support for U.S. basing do not reveal whose pockets the Pentagon dollars go into. Instead of flowing to large numbers of local workers, most Pentagon tax dollars land in the hands of a few military contractors, U.S. companies that supply American products to soldiers, and the wealthiest local business owners. Where heavy metals and explosives taint soil and water and children are born with neurological and other deformities, moreover, who dares put a price on those burdens? The power of local business elites and of the military, however, means that this quite partial story of economic impact is heard to the exclusion of more complete and nuanced ones.

Finally, U.S. bases are often brought in after trade and investment deal inducements have been given to local governments. As Irving et al. have noted:

> Base agreements often come with sweeteners for national governments, including U.S. investment and trade treaties. But these can tie countries into U.S. models of trade relations, liberalisation and privatisation, which are of dubious benefit to host nations. In the Philippines, for example, military agreements were tied to economic deals that gave U.S. and Filipino investors equal rights in one another's markets. But how many Filipino investors benefited from access to the USA, while U.S. companies ... made a quick killing from buying [Filipino companies] up at bargain prices? (Irving, van der Zeijden and Reyes 2007)

In some countries, people have felt convinced that there would be a dangerous increase in the potential for attack by a neighbor if the U.S. bases left. So some older Koreans feel that the U.S. bases help deter a North Korean attack that the South Koreans could not prevent or repel themselves. In Guam, a colony of the United States since 1898 with a brief Japanese occupation during World War II, the military government of the late 1940s brought in thousands of immigrant Filipino and Korean laborers to build the post-war bases. When all residents were made U.S. citizens in 1950, the native Chamorro people became a minority in their own country, and this made resistance to the bases a minority proposition as well. As in Okinawa, Guam had a devastating experience during World War II, one which led many to see the United States as a liberator on the one hand, and a powerful occupying army on the other. To support the military might have seemed the only safe course in such traumatized circumstances, as well as helping solidify one's identity as a loyal American in the face of the suspicion, racially based, that one is not (Diaz 2001). The high rates of social dysfunction common to long-colonized societies, including high rates of drug use and mental illness, have also been obstacles to organizing against the bases, as has the control of local media by U.S. nationals supportive of the U.S. military.

Objections to U.S. bases have been voiced since their inception. The attempt to take the Philippines from Spain in 1898 led to a drawn-out guerilla war for independence that required 126,000 American occupation troops to stifle. After World War II, there were multiple calls for return of the bases or of the land on which the radically expanded U.S. military presence stood. Voiced both by former colonial rulers like France and Britain, and by the land's original inhabitants, these efforts contributed to the eviction of U.S. bases as noted above. Most recently, they were evicted from Panama in 1999, although there are continuing efforts to deal with the failure of the United States to clean up its toxic and explosive remains, including more than 100,000 rounds of unexploded ordnance on firing ranges, despite a Canal Treaty provision for removing such dangers.

Oftentimes host nations are compelled to protect the U.S. military's rights to lands and commit violent acts against their own citizens. In South Korea, bloody battles between civilian protesters and the Korean military were waged in 2006 in response to the United States' global repositioning efforts there. In 2004, the Korean government agreed to U.S. plans to expand Camp Humphreys near Pyeongtaek, currently 3,700 acres, by an additional 2,900 acres. The surrounding area, including the towns of Doduri and Daechuri, was home to some 1,372 people, many elderly farmers. In 2005, residents and activists began a peace camp at the village of Daechuri. While they declared autonomy from Korea on February 7, 2006, vowing to resist expulsion from the expanded base area, the Korean government eventually forcibly evicted all from their homes and demolished the Daechuri primary school, which had been an organizing center for the resisting farmers.

Farmer resisting eviction from her land for expansion of the United States' Camp Humphreys near Pyeongtaek, South Korea, 2006.

Protest at U.S. foreign military presence was muted in the pre-1991 period by the Cold War's anti-communist climate, and by the authoritarianism of many of the allied regimes hosting U.S. bases, as in South Korea and the Philippines. These factors not only violently repressed the development of the movements but shaped their focus on what were seen as the prior but interconnected problems of democratization in South Korea and the Philippines, and of internal colonialism in the case of Okinawa and Guam (see Simbulan, this volume). Nonetheless, anti-militarist movements in Japan had drawn attention to the bases. In the 1980s, the anti-nuclear movement, spurred particularly by the U.S./NATO move to introduce cruise missiles into Europe, drew attention to the nuclear weapons stored across the continent and spurred similar interrogation and protests at the nuclear weapons on U.S. bases in Australia. That movement continues today to call for the removal of the 480 U.S. nuclear weapons still scattered across Europe (see Heller and Lammerant, this volume).

With the end of the Cold War, the central pretext used for most U.S. bases evaporated, and calls for their return were renewed. Democratization efforts in Korea, the Philippines, and elsewhere had meanwhile succeeded, and would allow for more energetic calls for redress of grievances against the U.S. military. So, as Simbulan describes in his chapter, the Philippine movement to oust the bases was successful in 1991, based first in the charter provided by a new post-Marcos constitution that declared: "foreign military bases, troops or facilities shall not be allowed in the Philippines except under a treaty duly concurred in by the Senate and, when the Congress so requires, ratified by a majority of the votes cast by the people in a national referendum held for that purpose."

With the onset of the Bush administration's declaration of a war on terror and of the right to preemptive war, the number of countries into which the United States inserted and based troops radically expanded, as Gerson details in the next chapter (see also Magdoff et al. 2002). Aggressive campaigns of coercion and financial enticement succeeded in putting U.S. soldiers in many new places, particularly where the military aid provided as quid pro quo fulfilled local elite aspirations to military hardware and military control over their own population or regional status as a military power.

Nine/eleven notwithstanding, sustained campaigns of direct action and political lobbying resulted in the 2003 removal of the U.S. Navy from Vieques. As McCaffrey notes in her chapter and elsewhere (McCaffrey 2002), the success of this anti-base campaign where others had failed hinged in part on use of arguments about the environmental and health damage of the military's activities. This also remains the centerpiece of resistance to military activities on and around domestic bases. The efforts, networked by the Military Toxics Project, have focused on the military's role in polluting soil, air, and groundwater around bases with PCBs, lead, fuel, agents orange, blue, purple, and white and DDT, among many others (Castro 2007). They have documented the resulting clusters of people with cancers and other diseases. These movements have drawn attention to the role of many bases in testing and storing weapons, including nuclear bombs, depleted uranium weapons, and nerve gas.

An unprecedented global mobilization of peace movements arose in the wake of the terror attacks and counter-attacks from 2001 forward. Gerson gives a brief history of that global emergence as well, and most of the chapters of this book give rich detail on what those movements have attempted and achieved in myriad places around the world. While their work is often entwined in other local disagreements over goals and tactics, the work to expel overseas U.S. military bases is considered by many, including an international body that met in Indonesia in 2003, to be one of the four pivotal goals of the global peace movement.[22]

The United States has responded to anti-bases organizing, on the other hand, by a renewed emphasis on "force protection," in some cases enforcing curfews on soldiers, and cutting back on events that bring local people onto base property. The Department of Defense has also engaged in the time-honored practice of renaming: clusters of soldiers, buildings, and equipment have become "defense staging posts" or "forward operating locations" rather than military bases. The regulating documents become "visiting forces agreements," not "status of forces agreements," or remain entirely secret. While major reorganization of bases is under way for a host of reasons, including a desire to create a more mobile force with greater access to the Middle East, Eastern Europe, and Central Asia, the motives also include an attempt to derail or prevent political momentum of the sort that ended U.S. use of Vieques and the Philippine bases. The U.S. attempt to gain permanent basing in Iraq foundered in 2008 on the objections of forces in both Iraq and the U.S. (see Engelhardt, this volume). It is unlikely that a change of U.S. administration will make for an immediate dismantling of those bases, however, for all the reasons this brief history of U.S. bases and empire suggests.

The Chapters to Come

The contributors to this volume consider U.S. bases and social movement responses to them from areas around the world with which they are intimately familiar. They address the following questions: What is the current state of organized activism and everyday political sentiment about U.S. military bases today? How does this emerge from a longer local or regional history of concern with questions of political and economic development, sovereignty, and militarization? What are the ranges of strategies and tactics used by local movements? What understandings of the problem (e.g. as one of militarism, sovereignty, imperialism, security threats, and/or crime) have currency, and which dominate? What is the movements' relationship to popular opinion more generally, to the media, to local and national government? What specific new challenges are presented by changes in U.S. military base locations, base daily operations and practices, and U.S. military and civilian relationships to local governments? The contributors have diverse backgrounds in anthropology, law, gender studies, political science, and activism, and include young activists and scholars alongside distinguished experts in peace and demilitarization. This interdisciplinary approach provides exciting and wide-ranging analyses of this globally important issue.

The central political problem of the coming decade(s) is massive and growing global inequality. Central to the construction and maintenance of that inequality and the capitalist social relations that produce it are vast investments in military power by the sole superpower, the United States, and their deployment in increasingly offensive positions under a doctrine of preemption in the name of eliminating any aspirants to military parity in the global arena. To pursue these goals has involved the major relocation and growth of U.S. military overseas basing, particularly in the last few years. The social disruptions and conflicts precipitated by these imperial projects are legion, central to the fate of empire, but yet are geographically scattered and poorly understood. These chapters begin the process of tracing those disruptions, conflicts, and contestations. They have the additional goal of attempting to facilitate understanding between widely dispersed groups facing the bases, and identifying the lessons learned about the challenges and successes of the global movement to evict these bases. The overarching goal is a call, through the visibility and sharp analysis these chapters provide, for justice for those living in the toxic, dangerous, and often arrogant shadow of U.S. military posts, and recognition of the power and cooperative achievements of the social movements working to that end.

Notes

1. Department of Defense (2007) Base Structure Report: Fiscal Year 2007 Baseline Report, available online at www.defenselink.mil/pubs/BSR_2007_Baseline.pdf. Date last accessed June 5, 2008. These official numbers far undercount the facilities in use by the U.S. military. To minimize the total, public knowledge, and political objections, the Department of Defense sets minimum troop numbers, acreage covered, or dollar values of an installation, or counts all facilities within a certain geographic radius as a single base.

2. The major current concentrations of U.S. sites outside those war zones are in South Korea, with 106 sites and 29,000 troops (which will be reduced by a third by 2008), Japan with 130 sites and 49,000 troops, most concentrated in Okinawa, and Germany with 287 sites and 64,000 troops. Guam with 28 facilities, covering a third of the island's land area, has nearly 6,600 airmen and soldiers and is slated to radically expand over the next several years (Base Structure Report FY2007).

3. Funding for the International Military Education and Training (IMET) Program rose 400 percent in just eight years from 1994 to 2002 (Lumpe 2002).

4. The deadliness of its armaments matches that of every other empire and every other contemporary military combined (CDI 2002). This involves not just its nuclear arsenal, but an array of others, such as daisy-cutter and incendiary bombs.

5. A variety of theories have argued for the relationship between foreign military power and bases and the fate of states, including long cycle theory (Harkavy 1999), world systems theory (Wallerstein 2003), and neo-Marxism (Magdoff 2003).

6. Donald Rumsfeld, "Department of Defense Office of the Executive Secretary: Annual Report to the President and Congress," 2002, p. 19, available online at www.dod.mil/execsec/adr2002/toc2002. htm. Date last accessed October 8, 2007.

7. Between 1947 and 1988, the United States left 62 countries, 40 of them outside the Pacific Islands (Blaker 1990:34).

8. Luis Nuno Rodrigues, "Trading 'Human Rights' for 'Base Rights': Kennedy, Africa, and the Azores," manuscript in possession of the author, March 2006.

9. Harkavy (1982:337) calls this the "arms–transfer–basing nexus" and sees the U.S. weaponry as having been key to maintaining both basing access and control over the client states in which the bases are located. Granting basing rights is not the only way to acquire advanced weaponry, however. Many countries purchased arms from both superpowers during the Cold War, and they are less likely to have U.S. bases on their soil.

10. *Atlantic Monthly*, June 2005.

11. Available online at www.whitehouse.gov. Date last accessed October 14, 2007.

12. This statement appeared in an article on the U.S.–Oman Free Trade Agreement, available online at www.heritage.org/Research/MiddleEast/wm1158.cfm. Date last accessed October 14, 2007.

13. Available online at www.globalsecurity.org/military/facility/diego-garcia.htm. Date last accessed October 14, 2007.

14. Conn Hallinan, "Into Africa," *Foreign Policy in Focus*, March 15, 2007, available online at www.fpif.org/fpiftxt/4079. Date last accessed August 10, 2007.

15. *Financial Times*, July 21, 2006; *Business Week*, July 24, 2006.

16. This has not prevented bases from being established in "white nations," of course, including Western and Eastern Europe and Australia, on other grounds.

17. For other studies documenting the effects of and responses to U.S. military bases, beyond this volume, see Simbulan (1985); Hayes, Zarsky, and Bello (1987); Gerson and Birchard (1991); Soroko (2006).

18. On the latter, see *New Statesman*, October 8, 2002.

19. "Global Views 2004: Comparing South Korean and American Public Opinion." Topline data from South Korean Public Survey, September 2004. Chicago: Chicago Council on Foreign Relations, East Asia Institute, p. 12.

20. *Common Dreams*, February 19, 2007, available online at www.commondreams.org/headlines07/0219-02.htm. Date last accessed August 10, 2007.

21. See Lutz (2001) and *Los Angeles Times*, August 25, 2005.
22. The Jakarta Peace Consensus. Electronic document, available online at www.focusweb.org/publications/2003/jakarta-consensus.pdf. Date last accessed April 26, 2005.

References

Aguon, Julian (2006) *Just Left of the Setting Sun* (Tokyo: Blue Ocean Press).

Baker, Anni (2004) *American Soldiers Overseas: The Global Military Presence* (Westport, CT: Praeger).

Blaker, James R. (1990) *United States Overseas Basing: An Anatomy of the Dilemma* (New York: Praeger).

Bloomfield, Lincoln P. (2006) "Politics and Diplomacy of the Global Defense Posture Review," in Carnes Lord (ed.) *Reposturing the Force: U.S. Overseas Presence in the Twenty-First Century* (Newport: Naval War College).

Blum, William (1995) *Killing Hope: U.S. Military and CIA Interventions since World War II* (Monroe, ME: Common Courage Press).

Campbell, Kurt M. and Ward, Celeste Johnson (2003) "New Battle Stations?" *Foreign Affairs*, Vol. 82, No. 5.

Castro, Fanai (2007) "Health Hazards: Guam," in Irving, van der Zeijden and Reyes (2007).

Cheng, Sealing (2003) "'R and R' on a 'Hardship Tour': GIs and Filipina Entertainers in South Korea," National Sexuality Resource Center. Available online at www.nsrc.sfsu.edu. Date last accessed October 14, 2007.

Cliff, Roger and Shapiro, Jeremy (2003) "The Shift to Asia: Implications for U.S. Land Power," in Davis and Shapiro (2003).

Cooley, Alexander (2008) *Base Politics: Domestic Institutional Change and Security Contracts in the American Periphery* (Ithaca, NY: Cornell University Press).

Davis, Lynn E. and Shapiro, Jeremy (eds.) (2003) *The U.S. Army and the New National Security Strategy* (Santa Monica, CA: RAND).

Department of Chamorro Affairs (2002) *Issues in Guam's Political Development: The Chamorro Perspective* (Guam: Department of Chamorro Affairs).

Diaz, Vicente (2001) "Deliberating Liberation Day: Memory, Culture and History in Guam," in Takashi Fujitani, Geoff White and Lisa Yoneyami (eds.) *Perilous Memories: the Asia Pacific War(s)* (Durham: Duke University Press).

Donnelly, Thomas et al. (2000) *Rebuilding America's Defenses: Strategy, Forces and Resources for a New Century*. A Report of The Project for the New American Century. www.newamericancentury.org/RebuildingAmericasDefenses.pdf. Date last accessed October 8, 2007.

Dower, John (1987) *War Without Mercy: Race and Power in the Pacific War* (New York: Pantheon Books).

Erickson, Andrew S. and Mikolay, Justin D. (2006) "A Place *and* a Base: Guam and the American Presence in East Asia," in Carnes Lord (ed.) *Reposturing the Force: U.S. Overseas Presence in the Twenty-First Century* (Newport: Naval War College).

Gerson, Joseph and Birchard, Bruce (1991) *The Sun Never Sets* (Boston: South End Press).

Gusterson, Hugh (1999) "Nuclear weapons and the other in the Western imagination," *Cultural Anthropology*, Vol. 14, No. 1, pp. 111–143.

Harkavy, Robert E. (1982) *Great Power Competition for Overseas Bases: The Geopolitics of Access Diplomacy* (New York: Pergamon Press).

—— (1989) *Bases Abroad: The Global Foreign Military Presence* (Oxford: Oxford University Press).

—— (1999) "Long cycle theory and the hegemonic powers' basing networks," *Political Geography*, Vol. 18, No. 8, pp. 941–972.

—— (2006) "Thinking about Basing," in Carnes Lord (ed.) *Reposturing the Force: U.S. Overseas Presence in the Twenty-First Century* (Newport: Naval War College).

Hayes, Peter, Zarsky, Lyuba, and Bello, Walden (1987) *American Lake: Nuclear Peril in the Pacific* (New York: Penguin).

Henry, Ryan (2006) "Transforming the U.S. Global Defense Posture," in Carnes Lord (ed.) *Reposturing the Force: U.S. Overseas Presence in the Twenty-First Century* (Newport: Naval War College).

Inoue, Masamichi S. (2004) "'We Are Okinawans But of a Different Kind': New/Old Social Movements and the U.S. Military in Okinawa," *Current Anthropology*, Vol. 45, No. 1.

Irving, Sarah, van der Zeijden, Wilbert and Reyes, Oscar (2007) *Outposts of Empire: The Case against Foreign Military Bases* (Amsterdam: Transnational Institute).

Johnson, Chalmers (2000) *Blowback* (New York: Henry Holt).

—— (2004) *The Sorrows of Empire: Militarism, Secrecy, and the End of the Republic* (New York: Metropolitan).

Kennedy, Paul M. (1987) *The Rise and Fall of Great Powers: Economic Change and Military Conflict from 1500 to 2000* (New York: Random House).

Lindsay-Poland, John (2003) *Emperors in the Jungle: The Hidden History of the U.S. in Panama* (Durham: Duke University Press).

Lens, Sidney (1987) *Permanent War: The Militarization of America* (New York: Schocken).

Lumpe, Lora (2002) *U.S. Foreign Military Training: Global Reach, Global Power, and Oversight Issues.* Foreign Policy in Focus Special Report, May.

Lutz, Catherine (2001) *Homefront: A Military City and the American Twentieth Century* (Boston: Beacon Press).

McCaffrey, Katherine T. (2002) *Military Power and Popular Protest: The U.S. Navy in Vieques, Puerto Rico* (New Brunswick, NJ: Rutgers University Press).

Magdoff, Harry (2003) *Imperialism Without Colonies* (New York: Monthly Review Press).

—— Foster, John Bellamy, McChesney, Robert W. and Sweezy, Paul (2002) "U.S. Military Bases and Empire," *Monthly Review*, Vol. 53, No. 10.

Overseas Basing Commission (2005) "Commission on Review of the Overseas Military Facility Structure of the United States: Report to the President and to Congress," August 15.

Robinson, Ronald, Gallagher, John and Denny, Alice (1961) *Africa and the Victorians: The Official Mind of Imperialism* (London: Macmillan).

Roncken, Theo (2004) *La Lucha Contra Las Drogas y la Proyeccion Militar de Estados Unidos: Centros Operativos de Avandzada en America Latina y el Caribe* (Quito, Ecuador: Abya Yala).

Scanlan, Tom, ed. (1963) *Army Times Guide to Army Posts* (Harrisburg: Stackpole).

Sherry, Michael S. (1995) *In the Shadow of War: The United States Since the 1930s* (New Haven: Yale University Press).

Shy, John (1976) *A People Armed and Numerous: Reflections on the Military Struggle for American Independence* (New York: Oxford University Press).

Simbulan, Roland (1985) *The Bases of Our Insecurity: A Study of the U.S. Military Bases in the Philippines* (Manila, Philippines: BALAI Fellowship).

Smith, Neil (2003) *American Empire: Roosevelt's Geographer and the Prelude to Globalization* (Berkeley: University of California Press).

Soroko, Jennifer (2006) "Water at the intersection of militarization, development, and democracy on Kwajalein Atoll, in the Republic of the Marshall Islands," MA thesis, Department of Anthropology, Brown University.

Sturdevant, Saundra Pollock and Stoltzfus, Brenda (1993) *Let the Good Times Roll: Prostitution and the U.S. Military in Asia* (New York: New Press).

Theweleit, Klaus (1987) *Male Fantasies, vol. 1: Women, Floods, Bodies, History*, trans. Steven Conway (Minneapolis: University of Minnesota Press).

U.S. Defense Department (2004) "Strengthening U.S. Global Defense Posture," report to Congress (Washington, D.C.).

Van Evera, Stephen (2001) Militarism (Cambridge, MA: MIT). Available online at http://web.mit.edu/polisci/research/vanevera/militarism.pdf. Date last accessed October 8, 2007.

Wallerstein, Immanuel (2003) *The Decline of American Power* (New York: New Press).

Weigley, Russell Frank (1984) *History of the United States Army* (Bloomington, IN: Indiana University Press).

Weiner, Tim (1990) *Blank Check: The Pentagon's Black Budget* (NY: Warner Books).

Part I

Mapping U.S. Power

1

U.S. FOREIGN MILITARY BASES AND MILITARY COLONIALISM: PERSONAL AND ANALYTICAL PERSPECTIVES

Joseph Gerson

In May 2005, with more than 100,000 U.S. troops at war in Iraq as they sought to enforce the U.S. military occupation of that oil-rich nation, and with confrontations growing over North Korean and Iranian nuclear programs, the *Washington Post* carried a disturbing report about U.S. preparations for its next war. In response to Secretary of Defense Donald Rumsfeld's top secret "Interim Global Strike Alert Order," the Pentagon's Strategic Command had, it was reported, developed a "full-spectrum global strike ... capability to deliver rapid, extended range precision kinetic (nuclear and conventional) and non-kinetic (elements of space and information operations) effects in support of theater and national objectives" (Arkin 2005). In plain English, this meant that even as U.S. forces were bogged down in Iraq, the Pentagon claimed to have established the ability to launch offensive military attacks – "conventional" or nuclear – "in any dark corner of the world" including North Korea, Iran, or China "at any moment's notice."

"American imperial power," former National Security Adviser Zbigniew Brzezinski once wrote, derives "in large measure from superior organization, from the ability to mobilize vast economic and technological resources promptly for military purposes" (Brzezinski 1998). Like the wars the United States has fought to create and then to maintain its global and regional hegemonies, from World War II and the Bushes' Iraq wars, to Vietnam, Nicaragua, and Kosovo, the Pentagon's twenty-first century "global strike" doctrine depends on the organization of military violence supported by a historically unprecedented U.S. global infrastructure of foreign military bases. Without its foreign fortresses, the United States could not have been an "Asian power," or established hegemony in the Middle East – "the jugular vein" of global capitalism. If U.S. military forces had not guaranteed the survival of the Saudi monarchy, and maintained bases near Mecca and Medina, cities revered by Moslems, the world might never have heard of Osama Bin Laden. September 11 might still be remembered as the day Chilean president Salvador Allende was overthrown and died in General Pinochet's CIA-backed coup d'état. Similarly, the Monroe Doctrine that declares all of Latin America and the Caribbean to be within the U.S. "sphere of interest" could not have been enforced without repeated invasions and other acts of subversion over almost two centuries.

Even as it suffers setbacks in the Middle East and Central Asia, the U.S. goal is to colonize time as well as space in order to guarantee U.S. military, economic, and political dominance for the century to come. This military colonialism claims its tolls of human lives and hopes, the environment, sovereignty, and national independence even without shots being fired, missiles launched, or countries invaded. More than 200 years ago the U.S. *Declaration of Independence* decried the "abuses and usurpations" caused by the "Standing Armies" that King George III "kept among us, in times of peace." Today the "abuses and usurpations" are far more intrusive and destructive than those that fueled the U.S. war of independence. They include more than rape, murder, sexual harassment, robbery, other common crimes, seizure of people's lands, destruction of property, and the cultural imperialism that have accompanied foreign armies since time immemorial. They now include terrorizing jet blasts of frequent low altitude and night-landing exercises, helicopters and warplanes crashing into homes and schools, and the poisoning of environments and communities with military toxics; and they transform "host" communities into targets for genocidal nuclear as well as for "conventional" attacks.

As Cynthia Enloe (1989) helped us understand, U.S. military bases and their "host" communities are complex and dynamic social systems that extend beyond their gates. Inside there is housing for the troops and their dependants. There are schools, shops, bowling alleys, and movie theaters as well as firing ranges, runways, and ammunition depots. To greater and lesser degrees bases engage the people of "host" communities, serving as sources of employment, goods, culture, and more.

But "abuses and usurpations" are essential to these complex social relations. Take Kin Town in Okinawa, which abuts the Marine Base at Camp Hansen. Its small commercial district is marked by seedy restaurants and businesses that serve GIs. Before the dollar's decline, prostitution was rife, and before the nonviolent Okinawan uprising in 1995 and 1996 that forced the United States to commit itself to reducing the size of its "footprint" on Okinawa, the explosions of live-fire artillery exercises regularly reverberated across this otherwise quiet community, occasionally landing in people's homes, farm land, and roads.

Sixty years after the United States first occupied Okinawa, and a decade and a half after the end of the Cold War, something remarkable, but largely unnoticed, occurred in Kin. On the day that baseball practice resumed in schools across Japan, I found myself in a schoolyard, waiting to meet an authority on the impacts of the nearby bases on the community. Children and teenagers were taking their turns fielding ground balls and taking their first swings in batting practice. But, as they worked at developing their athletic skills and strength, the hillsides echoed with the gunfire of marines training for war, and the children and coaches continued baseball practice as if nothing unusual or dangerous was happening.

Marine gunfire has become a part of Kin Town's natural environment and daily life.

Military colonialism, hard and soft, persists in Okinawa and elsewhere in other nearly invisible ways. A century ago European powers consolidated their colonial power over and continued privileged presence in East Asian nations through "unequal treaties," such as those dictated to Japan, Korea, China, and Indochina. With Japan's brutal invasions of these colonies and with the destruction of colonialism's remaining foundations in the course of World War II and the Chinese revolution, these unequal treaties were consigned to the dustbin of history. But, in the immediate aftermath of the war, the unequal treaties returned in a new guise: military alliances and Status of Forces Agreements imposed by the United States on Japan and on many of these formerly colonized nations which have provided the "legal" foundations for the continued presence of U.S. "standing armies" for the past six decades.

The "soft" side of military colonialism expresses itself in food, cultural tastes, and markets. Inexpensive and plentiful food on and around U.S. bases in Okinawa – especially during the 25-year formal military occupation (1945–72) – permeated Okinawan culture, changing tastes and creating markets for companies like McDonalds, Burger King, and Mattel Toys. Until recently Okinawans, who "host" three-quarters of U.S. troops based in Japan on 0.6 percent of the nation's territory, enjoyed the longest life expectancies of any Japanese, with the primary cause being Okinawans' unique diet. Today in Naha, Okinawa's capital, people spend 46 percent more on hamburgers than people do in other Japanese prefectural capitals. They spend 60 percent more on bacon, and 300 percent more on processed meats, while spending 49 percent less on salad and 71 percent less on sushi. Okinawan men are paying the greatest price. While Okinawan women remain the longest lived in Japan, Okinawan men's longevity has fallen to 26th among Japan's 47 prefectures (Onishi 2004). Military colonialism brings structural violence.

U.S. military colonialism is hardly limited to Okinawa. Despite its reputation as a tourist haven, one quarter of Hawai'i's main island, Oahu, is occupied with U.S. military bases, much of it, as Kyle Kajihiro (this volume) shows, on Native Hawai'ian sacred lands. Elsewhere Uzbeks complained that "security" near U.S. bases created in their country to launch the 2001 invasion of Afghanistan was more repressive than it was under Soviet rule. In Scandinavia, young activists have been discovering new illegal intelligence bases in Norway and a spy base in Sweden that violates Stockholm's long honored neutrality. And Guantánamo Bay in Cuba has become a U.S. military prison colony renowned for torture.

Learning about the scale and impact of U.S. foreign military bases is no easy task. The Pentagon doesn't go out of its way to inform the U.S. or "host" nation publics about the number, missions, or impacts of its web of foreign fortresses that surpass those created by Genghis Khan, Julius Caesar, Alexander the Great, or Queen Victoria. Progressive institutions and movements with their limited resources are already overextended as they labor to anticipate, prevent, or overcome the effects of empire, from its assaults on the New Deal and Great Society safety nets to the onslaughts of globalizing corporate capitalism and the next U.S. invasion.

I had the good fortune of being introduced to the history and roles of U.S. military bases while studying the history of U.S. diplomacy as an undergraduate being prepared for the U.S. Foreign Service. Professor Jules Davids explained that in the 1890s men like Theodore Roosevelt, Captain Alfred Mahan, and Henry Cabot Lodge had perceived the possibility of the United States replacing Britain as the world's dominant power and then built the blue water navy needed to do it. Professor Davids described how the navies and merchant steamships of that era were fueled by coal and required coaling stations in strategic locations if they were to traverse large bodies of water like the Pacific Ocean. He went on to explain how the founders of the United States' overseas empire laid the foundations for conquering markets in China and Latin America and for challenging its colonial competitors with their conquests in the Spanish–American War at the cost of hundreds of thousands of lives – especially in the Philippines where nationalist resistance was particularly strong. Davids explained that it was under the cover of the Spanish–American War that McKinley finally moved to annex Hawai'i, after being on the military's wish list since 1873.

Although I had worked with exiled and other Filipinos working to free their country of both the Marcos dictatorship and U.S. bases, the scale and impacts of U.S. bases did not penetrate my consciousness until the early 1980s, when I participated in a major nuclear disarmament conference in Hiroshima. There, in addition to being exposed to and devastated by what U.S. nuclear weapons had done to fellow human beings and to two cities, I was amazed to learn that the United States still had (and has) more than 100 military bases and installations across that island nation.

I was shaken by Okinawan and other Japanese descriptions of what it means to live in communities routinely terrorized by low altitude and night landing exercises, by crimes committed by GIs that regularly go unpunished, and about how people's land had been seized to make way for U.S. bases and how these bases block economic and social development. I was upset by reports of the pervasiveness of prostitution and of seemingly endless sexual harassment and violence near U.S. bases. People shared their agonizing memories of military accidents: planes falling into schools, drunken military drivers who caused deadly accidents, and the destruction of people's homes and property during military exercises.

People also spoke of their shame at being complicit in U.S. wars and aggressions, especially the savaging of Vietnam. U.S. bombers and warships were launched from their communities, and much of Okinawa still serves as a jungle warfare training base. As people scarred by war and massive aerial bombardments, they could identify with the pain, suffering, and losses of other innocent Asians terrorized by the tsunami of U.S. bombs and military might. I also learned about the political context: the unequal U.S.–Japan Military Alliance that was secretly imposed by the United States on the Japanese people as the price for ending the formal military occupation in 1952, and the resulting loss of national sovereignty. Left unsaid was how the U.S. bases in Japan – some of which are still located in the nation's capital – are designed to contain Japanese militarism which the United States has re-legitimated and revitalized over the decades as part of Washington's global Cold War and post-Cold War strategies.

That conference also included representatives of the Guam Landowners Association. Their presentation featured two maps they had brought with them. One showed the locations of the island's best fishing grounds, its best agricultural land, and its best drinking water. The other showed the locations of the U.S. military bases, installations, and military exercises. The two maps were identical.

Filipinos had also come to the conference, not only to share what they knew about U.S. nuclear weapons based in and transiting through their country, but also to urge leading peace activists from around the world to find ways to act in solidarity with their struggle to end U.S. military colonialism and the deadly Marcos dictatorship.

European peace activists at the conference who had come from Britain, Germany, and Russia were terrified by the Reagan administration's plans to deploy nuclear armed Tomahawk Cruise and Pershing II missiles in bases across Europe. The Pershing IIs were designed to destroy the Kremlin and "decapitate" Soviet leadership from its military within eight minutes of the missiles being launched. This, in turn, was leading Moscow to adopt the policy of "launch on warning," in which machines would automatically send Soviet (now Russian) missiles in a retaliatory attack within minutes of detecting incoming missiles. Launch on warning still prevails, making Europe and all of humanity vulnerable to human miscalculations and technological glitches, including confusing the launch of a Norwegian weather satellite or flocks of geese for incoming missiles. Global efforts from women's encampments outside U.S. bases in Britain, the Nuclear Weapons Freeze movement in the United States, and enlightened diplomacy by Soviet president Mikhail Gorbachev prevented the deployment of the Pershing IIs, but the struggle against U.S. nuclear weapons and bases in Europe still continues (see Heller and Lammerant, this volume).

Since then, it has been my humbling, sometimes painful, and often inspiring privilege to meet and to learn from people who have been victimized by and who are resisting U.S. military bases in many countries from Iceland to Guam, from Korea to Ecuador.

Each case is different. Each base brings calamitous "abuses and usurpations." And each brings resistance.

Etched in my memory is the face of an Okinawan woman who described how, when she was a child, her entire generation of girls – now middle-aged women – was terrorized by the brutal GI rape and killing of a young girl. Other faces are there too: the agony of a young Korean describing life within and around the Maehyang-ri bombing range and how people living there continued to suffer frequent live-fire practice bombings in what was for them the never-ending Korean War. There is the memory of another intense young Korean who insisted that I look at a CD his organization had made about Shin Hyo-soon and Shim Mi-sun, two young schoolgirls who were killed by a U.S. tank as they walked to a party – a military crime, like so many others, for which no one in the U.S. military was ever held legally accountable.

There are also more hopeful life-affirming memories, such as the image of older Okinawan farmers – each wearing a headband declaring that "Life is Sacred" – conducting a sit-in outside the courthouse in Naha, demanding the return of their land.

Bases bring insecurity: the loss of self-determination, human rights, and sovereignty. They degrade the culture, values, health, and environment of host nations – and of the United States. And, they make catastrophic wars possible.

Missions of Bases

Catherine Lutz's introduction outlines some prevailing myths about U.S. military bases. Their actual purposes, succinctly listed, include the following:

- They reinforce the status quo. For example, U.S. bases in the Middle East (including secret bases in Israel) and Central Asia are designed to ensure continued U.S. privileged access to, and control of, those regions' oil. U.S. forces in Europe and Japan serve to maintain the hierarchy of power and privilege created as a result of World War II.

- They encircle enemies. This was the case with the Soviet Union and China during the Cold War and it continues with China, which is seen as the emerging rival power that is most likely to become a "strategic competitor." U.S. bases in Korea, Japan, Guam, Australia, and in Central Asia, augmented by access agreements with the Philippines and Singapore, and the emerging U.S. alliance with India, are all designed to contain China. Another dimension of encirclement is so-called "missile defenses" – which the Chinese describe as the shield being built to complement Washington's first-strike nuclear swords. In addition to their deployments at sea and in space, missile defense weapons and support systems are being deployed in Greenland, Poland, the Czech Republic, Israel, Korea, and Japan. Encirclement is also a role played by U.S. bases in Europe, the Mediterranean, and the Middle East.
- U.S. bases serve interventionist aircraft carriers, destroyers, nuclear armed submarines, and other U.S. warships. This includes bases in Spain, Italy, Israel, Bahrain, Qatar, and Japan, and "access" agreements in Israel, the Philippines, Singapore, and other countries.
- Bases in Germany and Britain have long served as training centers for U.S. forces, as was long the case in Vieques for bombardiers. Jungle war-fighting, live-fire, low-altitude, and other training continues across Okinawa and elsewhere in Japan and is being brought to Guam.
- Bases can function as jumping-off points for U.S. foreign military interventions. With NATO's new "out-of-area operations" doctrine, the United States has reinforced its ability to use bases across Europe for launching attacks and wars against North African, Middle Eastern, and Central Asian nations. Bases in Okinawa and elsewhere in Japan were essential to the U.S. wars in Korea, Vietnam, and the Persian Gulf. This is also a function of the U.S. bases in Kuwait, Bahrain, Ecuador, and Honduras.
- Bases facilitate C4I, command, control, computers, communications, and intelligence for both "conventional"

and nuclear war. This includes the use of space for spying and actual warfare, as we saw in the wars against Serbia, Afghanistan, and Iraq. U.S. bases in Britain, Italy, Scandinavia, Australia, Japan, Qatar, among others, serve these functions.

- In Eastern Europe, Central Asia, the Middle East, Africa, and Latin America, U.S. bases are increasingly being used to secure and protect oil and gas pipelines, ensuring fuel for the U.S. economy and its war machines while attempting to control the energy supplies of allied and competitor nations.

- U.S. bases serve to control or influence the governments and political dynamics of host nations. Japan, Korea (where U.S. military forces were deeply involved in successive military coups), Germany, Saudi Arabia, and Iraq begin the list.

- As in the cases of Tajikistan and Iceland, small bases and installations have served as a way to "show the U.S. flag," demonstrating the United States' commitment to be taken seriously as a power in a particular country or region.

- Guantánamo in Cuba and Bagram Air Base in Afghanistan have served as notorious torture centers. It is believed that Diego Garcia and U.S. bases in Europe have served as transit bases for the secret U.S. prison and interrogation system.

- While it is too early to call them military bases, U.S. military power has moved to dominate space, as detailed in the Pentagon's "Vision 2020." Tomorrow we may well see a base on the moon for war fighting on earth, to control the moon–earth "space well," and as a base for the colonization of the solar system.

Twenty-first Century Contexts

In what the Bush II White House described as "the most comprehensive restructuring of U.S. military bases overseas since the end of the Korean War," Secretary Rumsfeld launched the reconfiguration and revitalization of U.S. forward military deployments and their global military infrastructure.[1] It was explained that the redesign was undertaken to address the challenges of the post-Cold War and post-9/11 world in which terrorists, nuclear, and near-nuclear powers threaten the U.S. "homeland." This was true in part, but the restructuring is better understood as a pillar of U.S. ambitions to threaten and fight offensive wars to consolidate the U.S. global empire into and through the power vacuums left in the wake of the Soviet Union's collapse and to ensure China's integration into U.S.- and Japanese-dominated systems.

While the reckless unilateralism of the Bush–Cheney administration was widely regarded as a radical departure from more complex and nuanced methods of maintaining the empire, it reflected more continuity than change. During World War II, U.S. strategic planners envisioned "the Grand Area," a single global market economy that would be dominated by the United States. That dream was frustrated by the rise of Soviet power and the Cold War. With their collapse, the way appeared to open for the establishment of that global empire in the form of "the arrangement for the twenty-first century."

Following the initial uncertainty that accompanied the collapse of the Berlin Wall – a time when most military alliances had lost their *raisons d'être* and when hopes that military budgets could be transformed into "peace dividends" were widespread – the first Bush administration responded to Iraq's invasion of Kuwait with the Desert Storm war. Mobilizing popular and global support by stressing the illegality of Saddam Hussein's invasion of the oil-rich sheikdom, Washington's goal was to create a "new world order" in which "what we say goes." The first rationale embraced and reinforced the United Nations' Charter, but the second reflected Washington's whims and the Pentagon's power, replacing international law as the new foundation of international relations.

Yet, even this was not entirely new. Desert Storm was in large measure a reaffirmation of what Noam Chomsky has called "Political Axiom #1": that the United States will never permit its enemies, *nor its allies*, to gain independent access to Middle East oil, which Winston Churchill called "The Prize" (Chomsky 1978: 27; Yergin 1991).

In addition to being designed to drive Saddam Hussein's forces from Kuwait, the war was to serve as a demonstration war. The conflagration in which one of the Arab world's most advanced nations was, as the United Nations later reported, bombed back into the "pre-industrial age," with hundreds of thousands of people ultimately dying from its after-effects, was also inflicted to serve as a warning to other nations, and even to China, that this would be their fate if they challenged U.S. hegemony.

Preparations for the war also served as the occasion to discipline U.S. allies. With Desert Storm, NATO was turned toward "out of area" operations, with bases in Britain and Germany used as staging areas and jumping-off points. Even placid Shannon Airport in Dublin was forced to accommodate U.S. warplanes to remind the Irish that they live in what Zbigniew Brzezinski (1998) called a "vassal state." The United States successfully insisted that $13 billion and the use of U.S. bases from Okinawa to Hokkaido for the war were not sufficient Japanese contributions. In the future, Japan would be expected to "show its flag" by deploying its troops to war zones in violation of its war-renouncing constitution.

Similarly, in North Africa and the Middle East, the war was used to exercise formal and informal alliances, to re-legitimate the presence and use of U.S. military bases in Egypt and the Persian Gulf, and to build new military bases in strategically important Saudi Arabia, Djibouti, Qatar, and Kuwait. With the nuclear threats made by the United States and Britain during the Desert Shield phase of the war and with the encirclement of Iraq with as many as 700 nuclear weapons to back up those threats, the first Bush administration attempted to re-legitimate the U.S. nuclear arsenal and the practice of nuclear blackmail – at least in elite U.S. circles – for the post-Cold War period (Bundy 1991: 83; Peden, Butcher, and Plesch 1990). Essential pillars of these threats and those in the run-up to the 2003 U.S. invasion of Iraq were the military bases in Britain, Belgium, Holland, Spain, Japan, and other nations where U.S. nuclear weapons are stored, where U.S. nuclear-capable ships are based or make port calls, and which host nuclear-war-fighting C4I functions.

Compared to the Bush administrations, the Clinton 1990s are often thought of as a relatively peaceful era for the United States, if not for Rwanda, the Congo, or Haiti. In truth, however, the Clinton administration's "bridge to the twenty-first century" was the span linking one aggressive Bush administration with another. In Europe, Assistant Secretary of State Strobe Talbott and the U.S. military did their best to re-divide and contain the continent (Talbott 2002). They pressed for the inclusion of nearly all of Eastern Europe into an enlarged NATO to augment U.S. interventionary power targeted against the Middle East, Russia, and other successor states of the Soviet Union and to counter growing French and German ambitions. The United States led NATO in fighting the Kosovo war against Serbia in violation of the United Nations Charter, and the Pentagon emerged from the war with a new and massive military base, Camp Bondsteel, the first of what the Pentagon hoped would become a new system of U.S. Eastern European military bases.

The Bush II administration came to power with the commitment to impose what Vice President Cheney called "the arrangement for the twenty-first century" to ensure that "the United States will continue to be the dominant political, economic, and military power in the world." The so-called "Revolution in Military Affairs" – the near complete integration of information technologies into U.S. war-fighting doctrines and its air-, land-, sea-, and space-based systems, was envisioned as an essential pillar of "the arrangement."

Even before the September 11 attacks, the administration was preparing popular opinion for a more aggressive military. In an interview with the *New Yorker*, Deputy National Security Advisor Stephen Hadley was clear that the United States would "have the military ability to act at any time, anywhere, in defense of what it sees as its global interests." As Deputy Assistant Secretary of Defense Andrew Hoehm later observed, "Transformation is more than just new capabilities, inherent in transformation is a physical change of the global military posture." The "new world" would transcend traditional, and what the administration saw as outmoded, concepts of national sovereignty (Lemann 2002).

Rumsfeld's Restructuring

Pre-inaugural reports in 2000, prepared under the direction of (later to be) Assistant Secretary of State Armitage and Ambassador Khalilzad, recommended "diversification" of U.S. military bases: reconfiguring the bases' Cold War global architecture to meet the demands of twenty-first-century war fighting and intimidation. Their plans, as implemented, called for the withdrawal of two army divisions from Germany and 12,000 troops from South Korea to "afford maximum flexibility in sending forces to the Middle East, Central Asia and other potential battlegrounds" (Gordon 2004). Over the next decade, some bases will be closed, some merged. But, the consistent goal will be to maximize U.S. war-fighting capabilities by increasing the agility, flexibility, and speed of U.S. fighting forces. With "diversification" of U.S. forces in East Asia and the Pacific, China will be more completely encircled. The likely number of U.S. casualties in a second Korean War will be reduced. And U.S. military power in the Middle East and the increasingly important oil-rich recesses of Central Asia is to be augmented.

When Spain precipitously withdrew from the shrinking U.S. coalition in Iraq, Madrid was punished by identifying Italy, not Spain, as the new home for the Navy's European headquarters, which was to be moved from Britain closer to the Middle East's oil reserves. With the Fulda Gap in Germany no longer a geopolitical center of the struggle for world power, the lion's share of the U.S. bases were to be closed and troops would be withdrawn from Germany. Although the United States' major air base at Ramstein would remain, other U.S. forces were to be transferred from Germany to Romania, Bulgaria, and Turkey. This movement of U.S. forces reflects more than simply moving U.S. forces closer to potential battlefields; it is also to ensure that "Old Europe" cannot inhibit Washington's use of force when it next opts for unilateral attack.

To the south, under cover of preparations for the Iraq war, the Pentagon removed one of the precipitating causes of the 9/11 attacks: the majority of U.S. troops and bases in Saudi Arabia, which many Moslems experienced as sullying Islam's holiest land. These troops, bases, and functions were transferred to Qatar, Kuwait, Djibouti, and Bahrain. The Bush–Cheney agenda for Iraq was not limited to gaining greater influence over its vast oil reserves, which serve U.S. "national interests" by fueling the U.S. economy and providing a means to leverage accommodations from Saudi Arabia and OPEC. With bases like Camp Victory in Baghdad, which hosts two strategically important headquarters and more than 14,000 troops and 13 other "enduring" U.S. military bases, Washington's military planners envisioned Iraq as a bastion of U.S. military power in the Middle East, which will also, for decades to come, augment Washington's ability to project force into Central Asia.

In the Asia Pacific, the news is that now "all of the Pentagon road maps lead to Guam," which is to "become one of two or three major hubs of U.S. activity in the world" (Gerson 2004). Japan, which has been the keystone of U.S. Asia Pacific power since 1945, is being given an augmented role which is being negotiated between the United States and Japan. As part of the decade-old effort to pacify popular opinion in Okinawa, the Pentagon's plan calls for either moving Futenma Air Base, which has long tormented Ginowan City which surrounds it, to a more remote site on the island or integrating it into the vast Kadena Air Base. It also calls for moving 8,000 marines based in Okinawa to Guam. Meanwhile, a number of command functions, a second aircraft carrier, and other forces are to be transferred from the United States' west coast and Guam to Japan, bringing them closer to China and North Korea.

South Korea is being pressed to assume greater "burden sharing," not only on the Korean Peninsula, but globally, as was the case with Seoul's grudging deployment of 3,000 South Korean soldiers to Iraq and a smaller deployment to Afghanistan. As part of the "diversification," U.S. troops are also being redeployed from the Demilitarized Zone along the 38th parallel – perhaps the most militarized piece of real estate in the world – to less vulnerable bases south of Seoul.

Elsewhere in the Asia Pacific region, U.S. bases in Australia are being augmented. The "Visiting Forces" and access agreements with the Philippines and Singapore are being expanded, and Indian Ocean tsunami relief operations in 2005 helped to open the way for U.S. forces to return to Thailand and for greater cooperation with the Indonesian military. The Philippine press reports that U.S. military officials are in process of trying to reestablish bases in the former colony.

The Bush administration's invasion of Afghanistan opened the way for U.S. bases in Central Asia where, as General Wald of the European Command put it, "In the Caspian Sea you have a large mineral [i.e. petroleum] reserve. We want to assure the long term viability of those resources" (Klare 2005). Following the September 11, 2001, terrorist attacks on New York and the Pentagon, the Bush administration used its "for us or against us" doctrine to force dictatorships in Pakistan, Uzbekistan, Kyrgyzstan, and Tajikistan to surrender sovereignty and to permit construction of what the Pentagon hoped would become permanent U.S. military bases. Bases were established and enlarged in Afghanistan, Uzbekistan, and Kyrgyzstan – while access and overflight agreements were negotiated with Kazakhstan, and Tajikistan Turkmenistan. These were designed not only to keep the (repressive) peace within the region, but to augment the encirclement of both China and Iran.

Years after ousting the Taliban from power, U.S. bases remain in Kyrgyzstan and Afghanistan.

Africa, which the Pentagon expects to become the source of up to 25 percent of the U.S. oil supply by 2015, has been the focus of a major U.S. military build-up, reinforced by the newly created Africa Command. With bases in Algeria and Djibouti and access agreements in Morocco and Egypt, the new focus is south of the Sahara, where a "family" of military bases is being created. This "family" includes major installations for brigades of up to 5,000 troops "that could be robustly used" (Schmitt 2003). The family will also include "lightly equipped bases available in crises to special forces or Marines." "Host" nations for the new family are to include Cameroon, Guinea (which has also been targeted as a major source of oil), Mali, and São Tomé and Principe, with Senegal and Uganda providing refueling installations for the air force.

And, Washington has not forgotten what used to be its own "backyard," Latin America. Although the Puerto Rican people's 50-year struggle to close the base at Vieques has prevailed, new military bases are now sprouting across Andean nations, and the United States is increasingly militarizing the Caribbean, as Lindsay-Poland's and McCaffrey's chapters detail.

The "restructuring" of the United States' unprecedented infrastructure of global military power is being built on several conceptual pillars, foremost among them agility, flexibility, and speed. In addition to training U.S. forces and developing new weapons that are "fast, small, dispersed" and which can be easily "decentralized," the Pentagon is working to "reconfigure" the locations and functions of its bases, installations, and access agreements to serve its new priorities.

Military planners want total "freedom of action." If Germany or another state is reluctant to permit U.S. use of military bases and installations in a given war, the Pentagon wants to be sure that bases in other countries will be immediately available. The plan for South Korea is illustrative of the multiple purposes it wants a greater number of bases to be able to play. While the primary role of U.S. forces in the Republic of Korea will continue to be to help ensure that North Korea is not tempted to take reckless military actions, their presence and the ability to threaten their complete withdrawal will be used to influence South Korean foreign and domestic policies. Despite objections raised by former president Roh Moo Hyun, U.S. troops deployed in South Korea can be used during confrontations and possible conflicts with China and elsewhere in East Asia. And, as in the case of their being dispatched to invade and occupy Iraq, U.S. South Korean-based forces are to be available for interventions as far afield as the Persian Gulf. At considerable expense, bases in Japan, Ecuador, Guinea, Iraq, Afghanistan, Romania, and elsewhere are being similarly prepared for multi-tasking.

Speed has been as important as flexibility. With more troops and major bases being positioned closer to anticipated war zones, with new technologies, and with new "lily pad" bases, the Pentagon is preparing to strike before the target of its attack can prepare its defenses or a long-term strategy of resistance. The perhaps unwarranted hope is that "shock and awe" will work in future wars.

Ending "Abuses and Usurpations"

How will we end the plagues of imperial wars made possible by Washington's global infrastructure of foreign military bases and the "abuses and usurpations" that inevitably accompany its foreign legions? How do people in the United States who believe that freedom and security are essential human rights make common cause and act in solidarity with people in other nations who are struggling to liberate their nations from U.S. military colonialism?

There are no easy answers, but we do well to remember the words of the abolitionist leader Frederick Douglass, who taught that power yields nothing without a struggle. Such struggle takes place at many levels of human activity: political, intellectual cultural, economic, and spiritual in addition to what are usually the pyrrhic victories of armed resistance.

The Roman, Spanish, and most British legions came home with the decline and fall of their empires. Like the inspiring victory of the people of Vieques in Puerto Rico, we may succeed in time by focusing on the withdrawal of particular bases, but the 100 years to win true independence and the withdrawal of Subic and Clark bases, as well as the struggles of the Okinawan and Japanese movements may provide a better model: integrating anti-bases campaigns into broader struggles for democracy and national self-determination.

It should be borne in mind that the United States is increasingly an isolated and unpopular nation that depends on European, Asian, and oil-rich Middle Eastern nations to maintain its empire. Both the national debt which is subsidized by Japanese, Chinese, and other nations' massive purchase of U.S. Treasury bonds, and the United States' seemingly irreversible balance of payments deficits are placing hundreds of billions of dollars in foreign hands. Wealth is power, and in time states and political forces seeking to contain or offset U.S. power will decide when it is time to literally cash in their chips. At some point, as the former head of the Dutch Foreign Ministry told me shortly before the United States invaded Iraq or He Fan of the Chinese Academy of Social Sciences has advised, some of these nations will conclude that they have had enough. By selling off their bonds or selectively disinvesting in U.S.-based multinational corporations, Asian or Middle Eastern nations could at the very least send a powerful signal to the U.S. establishment. They might even have the power to bring down the U.S. house of cards, much as states, private institutions, and individuals did in the 1970s and 1980s to help end South African apartheid. Of course, there would be negative consequences for all involved, but the results can be liberating as well as painful.

In building the political forces within the United States and internationally to win withdrawal of U.S. bases, we should not underestimate the importance of intellectual and analytical work that can be done by scholars, journalists, and community-based activists. Few in U.S. academic circles outside of the war colleges, and certainly not the wider public, have any good sense of the scale, roles, and impacts of U.S. foreign military bases or the need to repatriate them. The foundation of any political movement is knowledge and information that touch people's moral imaginations, that contribute to popular understandings of the world and how it operates, and that support or lead to action. Hopefully, like the largely invisible and demanding intellectual work that prepared the way for the Civil Rights struggles of the 1950s and 1960s, the Vietnam-era peace and feminist movements, and the Nuclear Freeze and Central America solidarity movements of the 1980s, scholarly and analytical work being done today will fuel popular movements in abused host nations and open the way for U.S. Americans to assume our roles in bringing our troops, bases, and war machines home and restoring our respect for other peoples and nations.

As this book's introduction notes, recent years have witnessed a growing wave of anti-bases education and organizing around the world. Most impressive is the global anti-bases network that began in East Asia under the tutelage of Focus on the Global South, an international NGO based in Bangkok, which is devoted to "development, policy research, analysis and action." Beginning with a small meeting in Seoul in 1999, anti-bases activists from the Philippines, Thailand, Japan, Korea, and the United States began sharing information and exploring possible collaborations. Subsequent meetings, involving activists from as many as 35 nations, were held in Jakarta and Seoul, and World Social Forums in Mumbai, India and Porto Alegre, Brazil, all of which built toward the founding of the International Network for the Abolition of Foreign Military Bases during a 2007 assembly welcomed by the anti-bases Correa government in Quito and Manta, Ecuador. The Network serves organizations, movements, and individuals across the world, and is beginning to provide support for local struggles and national movements. Its listserves and web pages are a constantly updated source of information for activists, scholars, and the media, and its International Organizing Committee is charged with reaching out to movements not yet associated with the network, establishing and deepening strategic alliances with other movements and institutions, and generating resources to build the global movement.

The Asia Pacific region continues to be the center of the most steadfast nonviolent resistance to the U.S. bases. The candlelight vigils protesting the killings of Shin Hyo-soon and Shim Mi Sun and the refusal of U.S. authorities to hold anyone accountable transformed Korea's political landscape and played a major role in the election of human rights lawyer Roh Moo Hyun as president from 2003 to 2008. A new and more independent generation, which looks critically at the continued U.S. military presence in Korea, has assumed power.

In Okinawa, decades of popular opposition are forcing the Pentagon to draw down the numbers of troops based there. The courageous resistance of the people of the small remote town of Nago in northern Okinawa to the construction of a new air base on a reef just beyond Haneko Beach has placed numerous roadblocks in the way of Washington's and Tokyo's paths to reconsolidating the U.S. presence there. While the struggle of the people of Nago was supported by people from across Okinawa, including base opponents in Ginowan City, which surrounds the Futenma base, the resistance was led by grandmothers and grandfathers in their eighties, and the symbol of their resistance was a friendly *dugong*, representing the manatees whose feeding grounds are threatened by the proposed base construction.

Further east, Native Hawai'ians, for whom land and respect for Creation are essential to their identity and ways of life, are struggling to prevent base expansions and to win back their sacred lands. Like the people of Vieques, they have occupied live-fire sites, lived in the open, and challenged the Pentagon in the courts and in the court of public opinion.

Equally courageous are the banished people of Diego Garcia who are struggling to return home and to end their years of suffering and marginalization as foreign outcasts. With activist allies in New Zealand and the help of leading journalists, human rights organizations, and jurists in Britain, they have risen from oblivion and won one case after another in the British courts. In the Americas, resistance to U.S. bases helped to elect Rafael Correa president of Ecuador, and even before Lula assumed power in Brazil, Latin America's rising economic power refused Washington's demands to transform its space center into a U.S. base. Across the Atlantic, activists in Europe are committing civil disobedience at U.S. and NATO nuclear weapons bases and forcing their governments and political parties to begin demanding that the United States withdraw the nuclear weapons that are still based in Belgium, Britain, Germany, Holland, Italy, and Turkey. And, in the northern reaches of Scandinavia, a lively network of young Scandinavians is scouting out and protesting the presence of secret bases in Norway and Sweden.

Reality is, of course, dynamic. Catastrophes as well as the routine operations of militarized systems will continue to provide major openings for anti-bases movements, as they have in the past. Hegel's moment of history will make itself felt when we least expect it. Recall the global outrage that followed the killing of twenty-two Italians when joy-riding U.S. pilots sliced the ski towline at an alpine resort. Remember the world-wide identity with the Okinawan people in the aftermath of the 1995 kidnapping and rape of a twelve-year-old schoolgirl by three marines and the solidarity that flowed toward the popular nonviolent Okinawan uprising. The following year business as usual presented another opportunity when the G8 met in Okinawa. They were greeted by a five-mile-long human chain around Kadena Air Base and by a full-page advertisement in the prefecture's newspaper, signed by hundreds of U.S. Americans, calling for the withdrawal of U.S. bases.

Child with neurological damage from U.S. military toxins in water supply, Clark AFB, Philippines (Catherine Lutz).

It was the unexpected synthesis of the mainland competition for the growing Latino vote and of decades of courageous organizing and action that forced the closing of Vieques' dangerous and still badly polluted base. And, it was Dictator Marcos' murder of Benigno Aquino that sparked the EDSA revolution and fueled the resistance that resulted in the withdrawal of the U.S. bases from the Philippines.

Those of us in the United States must be persistent and use our imaginations in exploring ways in which we can act in solidarity with movements working to liberate their communities and countries from the "abuses and usurpations" of U.S. bases. Even small acts of human solidarity, the sending of a letter or statement, assisting with research, or traveling to communicate concern and remorse, can help to buoy movements and have wide reverberations. As Roland Simbulan, Walden Bello, Cookie Djokno and other leaders of the movement that won the withdrawal of U.S. bases from the Philippines have remarked, the tiny network of U.S. activists that called themselves "Friends of the Filipino People" played a vital role in the successful Philippine struggle. Timely advertisements and statements of remorse and solidarity have contributed to the Okinawan movement. Exposure and speaking tours, videos, and publications have helped to raise issues and build movements within the United States. And we should never underestimate the importance of material assistance. Scientific research in Massachusetts and California about the human and environmental consequences of military toxics has been valuable to base opponents around the world. Even small financial contributions can help to pay for the leaflets, sound systems, and travel that are essential to popular movements anywhere in the world. And a dollar will pay to have far more leaflets printed in Ecuador or São Tomé than in New York or New Mexico.

Finally, there is the importance of vision. The World Social Forum and the world's anti-bases movements remind us that "another world is possible." The Bible tells us that "A people without vision will perish." This is not utopian idealism but serious realism. What was true in the first years of the Cold War still applies in the twenty-first century: "Military power in today's world is incompatible with freedom. Incompatible with providing security, and ineffective in dealing with evil" (American Friends Service Committee 1955).

Notes

1. State Department. "Bush Announces Largest U.S. Force Restructuring in 50 Years," August 16, 2004, available at www.america.gov/st/washfile-english/2004/August/20040816174727frllehctim0.490597.html. Accessed April 19, 2008.

References

American Friends Service Committee (1955) "Speak Truth to Power: A Quaker Search for an Alternative to Violence," March 2. Available at www.quaker.org/sttp.html.

Arkin, William (2005) "Not Just a Last Resort? A Global Strike Plan, With a Nuclear Option." *Washington Post*, May 15.

Brzezinski, Zbigniew (1998) *The Grand Chessboard: American Primacy and Its Geostrategic Imperatives* (New York: Basic Books).

Bundy, McGeorge (1991) "Nuclear Weapons and the Gulf," *Foreign Affairs*, Fall.

Chomsky, Noam (1978) "The Drift Towards War and the Alternatives," in Peggy Duff (ed.) *War or Peace in the Middle East?* (London: Spokesman Books).

Enloe, Cynthia (1989) *Bananas, Beaches, and Bases: Making Feminist Sense of International Politics* (Berkeley: University of California Press).

Gerson, Joseph (2004) "Empire and Resistance in an Increasingly Dangerous Era," *ZNet*, December 1, www.zmag.org/content/showarticle.cfm?ItemID=6769.

Gordon, Michael R. (2004) "A Pentagon Plan to Sharply Cut GIs in Germany," *New York Times*, June 4.

Klare, Michael T. (2005) "Imperial Reach: The Pentagon's new basing strategy," *The Nation*, April 25.

Lemann, Nicholas (2002) "The Next World Order," *New Yorker*, April 1.

Onishi, Norimitu (2004) "On U.S. Fast Food, Okinawans Are Super-Sized," *New York Times*, March 30.

Peden, William, Butcher, Martin, and Plesch, Dan (1990) "Environmental Dangers of the Gulf Crisis: Nuclear Weapons in a War Zone," BASIC Report 90.6.

Schmitt, Eric (2003) "Threats and Responses: Expanding U.S. Presence; Pentagon Seeking New Access Pacts for Africa Bases," *New York Times*, July 5.

Talbott, Strobe (2002) *The Russia Hand: A Memoir of Presidential Diplomacy* (New York: Random House).

Yergin, Daniel (1991) *The Prize* (New York: Simon & Schuster).

2

U.S. MILITARY BASES IN LATIN AMERICA AND THE CARIBBEAN

John Lindsay-Poland

The United States has operated military bases in Latin America since the beginning of the 1900s, when it first established army camps in Cuba during the Spanish–American War and in Panama at the beginning of U.S. canal construction there. These bases have served explicitly to project and protect U.S. government and commercial interests in the region, as part of a project of empire. More recently, the explosion of U.S. military interest and funding for Plan Colombia, occurring in the wake of the United States' withdrawal from military bases in Panama in December 1999, gave rise to a proliferation of new U.S. bases and military access agreements in the region. The growth of bases constituted a decentralization of the U.S. military presence in the region, Washington's response to regional leaders' reluctance to allow large U.S. military bases or complexes while maintaining a broader military foothold.

What Southern Command (Southcom) calls "theater architecture" is a complex web of U.S. military facilities and functions in the region. That interlocking structure has been in transition, reflecting changes prompted in many cases by social movements and other opposition to U.S. dominance. These facilities represent tangible commitments to U.S. policy priorities, such as ensuring access to strategic resources, especially oil and natural gas, and to a supply-side drug war that holds foreigners responsible for domestic addiction to illegal drugs.

The Pentagon has invested in new infrastructure in the region, with four new military bases in Manta (Ecuador), Aruba, Curaçao, and Comalapa (El Salvador), which it has dubbed "Forward Operating Locations," or FOLs. Military officials said the new sites actually increased the reach of its surveillance from what was possible from Howard Air Base in Panama.[1] Washington signed ten-year agreements with Ecuador, the Netherlands (for Aruba and Curaçao), and El Salvador, and appropriated $116 million in 2001 for the renovation of air facilities in Ecuador, Aruba, and Curaçao. Southcom also operates some 17 radar sites, mostly in Peru and Colombia, each typically staffed by about 35 personnel.[2]

The FOL and radar facilities monitor the skies and waters of the region and are key to increased surveillance operations in the United States' Andean drug and "counter-terror" war. Part of the growing U.S. military contribution to Plan Colombia, they constitute a cordon around Colombia. AWACS aircraft operate from an airbase in the port city of Manta, Ecuador, since October 2001, when renovation of the base runway was completed. Approved by the short-lived Mahuad government in November 1999, the base in Manta hosts up to 475 U.S. personnel. The agreement designated "aerial detection, monitoring, tracking and control of illegal narcotics activity" as the purpose of U.S. control of the air base.[3] But an operative agreement for the bases in Manta, Aruba, Curaçao, and El Salvador states explicitly that use of facilities there "is not prohibited for other type DOD organizations" provided they obtain approval from the local air force (for Manta, Aruba, and Curaçao) or navy (for El Salvador).[4]

Aircraft operating from the U.S. base in Manta have since been used to monitor and even, reportedly, attack boats off Ecuador transporting undocumented immigrants. A public declaration by the U.S. commander of the base in 2006 that it was key for Plan Colombia generated controversy. Rafael Correa, inaugurated as president in early 2007, ran on a pledge to close the Manta base when its lease is up for renewal in 2009. He ratified the pledge once in office, and the United States reportedly began discussions with Colombia and Peru to move the operations to one of those countries.

The Pentagon is moving to outsource much of the operation and maintenance of military bases to private contractors. The air force contracted out much of the operation of the Manta base to Dyncorp, a U.S.-based company that receives some $2 billion a year in contracts from the Pentagon and the State Department for operations in countries around the world. Even "host nation riders" who accompany military flights over Colombia as part of drug interdiction efforts were to be "outsourced" to a private U.S. military contractor, according to the implementation plan for the base.[5]

These bases are in addition to existing ones in Soto Cano, Honduras, a joint command base since 1984 which provides support for training and helicopter sorties, and in Guantánamo, Cuba, which enjoys a lease with no termination date. With a U.S. presence since 1903, Guantánamo has served as an R&R site for sailors and marines, a refueling site for coast guard ships, and a temporary camp for Haitian refugees. These activities have been overshadowed by the controversy over the U.S. military camp established for the detention of suspected Al Qaeda members, the camp's violation of Geneva Convention norms, and associated charges of torture and abuse.

"Puerto Rico has replaced Panama for forward basing headquarters in the region," then Southcom chief General Peter Pace told Congress in March 2001, with regional headquarters for the army, navy, and special forces, while Southcom headquarters itself is located in Miami. But the closure of the Vieques range in 2003 led the military to move the special forces and army headquarters for Latin America operations out of Puerto Rico entirely, to bases in Florida and Texas.

Historical Background

U.S. military bases in Latin America specifically have had at least nine identifiable missions: police interventions; tropical sanitation; Panama Canal defense, which often was interpreted liberally;

troop training; tests of weapons and other matériel; environmental engineering, particularly of the tropical environment; counterinsurgency warfare; counter-drug operations; and intelligence and communication tasks. Bases in Panama and Puerto Rico provided convenient platforms from which to launch interventions in Central American and Caribbean nations, which the United States did frequently from 1900 to 1933. Though limited in scale, especially by today's standards, the military interventions were always sufficient to determine the outcome of local conflicts, usually so as to favor U.S. commercial interests.[6]

The bases in Panama were also used for missions incidental to the United States' imperial project. In the bloom of conquest after the Spanish–American War, visions proliferated of whites settling tropical lands that were considered idle or vacant. Up to that time, U.S. military interventions in the region had been carried out from the sea by naval forces. When the United States obtained control over the unfinished canal works in Panama in 1903, through naval and diplomatic intimidation, it established army forts in the area. Both the canal construction workforce and U.S. soldiers would live in Panama and have to grapple with tropical diseases that had overcome the French effort to dig a canal. The chosen method was through military control of potential vectors of malaria and yellow fever, thus reinforcing the rationale for and control exercised by the foreign military presence. The army was also entrusted with overseeing the construction and management of the canal itself from 1907 until the very end of the U.S. tenure in 1999.

The existence of a complex of military bases in the Panama Canal area, including extensive tropical lands, and the clientelistic relationship between the U.S. and Panamanian states made the isthmus a convenient place to locate activities to help project U.S. power throughout the hemisphere and the Pacific. During World War II, the United States maintained as many as 63,000 troops in Panama and forced through an agreement to establish more than 100 military bases outside the Canal Zone in the interior of Panama, ostensibly to defend the canal. Some of these troops, however, were deployed for a project to test chemical weapons to see how they would behave in a tropical environment, in preparation for an anticipated chemical war with the Japanese in the Pacific. From late 1943 through 1947, the army's Chemical Warfare Service used San José Island – an unpopulated member of the Pearl Islands group – to fire or drop thousands of chemical munitions. The San José Project used soldiers, many of them Puerto Rican, as human subjects in the tests, exposing them to mustard gas and other agents to measure how well masks and ointments functioned and even, in one case, "to determine whether any difference existed in the sensitivity of Puerto Rican and Continental U.S. Troops to H gas [mustard]."[7]

Similarly, the United States dramatically expanded its military presence in Puerto Rico in the period leading up to and during World War II, establishing the vast Roosevelt Roads Naval Station and expropriating lands for the bombing ranges and maneuver area on the islands of Vieques and Culebra (the latter already in use as a firing range) (Beruff 1988:158–160). In fact, U.S. military facilities, especially airfields, were established during the war in many nations throughout much of the hemisphere (Ecuador, Peru, Guatemala, Costa Rica, Nicaragua, and in several British colonies in the Caribbean), an observation that bears comparison with the current growth of U.S. bases around the world in the "war on terror."[8] After the war, most of the U.S. bases in the region that had been set up for the war were closed, but the navy kept its bases in Puerto Rico.

During the Cold War, United States military doctrine for Latin America and the Caribbean focused on increasing the capacity of national militaries for "internal defense," i.e. combating forces within Latin American countries that challenged the existing order. The doctrine frequently did not distinguish between armed insurgency and peaceful agitation, or even civic opposition. Fort Gulick in Panama became host to a U.S. Army facility known as the School of the Americas, which trained 29,000 Latin American troops between 1949 and 1984, when the school was moved to Georgia. The air force and navy trained thousands of Latin American soldiers at other facilities in Panama (Arnold 1987:40). But the United States also trained and tested for its own military adventures, especially in Southeast Asia. The firing ranges and sites in Panama provided the central location for testing weapons (missiles, nerve agents, depleted uranium) and other military equipment under tropical conditions. A jungle operations training center on Fort Sherman in Panama was a key location for training infantry bound for Vietnam.

With the conclusion of the Cold War, the United States redefined the rationale for its military engagements in Latin America, with a primary focus on counter-narcotics missions. Within three months of the fall of the Berlin Wall in November 1989, with domestic constituencies already discussing possible substantial cuts in military spending as part of a "peace dividend," the United States launched "Operation Just Cause." Under the guise of the drug war, the U.S. invasion of Panama overthrew former CIA and U.S. Army client General Manuel Noriega, who had assumed dictatorial power. Using advanced transportation technology, the military carried out the invasion primarily using troops and equipment from bases in the United States. However, the Congress quickly passed a resolution calling for a renegotiation of the Panama Canal Treaties' provisions for closure of the U.S. bases by the end of 1999. The attempted reach of the bases to be renegotiated would extend well beyond Panama into the Andean region, which became the locus for the Southern Command's attention with the winding down of the civil wars in Central America. In 1995, Washington opened discussions with Panama to retain military bases in Panama beyond 1999 for a complex that would be called a Multinational Counter-narcotics Center. At its core, the United States sought the continued use of Howard Air Force Base for surveillance missions of the Andean countries and eastern Pacific.

Panamanian president Ernesto Pérez Balladares showed ambivalence toward the project from the beginning, saying there would be no bases without payment of rent. The "multinational" nature of the complex was largely a fig leaf designed to appease Panamanian nationalist sympathies; officials said other Latin American governments would participate in the center, but they were never involved in the negotiations. While Washington went through several negotiators, Panamanian nationalist, human rights, and environmental groups organized coalitions to oppose the continued presence of U.S. troops. They agitated in the media, on the street, and in the ruling Revolutionary Democratic Party against the negotiations. U.S. and Panamanian officials announced an agreement in December 1997, but when its details were leaked the following month, support for it evaporated. The agreement called for unpaid use of extensive facilities in the canal area, U.S. jurisdiction for crimes committed by U.S. soldiers, and a provision allowed for "other missions" besides counter-drug activity. The deal collapsed, and the United States would have to find new sites (Lindsay-Poland 1993:125–137).

Unlike U.S. bases in Panama, the function of navy training in Vieques had as much to do with U.S. military missions in Iraq and Europe as it did with operations in Latin America, since battle groups deployed directly from Puerto Rico to the Mediterranean and the Persian Gulf, where they conducted regular bombing runs even before the United States invaded Iraq in 2003.

Just as the U.S. forces were clearing out from the bases in Panama, most of them bound for bases in Puerto Rico, the opposition to bombing in Vieques erupted in April 1999 after a pilot training for operations in Kosovo dropped two bombs off-target on the Vieques range and killed a local civilian guard, David Sanes. Within days of the killing, protesters occupied sites on the bombing range's live impact area, where they would stay for more than a year in upwards of a dozen civil disobedience camps. The bombing resumed in May 2000, but within a month a group of women walked onto the range during the training, the opening of a civil disobedience campaign for which more than 1,500 people would be arrested. Vieques inspired a true mass movement, uniting all three of Puerto Rico's major political parties, and gave rise to the largest march in Puerto Rican history. The movement mobilized Puerto Ricans from all walks of life, on the island and across the diaspora, as well as considerable international solidarity. It included vibrant cultural expressions, savvy local and national political work in Puerto Rico and the United States, and relentless media efforts.

President Clinton struck a deal with Governor Pedro Rosselló in January 2000 to stop the bombing by May 2003, if Vieques residents voted to do so in a referendum, the date of which was to be set by the navy. The island municipality was to receive $50 million if they voted for the navy to stay and continue bombing, combined with another $40 million appropriated for works on the island regardless of the vote; this represented more than $15,000 per Vieques voter. However, with time the movement only grew in strength, as candidates favoring an immediate end to bombing won majorities in Vieques and Puerto Rico as a whole. A non-binding vote in Vieques showed that 70 percent of the population wanted the navy out, so military leaders asked Congress to cancel the referendum. Instead, Congress required the navy to certify that it had equal or better facilities elsewhere to train before it closed the range. It also required most lands used by the navy to be turned over to another federal agency, the Fish and Wildlife Service, to be maintained as a wildlife refuge and "wilderness area."

In January 2003, the Chief of Naval Operations, in certifying to Congress the availability of training facilities elsewhere, acknowledged the protesters' effectiveness. "Physical security at Vieques is becoming ever more difficult and costly to maintain given the civil unrest which accompanies the Navy's presence on the island," Admiral Vernon Clark wrote. "We have been successful in completing our training on the island only because of extremely aggressive and costly multi-agency security actions. Navy's departure from Vieques will relieve us from this burden."[9]

The operation and eventual closure of the Vieques bombing range demonstrated the web-like nature of apparently distinct military facilities. Besides the former land bombing range on Vieques, the navy also operated an "outer range" of nearly 200,000 square miles, which appears to be unaffected by the closure of the Vieques range, an underwater tracking range for submarines, and an electronic warfare range in waters near Vieques (Center for Naval Analyses 2002:57). The ranges are used by the navy and military contractors to test sophisticated ship and weapons systems. With the end of ship-to-shore and air-to-ground bombing in Vieques, the underwater tracking range, which had been located off the west coast of St. Croix, was moved to an area off Andros Island in the Bahamas, as part of the navy's Atlantic Undersea Test and Evaluation Center. The Bahamas already houses two coast guard sites with U.S. Army counter-drug helicopter operations.[10] A Pentagon report in 2004 said that the Andros Island facility presented a "serious limitation," and in 2006 the navy programmed funds to upgrade the range.[11]

Even more dramatic was the closure of the Roosevelt Roads Naval Station as a result of the Vieques range closure. After the navy certified its departure from Vieques, Atlantic Fleet Admiral Robert Natter told reporters that "without Vieques there is no way I need the Navy facilities at Roosevelt Roads – none. It's a drain on Defense Department and taxpayer dollars."[12] The base was closed in March 2004; most of the property was to be auctioned to private bidders, with the remainder going to Puerto Rican government agencies.[13] In Panama, all U.S. military forces left and bases were closed by treaty at the end of 1999. But the Pentagon continued to have access for military flights in and out of Panama, on a contract with Evergreen Air of Alaska to transport cargo and passengers between Honduras, Panama, and dirt strips in Colombia, on a daily basis.[14]

Table 2.1   Major US Bases in Latin America and the Caribbean

Location	Number of military personnel present/allowed
Guantánamo Bay, Cuba	850
Soto Cano, Honduras	550
Manta, Ecuador	475
Aruba	300, more typically 35
Curaçao	300, more typically 200–230
Comalapa, El Salvador	About 15, but no limit

Sources: Frida Berrigan and Jonathan Wing, 'The Bush Effect', November 5, 2005, World Policy Institute; texts of agreements between US and Dutch and Ecuadoran governments.

Bases or 'Presence'?

Bases belonging to Latin American militaries but built or used by U.S. soldiers are not considered U.S. bases, but often serve similar purposes. The Joint Peruvian Riverine Training Center in Iquitos, Peru has largely replaced the former riverine training base in Panama. The up to 1,400 U.S. military and contract personnel operating at any time in Colombia are also housed at nominally Colombian bases.

The U.S. military's presence increasingly takes form not in permanent installations, but through bilateral agreements for military operations and maneuvers. The Paraguayan Congress's authorization in May 2005 for 13 U.S. military exercises through December 2006 offers a pointed example of this phenomenon. The authorization granted diplomatic immunity to the U.S. troops, as well as exemption from import taxes and inspections. The U.S. troops operating in Paraguay were centered in a military base in Mariscal Estigarribia, constructed in the 1980s and with the longest runway in the country, although it is located in a remote area with a population of just 2,000. The air base sits close to the "tri-border area" of Paraguay, Argentina, and Brazil, which holds strategic economic value, particularly for its hydrological resources and proximity to Bolivia's gas reserves. In addition, the area has a sizable Arabic population, and ever since September 11, 2001, U.S. officials promoting an anti-terrorist lens for military activity in Latin America have pointed to the area as a possible focal point for Al Qaeda activity.

Four hundred U.S. troops landed in Paraguay in July 2005, followed within a week by an announcement that the FBI would set up shop in the country. Later that month, 300 parachutists simulated a takeover of the Itaipú Dam, and two weeks later the Treasury Department's top official for combating financing of terrorism asserted that "there is terrorism being financed" in the tri-border area of Paraguay, Argentina, and Brazil.[15] Most of the maneuvers carried out by U.S. troops in Paraguay are billed as humanitarian "medical readiness exercises" to benefit the local population. But an observation mission in July 2006 to three localities where exercises took place noted that medical attention was one-time only, and that U.S. personnel handed out unlabeled medicines indiscriminately, regardless of the differences in medical conditions. Other military personnel filmed local residents, and medical attention included questions about residents' affiliations with peasant organizations. Many of the exercises took place in areas where social conflict between peasant organizations and landowners had been acute.[16] "In Paraguay enormous infrastructures – such as the Mariscal Estigarribia airbase – are combined with humanitarian operations, small facilities, and internal militarization of the country," notes Uruguayan analyst Raúl Zibechi.[17]

The troop presence in Paraguay evoked widespread media attention and opposition from human rights groups. Some reports asserted that the United States aimed to establish a base at Mariscal Estigarribia,[18] and an international observation commission organized by human rights groups visited the area and produced a report in July 2006. As important as popular opposition, however, were the concerns of neighboring countries Brazil and Argentina. Both countries mobilized their own troops in response to the U.S. exercises: Brazil with an exercise by 700 soldiers near its Paraguay border in September 2005, while Argentina led a multinational military exercise in October 2006 "to recover an airport that has fallen under the control of an extra-continental power, being used to fly in and deploy troops into the area." Analysts observed that the United States is the only such power with the capacity and political wherewithal to fly in troops in such an operation. Paraguayan soldiers participated in the exercise, dubbed "Operación Hermandad (Operation Brotherhood)."[19]

It was regional neighbors' concerns about Paraguay's military collaboration with the United States that Paraguayan Foreign Minister Ruben Ramirez cited when he announced in October 2006 that Paraguay rescinded the immunity granted to U.S. soldiers for crimes committed in the country. The decision brought with it the cancellation of a cooperation agreement between the two countries' militaries for U.S. training of Paraguayan soldiers.[20]

Troop exercises in the Dominican Republic have also encountered renewed and broad social protest. In February 2006, hundreds of soldiers arrived in the southern province of Barahona for what the U.S. Embassy called "humanitarian" exercises: building roads and schools and digging wells.[21] The Dominican Republic has hosted or participated in many of these exercises since at least the 1990s.[22] This time, however, thousands of Dominicans marched to the military camp where troops were housed, leading to a tense confrontation with Dominican guards who pointed machine guns at the protesters. "You can't do humanitarian assistance with tanks and bombs," shouted the protesters. "If you want to build schools, build them in New Orleans where they are needed."[23] Activists pointed out that the exercises coincided with elections in neighboring Haiti, still in turmoil and occupied by a multinational military force. The exercises also carried special weight because of the two previous U.S. military invasions of the Dominican Republic: in 1965, and in 1916, when marines stayed for nine years.

U.S. officials directly denied any intention of establishing a base in the Dominican Republic. But as one critic observed, the New Horizons and other "humanitarian" exercises "are usually developed in very specific areas of strategic importance, typically near bases of operation or military facilities of the host country that serve as headquarters for training troops by the United States."[24] In effect, U.S. troops use the host countries' facilities for their own military training objectives, obviating the need for U.S. title to a facility that would make it a "U.S. base." Leftist, labor, and student groups demanded the immediate removal of the troops from the Dominican Republic.

The discomfort and opposition expressed by Latin American governments and civil societies to U.S. military presence in the region is inevitably tied to the unilateral nature of Washington's military policy, including the war in Iraq and attempts to exempt U.S. soldiers from jurisdiction of the International Criminal Court (ICC). In 2002, the United States established the "American Service-members' Protection Act," which prohibits certain kinds of military aid to countries that have ratified the Rome Statute establishing the ICC, unless they sign an agreement with the United States pledging not to seek prosecution of U.S. soldiers in the ICC. U.S. embassies around the world have exerted considerable pressure on other nations to sign such pledges, known as Article 98 agreements. Twenty-one countries have refused, and 12 of these are in Latin America and the Caribbean.[25]

Washington's resurgence of unilateral militarism had other expressions as well. In April 2006 the Pentagon approved a plan to allow the military to send special operations troops into a country for covert operations without the authorization even of the U.S. ambassador in the country or other State Department officials. The move reinforced a trend away from the rule of international law that has both governments and civil societies in Latin America concerned.[26]

Latin American governments have responded to popular movements against U.S. militarism in another important way as well: through public decisions not to send members of their own militaries to courses at the U.S. Army's Western Hemisphere Institute for Security Cooperation (WHINSEC, formerly known as the School of the Americas). The WHINSEC has come into extended controversy because many of its students have been implicated in human rights atrocities and military dictatorships at home after passing through the school's courses. In 1996, documents were released showing that the school had used a curriculum that sanctioned torture methods of interrogation, false imprisonment, and executions, and designated nonviolent political opposition as legitimate military enemies (Gill 2004:49). Since then, every November, thousands of people gather at the gates of Fort Benning, Georgia, where the school is located, to remember Latin Americans assassinated by graduates of the school and to call for its closure. Congressional votes to shutter the facility have been hotly debated and close.

Hugo Chavez's Venezuela was the first to announce, in 2004, that it would no longer send soldiers to the school. Uruguay, Argentina, and Costa Rica followed suit in 2006 and 2007, while Bolivia reduced the number of soldiers sent to the school.[27] The commitments by government officials responded to growing cross-border collaboration between activists from the United States and the Latin American countries involved.[28] In November 2006, groups in Latin America organized protests in eleven different Latin American cities in coordination with the annual protest at Fort Benning, Georgia.[29]

Problems with U.S. Bases in the Region

The soldiers and contract personnel that the U.S. military deploys to bases in Latin America and the Caribbean far outnumber personnel of U.S. civilian agencies in the region. The presence of so many personnel on military missions outside U.S. borders sends a message that the United States prefers force to diplomacy to settle the region's problems, including problems that involve conflict with the United States. In addition to their role in facilitating military operations, U.S. bases and maneuvers are a symbol of Washington's history of gunboat intervention, and of its use of local armies to control Latin populations and resources. Most U.S. bases in the Caribbean were explicitly acquired through conquests in the 1898 Spanish–American–Cuban War.

Besides evoking the past, the bases are contracted into a future beyond any imagined or articulated military mission. Plan Colombia was originally envisioned as a two-year "push" into guerrilla-occupied southern territories, with vague plans for subsequent years, but has been extended with little debate or evaluation. Even moves by the Democratic majority in Congress in 2007 to reduce the military component of Plan Colombia retained more than $440 million in military funds – about 65 percent of the total package.[30] In contrast, the ten-year leases in Ecuador, Curaçao, and Aruba are brief compared with the perpetuity claimed for the naval base in Guantánamo. This permanent infrastructure generates inequitable relations and in a crisis invites intervention by the United States or, more often, capitulation by Latin American governments, instead of negotiation.

The new FOLs, purportedly created to monitor drug traffic, have no mechanism for transparency or monitoring by civil society in the countries where they are located, and are thus subject to being used for other missions. Although some officials apparently interpreted the agreement with Ecuador for use of Manta as restricted to counter-drug missions, a State Department official said in 1999 that "the new counter-narcotics bases located in Ecuador, Aruba, and Curaçao will be strategic points for closely monitoring the steps of the [Colombian] guerrillas."[31] After the "war on terror" got under way, Congress loosened restrictions on Colombia's use of counter-drug assistance for use against insurgents. And consistent with General Pace's identification of illegal immigration as a central security threat, aircraft from the Manta base have been used to find and detain fishing boats with Ecuadorans aboard who were suspected of planning to enter the United States. Although the base agreement restricts such operations to the Ecuadoran navy, U.S. military ship personnel illegally boarded 45 local boats between 2001 and 2005, sinking or damaging eight of them.[32]

In 2005, even more incendiary military activities in Manta came to light, though it was unclear who approved them. A former employee of the U.S. military contractor Dyncorp in Manta named Jeffrey Shippy and his wife advertised a business that they claimed had recruited nearly 1,000 Colombian and Ecuadoran ex-soldiers to work for the United States as mercenaries in Iraq, reportedly paying them from $2,500 to $5,000 a month. The couple was ordered arrested, but they disappeared.[33]

These developments, the dramatically increased U.S. military involvement in Colombia, and the spillover of refugees and conflict in the border region have generated alarm among broad sectors of Ecuadoran society – including the military – over the potentially destabilizing role of the Manta base. One officer calls the base "the eyes and ears of Plan Colombia," and other opponents point out that Ecuador's Congress never considered or approved the agreement, as the constitution requires for treaties and military alliances. They also object to provisions exempting U.S. on-duty military personnel from Ecuadoran criminal jurisdiction. The Correa government's resistance to U.S. military impositions led Ecuador to withdraw as host of annual multinational naval exercises, known as UNITAS, in 2007.[34]

The FOL in Comalapa, El Salvador, operated by the navy, has no limit on the number of U.S. personnel, who have access to ports, air space, and unspecified government installations. The opposition FMLN party argued that the agreement affected Salvadoran sovereignty, and thus required more than a simple majority vote by the legislature for ratification, but it did not prevail in a legal challenge to the agreement. In 2005, the United States expanded its armed presence in Comalapa with the inauguration of the International Law Enforcement Academy, a hemispheric police training center, the posting of which Costa Rica had rejected two years earlier.

In Puerto Rico, military bases had additional meaning and political function. On an island where the FBI has compiled 1.8 million documents based on surveillance of independence activists and other political cases, the presence of large United States military bases played an important role in conditioning islanders' choices about the status of Puerto Rico. Many Puerto Ricans viewed the bases as a quid pro quo for the benefits that some received from the colonial relationship. But the bases also were an expression of who held overwhelming power in that relationship, and with the bases' closure, Puerto Ricans face market forces at least as powerful as the military in the struggle to claim their autonomy and identity. The continuing presence of military recruiters and JROTC programs in Puerto Rico show that U.S. militarism still pervades the island. Yet resistance to militarism and the Iraq War led 57 percent of Puerto Rican high school students to "opt out" of being contacted by military recruiters in 2007.[35]

The outsourcing of air transport, base construction, and maintenance and the "host nation" rider program, like that of other military activities overseas, diminishes the information available and accountability for actions sponsored by the United States outside its borders. Not until an enterprising reporter discovered an Internet-posted request for proposals did Panamanian civil society become aware that the Pentagon had been using airstrips in Panama for "transportation services" in and out of Colombia, even after U.S. troops had left. The contract had been held since

1997 by Evergreen Helicopters, which had a clandestine role in the 1989 U.S. invasion of Panama.

Many military bases in Latin America – like those in the United States and elsewhere – leave a devastating environmental legacy. In Panama, the military by its own estimate left behind more than 100,000 pieces of unexploded ordnance on firing ranges in the fast-growing canal area, despite a Canal Treaty provision for removing such dangers (Hunt 1999). On San José Island, an inspection team from the Organization for the Prohibition of Chemical Weapons – the implementing body of the Chemical Weapons Convention, which both the United States and Panama have ratified – verified in 2001 that the United States had abandoned seven mustard gas bombs on the island, which is now owned by a private consortium that aims to develop it for tourism. The convention requires countries that have abandoned chemical weapons on other nations' territories to declare and remove them, but the United States refused to do so, putting it in violation of the convention.

In Vieques, studies have found high rates of cadmium, lead, mercury, uranium, and other contaminants present in the soil, food chain, and human bodies of island residents. These contaminants have led to elevated rates of disease among Vieques residents, who have an incidence of cancer 27 percent higher than other Puerto Ricans.[36]

U.S. military bases outside the 50 states present special environmental problems, because the United States doesn't recognize the same obligations for cleanup as it does on domestic installations – which themselves suffer from widespread contamination and neglect. Once the Pentagon is gone, the United States abandons jurisdiction – and responsibility – for the contamination its military has caused. In Puerto Rico, the military is formally bound by U.S. environmental law, and cleanup funds are part of the same budgets as those appropriated for bases inside the United States. But the political influence that might ensure adequate funding for the cleanup and attention to health concerns in Vieques must be exercised indirectly, because as a colony Puerto Rico has no voting representatives in Congress.

Social Movements Respond

The grassroots movement in Puerto Rico that burst into the international media spotlight in 1999 against the naval bombing range in Vieques demonstrated determined local opposition as well as widespread international solidarity by using creative and often risky protests. This movement, with its dramatic and diverse tactics and its ultimate success in stopping the bombing and closing the naval range, has drawn most attention from military and civilian observers.

But movements and protest activity have also emerged in response to negotiations for renewal of bases in Panama, and for the establishment of an international police academy in Costa Rica, against military exercises in Argentina, against an extended U.S. troop presence in Paraguay, and against the U.S. bases in Manta, Ecuador. The broad movement in the United States to close the U.S. Army School of the Americas – at one time located on a U.S. base in Panama, now in Fort Benning, Georgia – has also drawn new connections with anti-militarist movements in Latin America.

The base in Manta has been the site of a growing conflict with peasants pushed off their land by Ecuadoran naval officials. The agreement with the United States gives the U.S. military access to a naval base adjacent to the port – including a live-fire range – with increasing claims to enormous extensions of land: more than 30,000 acres. Naval officials have told local farmers that the land does not belong to them, even though some of the farmers have documents proving title, while others have been working the land for many years. Some farmers, intimidated, have stopped farming or moved away. Ecuadoran human rights workers anticipate the day when the United States will make use of its access to these lands, while some farmers resist the base expansion by planting seeds on the contested land. Various sectors of Ecuador's civil society mobilized against the base and made it a national issue in the 2006 presidential elections. The victory of Rafael Correa Delgado raised hopes among anti-base groups, since Correa had pledged not to renew the base agreement when it expires in 2009. He joked that "we can negotiate with the U.S. about a base in Manta, if they let us put a military base in Miami; if there is no problem, we'll accept."[37] But keeping the air base in Manta was still on the table, in spite of President Correa's public statements, according to a senior Pentagon official. One arrangement reportedly being explored was allowing U.S. military or surveillance aircraft to land in Ecuador, but not at a fixed U.S. base. U.S. officials also might simply move the base operations within the region. In mid 2007, Colombia offered to host operations being run out of Manta, once the lease for the base there expired.[38] Similarly, when Ecuador withdrew from annual naval exercises led by the United States that were scheduled to be held off its coastline in May 2007, Southcom said that the exercises would be held instead in Malaga Bay on Colombia's Pacific coast, near Buenaventura.[39]

Growing connection and collaboration between anti-base movements promise to strengthen them. But such international networks also highlight the challenge anti-militarists face as they aim to affect the overall thrust of U.S. military projection in the region – of ending military activities and re-casting the policy that generates them, rather than simply moving bases and exercises to areas where they will be more politically acceptable.

Toward Inter-American Change

To live up to the democratic ideals of its people, the United States should adopt a new security doctrine in Latin America and the Caribbean. Such a doctrine would value ties with civilians more than ties with the military as the sphere where democratic decision making takes place. It would dedicate more resources to addressing the economic causes of conflict, rather than to building installations designed for the use of force. It would also commit the United States to transparency about the purposes, activities, and effects of existing U.S. military bases in the region, even if – especially if – that means the bases are eliminated by the will of a democratic polity.

U.S. military facilities represent tangible commitments to underlying policies that are outmoded, as in the case of Cuba, or perniciously expansionist. The command briefing guiding the army's military presence in the region, according to Southcom, highlights access to strategic resources in South America, especially oil, as well as other issues with social and political roots, such as immigration and narcotics (Transnational Institute 2003:10–11).

A different doctrine would redirect resources invested in military bases to civilian agencies whose charter is to address such social and political problems, including non-governmental organizations, local and regional agencies of the region's governments, and agencies of the United Nations. This would imply important changes for the Andean Counternarcotics Initiative, consistent with proposals to redirect military and police assistance to alternative crop and other development programs in the Andes and to drug treatment and health programs in the United States.

Short of such a re-examination of the policy foundations for military bases in the region, the United States should review existing agreements for overseas bases using democratic criteria. Bases should not be maintained or established without broad consultation and the agreement of the civil societies and legislatures in which these bases are located. Without such consultation and agreement, the bases are a usurpation of democratic control within the society. If local officials feel compelled to accept base agreements, bases should only be established for fixed periods of time with clearly defined missions, and require renewal by both U.S. and host congresses. In those instances, objectionable provisions, such as broad U.S. military access to the host nation's ports and air space, diplomatic immunity for U.S. military personnel, and prohibitions on access or inspections by local authorities, should be deleted. But the values of democracy and sovereignty for those who populate and work the land argue for foreign bases' abolition. The United States should also not attempt to establish military access or carry out controversial military missions through private means, such as the outsourcing of military operations. In Panama, the United

States should honor the substance of the Neutrality Treaty, which forbids stationing U.S. soldiers and bases in Panama, by refraining from using local airstrips for military sorties by either military or contract aircraft.

To ensure transparency and accountability to affected communities, base agreements should be amended to give the local public health and environmental officials and representatives of communities affected by U.S. bases the authority to inspect all base facilities on short notice. To address environmental problems generated at U.S. military bases in Latin America as well as in other regions, the United States should recognize its responsibility and Congress should establish an Overseas Defense Environmental Restoration Account. The account should provide for cleanup of both existing and former U.S. bases overseas to standards that protect neighboring populations and the environment from contamination and safety hazards, with adequate study of the affected lands and waters.

In Vieques, in the wake of more than 60 years of bombing, a cleanup is necessary for the protection of public health, and Congress should appropriate funds for it. Similarly, policy makers ought to heed the repeated appeals by Panama to remove the thousands of pieces of unexploded ordnance left in firing ranges in the canal area. Such measures of environmental responsibility would demonstrate the accountability and environmental leadership that is sorely needed. And enacting the range of changes described could begin to reverse the perception that U.S. leaders consider themselves outside law and mutual ethical obligation.

Notes

1. Marty Kauchak, "Eyes in the Sky," *Armed Forces Journal International*, April 2001.
2. This includes at least five radar sites in Colombia, all operated by the ITT corporation, as well as a "Forward Operating Site" in Apiay (See Department of State, "Report to Congress on Certain Counter-narcotics Activities in Colombia," available online at www.cipcol.org), where the U.S. Army 7th Special Forces Group trains thousands of Colombian soldiers every year. See Adam Isacson, "Counter-

drug military construction projects in 2005," October 27, 2006, available online at www.cipcol.org/archives/cat_us_policy.htm. Date last accessed October 13, 2007.

3. "Agreement of Cooperation Between the Government of the United States of America and the Government of the Republic of Ecuador Concerning United States Access to and Use of Installations at the Ecuadoran Air Force Base in Manta for Aerial Counter-Narcotics Activities," unpublished at time of writing, November 12, 1999.

4. Brig. Gen. James N. Soligan, "Memorandum for Director, Joint Staff, United States Southern Command, Change 1 to the Forward Operating Location Implementation Plan," unpublished, December 1, 1999, p. 11.

5. Ibid.

6. In many cases, such as in Nicaragua and Panama, the interventions were publicly rationalized as defending U.S. property. In Haiti, the Dominican Republic, and Honduras, national treasuries came under U.S. receivership in connection with military interventions (Schoultz 1998).

7. Secretary of Defense William Cohen to Representative José Serrano, "San José Project Report No. 24 Summary," unpublished letter, April 7, 1998. San José Island was only one of many places that utilized soldiers as human subjects in chemical weapons tests during and after World War II; others were in bases in the United States, while Allied militaries also conducted such tests in Australia (Pechura and Rall 1993; Goodwin 1998).

8. U.S. Army Caribbean Defense Command, "History of the Panama Canal Department," Panama C.Z.: 1946, Vol. 2, unpaginated chart.

9. Admiral Vernon Clark, "Cessation of Training at Vieques Naval Training Range," Memorandum for Secretary of the Navy, unpublished, December 10, 2002.

10. Available online at www.globalsecurity.org/military/agency/dot/district7.htm. Date last accessed October 13, 2007; Isacson, "Counter-drug military construction," 2006.

11. "Aerospace Daily and Defense Report," January 24, 2005. Department of the Navy, Fiscal Year 2007 Budget Estimates Submission, Justification of Estimates, Other Procurement Activity, February 2006, p. 16.

12. *Associated Press*, January 11, 2003.

13. *South Florida Sun Sentinel*, November 19, 2006.

14. *Panama News*, April 11, 2001; *LP*, April 18, 2001; Synopsis for Solicitation F11626-01-R0015, www.epa.gov.

15. Raúl Zibechi, "Paraguay: Platform for Hemispheric Hegemony," IRC Americas Program, August 29, 2006, available online at http://upsidedownworld.org/main/content/view/408/1/. Date last accessed October 13, 2007.
16. Campaña por la Desmilitarización de las Américas, "Conclusiones generales de la Misión Internacional de Observación," July 21, 2006, available online at www.alainet.org/active/12453&lang=es. Date last accessed October 13, 2007.
17. Zibechi, "Paraguay".
18. *Clarín*, June 13, 2005. A critical perspective on claims that the United States intends to establish a base in Mariscal Estigarribia is available online at www.globalsecurity.org/military/facility/mariscal-estigarribia.htm. Date last accessed October 13, 2007.
19. Raúl Zibechi, "Intense Dispute in the Heart of the Southern Cone," IRC Americas Program, November 1, 2006, available online at www.americas.irc-online.org. Date last accessed October 13, 2007.
20. *Reuters*, October 3, 2006; *Associated Press*, October 3, 2006.
21. The number of U.S. soldiers was disputed, as it has been in other nations. U.S. officials claimed 150 to 240 troops, while opposition activists said up to 800. The debate over numbers itself is instructive of attitudes about the U.S. presence. Opponents seek to show a large number of troops to illustrate the incursion onto national sovereignty. U.S. officials do not assert that more troops would bring more assistance. Instead they minimize the number of troops, and emphasize the work that they do. *El Nacional*, February 22, 2006.
22. Carlos Ernesto Motto, "Ejercicios militares de EUA en República Dominicana: Un eslabón más de la cadena imperial," *Observatorio Latinoamericano de Geopolítica*, 2006. Available online at www.geopolitica.ws. Date last accessed October 13, 2007.
23. H. Galván, "Reportaje marcha contra tropas extranjeras 27-F," available online at www.lainiciativa.org/Yankes/reportaje.html. Date last accessed October 7, 2007.
24. Motto, "Ejercicios militares de EUA," p. 3.
25. Latin America Working Group, "Tarnished Image: Latin America Perceives the United States," 2006, pp. 10–13, available online at www.lawg.org. Date last accessed October 13, 2007.
26. *Washington Post*, February 24, 2005; *Washington Post*, April 23, 2006.
27. *TIME*, June 13, 2006; "Costa Rica to Cease Training at SOA/WHINSEC," available online at www.soaw.org. Date last accessed October 13, 2007.
28. Lisa Sullivan, "The Shadow of SOA Looms over Latin America," October 2006, available online at www.soaw.org/new/article.php?id=1375. Date last accessed October 13, 2007.

29. Statement by Cristianos por la Paz con Justicia y Dignidad (Ecuador), November 16, 2006.
30. Adam Isacson, "A guide to House bill's proposed changes to Colombia aid," June 20, 2007, available online at www.cipcol.org. Date last accessed October 13, 2007.
31. *El Espectador*, June 4, 1999.
32. Fundación Regional de Asesoría en Derechos Humanos (INREDH), "Informe para el Grupo de Trabajo de Naciones Unidas sobre Mercenarios," Quito, August 2006, p. 6. For a full and moving account of these operations and the impacts on fisher families, see Juan Carlos Calderón, *Naufragio*, Quito, 2007.
33. Ibid., pp. 17–18.
34. "Ecuador no sera sede de las maniobras militares UNITAS," *Altercom*, May 3, 2007.
35. *Washington Post*, August 18, 2007.
36. Arturo Massol, Casa Pueblo, "Studies on Vieques Flora and Fauna: Summary of Findings," available online at www.viequeslibre.addr. com/articles/articles.htm. Date last accessed October 13, 2007; Erick Suárez, "Incidencia y Mortalidad de Cáncer en Vieques," presentation to the First Puerto Rican Conference on Public Health, San Juan, April 10, 2002.
37. Helga Serrano, No Bases Network (Quito), "No Bases News," No. 1, November 27, 2006.
38. *Bloomberg*, July 12, 2007; *El Tiempo*, July 12, 2007.
39. *El Comercio*, May 3, 2007.

References

Arnold, Captain Gary L., USAF (1988) "IMET in Latin America," *Military Review*, Vol. 67, No. 2.
Beruff, Jorge Rodríguez (1988) *Política Miltar y Dominación: Puerto Rico en el Contexto Latinoamericano* (San Juan: Ediciones Huracán).
Center for Naval Analyses (2002) *Future Training Environments* (Alexandria: CNA).
Gill, Leslie (2004) *The School of the Americas: Military Training and Political Violence in the Americas* (Durham: Duke University Press).
Goodwin, Bridget (1998) *Keen as Mustard: Britain's Horrific Chemical Warfare Experiments in Australia* (Queensland: University of Queensland Press).
Hunt, Col. David (1999) "Executive Summary: 1999 Range Clearance Activities," in Jorge Eduardo Ritter et al., *Memoria Cronológica: El Proceso de Saneamiento de las Bases Militares y Otras Areas Utilizadas por los Estados Unidos en la República de Panamá* (Panama).

Lindsay-Poland, John (2003) *Emperors in the Jungle: The Hidden History of the U.S. in Panama* (Durham: Duke University Press).

Pechura, Constance M. and Rall, David (eds.) (1993) *Veterans at Risk: The Health Effects of Mustard Gas and Lewisite* (Washington: National Academy Press).

Schoultz, Lars (1998) *Beneath the United States: A History of U.S. Policy toward Latin America* (Cambridge: Harvard).

Transnational Institute (2003) "Forward Operating Locations in Latin America: Transcending Drug Control," *Debate Papers* No. 8, available online at www.tni.org. Date last accessed October 14, 2007.

3

U.S. NUCLEAR WEAPONS BASES
IN EUROPE

David Heller and Hans Lammerant

Since World War II, the United States has maintained a network of
military installations across Europe. Throughout the 1980s, this
infrastructure supported several thousand tactical, intermediate-
range, and strategic nuclear weapons, as well as conventional
forces. Although the number of U.S. bases in Europe is now
significantly smaller than at the height of the Cold War, the U.S.
troops, weapons, communication systems, and other military infrastructure remain significant politically, socially, militarily, and often
economically for both the United States and the host country.

One of the most problematic parts of the U.S. forces currently
in Europe are the B61 tactical nuclear weapons (estimations
range between 350 and 480) based on the territory of its NATO
allies: secret, deadly, illegal, costly, militarily useless, politically
motivated, and deeply, deeply unpopular. This chapter deals
with the U.S. nuclear weapons that are based in Europe, as well
as other bases related to the functioning of the United States'
(nuclear-)war-fighting plans. It discusses the recent political and
social debates and protests within the host countries and the
United States regarding the continued presence of these weapons
– and the bases that support them.

Cold War Nuclear Weapon Stocks in Europe

During the Cold War stand-off with the Warsaw Pact, the United
States stationed nuclear weapons on the territory of a number

of European countries, many of which were NATO members. Information released under the Freedom of Information Act has revealed that the United States based nuclear weapons in Britain (from September 1954); West Germany (from March 1955); Italy (from April 1957); France (non-nuclear components, from August 1958); Turkey (from February 1959); Netherlands (from April 1960); Greece (from October 1960); and Belgium (from November 1963). Spain, not a NATO member at that point, also hosted nuclear weapons from March 1958. Nuclear weapons were stored on the Danish territory of Greenland from 1958 (Norris, Arkin, and Burr 1999).

The number of U.S. nuclear weapons based in Europe rose to a maximum of 7,300 land-, air-, and sea-based weapons in 1971, the majority of which were based in West Germany. The rationale for basing nuclear weapons in Europe was always double-sided. It was a clear signal towards the Soviet Union that an attack on a NATO member state would be met with an overwhelming military response. Involving NATO allies in the making of plans for the use of nuclear weapons, and discussions on when nuclear weapons would be used, also ensured that the NATO member states were linked to the alliance in a politically significant way. As such, nuclear sharing was an important political tool for maintaining links with NATO allies (Nassauer 2001).

The United States placed an emphasis on the ability to use tactical and intermediate range nuclear weapons to contain a war within the European arena. They believed that placing nuclear weapons with smaller yields and shorter ranges in Europe would give the capacity to respond to a Warsaw Pact attack, without the nuclear war necessarily escalating to an all out exchange of weapons. However, the European allies stressed that any hostile action against them, and the subsequent retaliation with tactical nuclear weapons, would inevitably lead to all-out nuclear war, and would thus deter attack (the so-called "extended deterrence").

In 1979, NATO decided on a dual approach to negotiations with the Soviet Union. They would negotiate for the withdrawal of SS-20 nuclear missiles from Eastern Europe, while at the same time preparing for the deployment of several hundred new intermediate range nuclear weapons on the territory of NATO member states.[1] If the Soviets withdrew the SS-20s, the NATO weapons would not be deployed.

Over the following few years, millions of people took to the streets of the capital cities of many NATO member states to demand that the new nuclear weapons not be deployed. The opposition to the new nuclear weapons in Europe was, however, not only expressed as a political opposition to the political decisions. Many nuclear weapon storage locations themselves became the site of bitter struggles, not least of which were the bases proposed for the storage of cruise and Pershing II intermediate range missiles with nuclear weapons. Among all these bases, it was Greenham Common which became a symbol across Europe and around the world of the new nuclear weapon deployments, and the struggle of the anti-nuclear movement.

Greenham Common: Cruise Missile Base and Site of Resistance

The United States deployed Ground Launched Cruise Missiles at several sites across Europe: Greenham Common and Molesworth in Britain, Comiso in Italy, Wuescheim in West Germany, and Florennes in Belgium. Pershing II missiles were stationed at Schwaebisch-Gmuend, Neu Ulm and Waldheide-Neckarsulm in West Germany. In 1983, Greenham Common became the first base in Europe to receive the new Ground Launched Cruise Missiles. The base covered an area of several square miles, and was located in the south of England approximately 50 miles east of London. It had been under U.S. control since the 1950s.

The arrival of 96 cruise missiles, scheduled for 1983, meant that an additional 1,200 U.S. personnel were stationed at the base. The 501st Tactical Missile Wing was activated at the base in 1982. The deployment of the missiles necessitated a great deal of construction, including building the large bunkers where the nuclear weapons and convoy vehicles were stored.

Although Greenham Common had been an airbase since World War II, and at one point had the longest runway in Europe, at

3,300 meters, the cruise missiles were not air launched. They were based on mobile delivery vehicles, which at times of heightened international tension would be moved up to 200 miles from the base to secret locations around the south of England to make the weapons less vulnerable to pre-emptive attack. During the period that the nuclear weapons were based at Greenham Common, regular exercises were held in which large convoys were moved around the country, to areas including the military training area of Salisbury Plain.

The resistance to the cruise missiles at Greenham Common was a milestone in resistance to nuclear weapons. The image of women living in makeshift encampments – outside a military base that was home to some of the most sophisticated and destructive weaponry on the planet threatened not only by nuclear war, and the brutality of the police and soldiers, but also by the elements – can be read as a story of marginalization and transgression. Depending on political bias, this position was something to be despised or celebrated (Cresswell 1996). However, there is another reading of the protests at Greenham which does not place them as marginal, but rather locates them as part of a creative and vibrant web of resistance, which after years of struggling and sharing, saw the nuclear weapons removed by 1991.

Following the decision to station nuclear weapons at Greenham, the "Women for Life on Earth" walk was organized from the Welsh capital of Cardiff to Greenham Common, arriving in September 1981. Following the walk a permanent peace camp was established at the base. Despite considerable local opposition, and the daily destruction of their camps following an eviction order in 1984, the Greenham women maintained a constant presence at the base from 1981 until 2000.

The resistance to nuclear weapons in the 1980s took many forms, and was inspired by many political, personal, and practical motivations. At the height of the struggle, separate camps, each with its own political and social character, were established at every one of the gates to the base. The camps also organized regular actions, ranging from spontaneous incursions into the base and the removal of large sections of the fence, to mass protests that brought together several thousands of women.

There were sections of the peace movement that remained critical of or obstructive towards the peace camps at Greenham, as a result of the ideological position of the camps. Criticism came as a result of the Greenham women's critical stance towards the Soviet Union's nuclear weapons, as well as the choice to remain a women's campaign. The model of organizing, based on anarchist and non-hierarchical methods, was also criticized by sections of the peace movement who saw this as alienating the majority of the working class, and especially the trade unions. Despite these criticisms, Greenham provided a visible focal point for the peace movement, and inspired permanent and temporary peace camps at many other nuclear weapon bases across Europe.

Maintaining a peace camp directly outside a nuclear weapons base highlighted many issues that would perhaps have remained hidden had the protests been restricted to the streets of London, or the debating chambers of Westminster. The presence of the camps directly adjacent to the base was a way of bearing a permanent witness to the horrors of nuclear warfare that could be unleashed from the missiles located just the other side of the fence. With Greenham Common placed firmly on the map by the protests and the peace camps, these were no longer abstract weapons, based in anonymous locations; these were very real weapons, with a very real location. Despite the clear territorialization of the issues in this way, the protests, and the spirit of the camps, certainly did not remain territorially bounded. The struggle was taken across Britain and around the world, buoyed up by the idea that "Greenham Women are Everywhere," and exhortations to "Carry Greenham Home."

As well as being labeled as a site that threatened a potential genocide, the presence of the nuclear missiles at Greenham made the area a certain target for attack in a nuclear war. The activities of the Greenham peace campers, and the "Cruisewatch" network of anti-nuclear activists who tracked and obstructed the exercises of the mobile carriers, highlighted the fact that hosting these missiles made the whole of the south of England a potential target in a nuclear war.

The image of an idyllic rural England, disrupted by the presence of a foreign body in the form of a huge U.S. military base and U.S. nuclear weapons, was successful in mobilizing a certain form of deep-rooted English nationalism. The fact that the land occupied by the base had formerly been common land, on which the local population traditionally had rights to graze cattle and collect firewood, added poignancy to this claim. In common with many other military bases around Britain, the area of Greenham Common Air Base was covered by bylaws drafted during the 1980s that were designed to curtail the rights of protesters. Many of these bylaws were successfully challenged, and had to be re-drafted.[2]

The fact that it was an exclusively women's action, and one which had resolutely chosen non-alignment and nonviolence as tactics, brought the links between capitalism, patriarchal power structures, and militarism to the fore. The power structures defended the U.S. military base at Greenham through the brutal treatment, surveillance, physical exclusion, and control of Greenham Women. In turn, these power structures depended for their survival upon the base and the nuclear weapons that it contained. These structures were revealed to be the same structures that defended (and depended upon) the oppression of women in wider society. The resistance that simultaneously revealed and undermined these structures of power has been described as a process of "practical deconstruction" (Emberley and Landry 1989).

The peace camps, the use of nonviolent direct action to disrupt the work of the base and the cruise missile exercises, as well as the regular incursions into the base, revealed that the base (and by extension the military–nuclear–industrial complex) was not a monolithic and impermeable structure, but rather more fragile and vulnerable than the military planners and politicians would have preferred people to believe (Haraway 1991).

Following the signing of the INF treaty between Reagan and Gorbachev in 1987, the cruise and Pershing II weapons were removed to the United States to be dismantled, and the remaining nuclear-related military equipment was moved to other U.S. bases in the region. The Greenham base was finally closed in 1992, with the departure of the last 400 U.S. soldiers who had remained after the withdrawal of the nuclear weapons.

Greenham Common was reopened to the public in 1997. Many parts of the former base have been officially designated "sites of special scientific interest (SSSI)," in recognition of the important flora and fauna that can be found there. It is ironic that the fences that were erected to protect and maintain the secrecy of weapons of mass destruction may have incidentally contributed to maintaining the biodiversity of the region. In an attempt to compensate for the economic impact following the closure of the base, the New Greenham Park business park, owned by Greenham Common Trust has been set up on part of the former base, and now plays a significant role in the local economy. Housing developments are planned for other parts of the site.[3] A monument to the peace campers and a peace park have been set up by former peace campers and supporters at the site of the "Yellow Gate" peace camp.

The "Forgotten" U.S. Tactical Nuclear Weapons in Europe

Greenham Common was one of 112 storage sites for U.S. nuclear weapons in Europe that were closed between 1985 and 1995 (Norris and Arkin 1995). During that time, the geopolitical landscape of Europe changed dramatically with the end of the Warsaw Pact, the reunification of Germany, and President George Bush proclaiming a "new world order" following the 1991 Gulf War.

However, despite these changes, the United States still retains an arsenal of up to 480 secret, and largely forgotten, tactical nuclear weapons in Europe. These weapons are all type B61, a free-fall nuclear bomb that is designed to be dropped from a fighter-bomber aircraft such as the F-15, F-16 or Tornado.

The weapons are stationed at eight Air Bases in six NATO countries, which stretch in an almost straight line across Europe.

Until June 2001, nuclear weapons were also stored at Araxos Air Force Base (AFB) in Greece. A further three sites, at Nörvenich AFB in Germany, and Akinci AFB and Balikesir AFB in Turkey, have the capacity to hold B61 nuclear weapons in "caretaker status," but are not hosting bombs at present. At this moment it is also unclear if there are still nuclear weapons in Ramstein or not.[4]

A U.S. Air Force document dealing with the upgrading of the storage facilities for U.S. nuclear weapons in Europe reveals that between February 1989 and April 1998 the U.S. engineering giant Bechtel installed 249 Weapons Storage and Security Systems (WS3) vaults at 15 sites in 7 European countries.[5] A sub-contract for the modernization of the vaults was awarded to Atlantic CommTech in 2002.[6]

The WS3 vaults are built in the ground of the Protective Aircraft Shelter (PAS). The vault rises up out of the floor of the aircraft shelter, and exposes the bomb. This arrangement makes it much easier to load or unload the bombs, as they do not have to be transported outside the hangar (PAS) where the plane is stationed. These vaults are designed to store nuclear weapons until at least 2018. When this date was made public, it caused serious concern that certain NATO allies would continue to host nuclear weapons for a relatively long period, without public debate on the issue.[7]

The issue of a possible end date for this arrangement of sharing nuclear weapons between NATO members has also been placed in the context of the replacements for the Tornado, F-15, and F-16 dual-capable aircraft that are currently tasked with the delivery of these weapons. Host nations will almost certainly need to order new planes before 2018, and the decision on whether a nuclear-capable model is ordered may determine whether the nuclear-sharing agreements can continue.[8]

A division can be made between those bases operated by the USAF (Aviano, Italy; Incirlik, Turkey; Lakenheath, England; Ramstein, Germany) and those operated by the air force of the host nation (Büchel, Germany; Ghedi Torre, Italy; Kleine Brogel, Belgium; Volkel, Netherlands). At the former, the nuclear weapons are in the custody of U.S. soldiers, and they are deployed to be loaded onto American planes, to be flown to their targets by

American pilots. In the latter bases, the nuclear weapons remain in the custody of a U.S. Munitions Support Squadron (MUNSS) until the weapons are loaded onto planes belonging to the host air force. At this point, they would be flown to their targets by pilots of the host country.

The nature of the relationship between the host nation and the United States varies depending on which of these systems is used. This difference is reflected in differences in the relationship between the host nation air force and the USAF, but also in terms of the impact the bases have on the local area and the host nation. Some of these differences can be illustrated by looking in more detail at two of these bases, Lakenheath (a USAF base in England) and Kleine Brogel (a Belgian air force base).[9] We turn first, however, to considering the common legal and political context of these bases, and the secrecy that surrounds them.

The NATO Nuclear Weapons in a Political and Legal Context

These nuclear weapons are a remnant of the Cold War strategy in which nuclear arms were used by NATO in a standoff with the Warsaw Pact, which was supposed to have a larger combined nuclear and conventional force. Since the end of the Cold War, and the demise of the Warsaw Pact, the military use for these weapons has changed. Although some see the nuclear weapons based in Turkey as possibly having a role in a preemptive strike against Iran, the NATO Strategic Concept makes it clear that the primary role of the nuclear weapons in Europe is political. This political role encompasses both the doctrine of deterrence (where the threat of nuclear weapons is seen as essentially a political task, rather than a military one) and also the role of U.S. nuclear weapons in maintaining links within the NATO alliance.

The Strategic Concept states:

62. The fundamental purpose of the nuclear forces of the Allies is political: to preserve peace and prevent coercion and any kind of war. They will continue to fulfil an essential role by ensuring uncertainty in the mind of any

aggressor about the nature of the Allies' response to military aggression. They demonstrate that aggression of any kind is not a rational option...

63. ... Nuclear forces based in Europe and committed to NATO provide an essential political and military link between the European and the North American members of the Alliance.[10]

As such, the continued deployment of U.S. nuclear weapons in Europe serves to symbolize the sharing of risks amongst the allies, and justifies the participation of NATO non-nuclear weapon states in nuclear decision making, and specifically the NATO Nuclear Planning Group. The NATO Nuclear Planning Group meets every six months, on the first day of the NATO defense ministers' summit, normally held at NATO headquarters in Brussels, Belgium. All NATO defense ministers, with the exception of France and Iceland, attend the meeting. The political decisions made here are translated into military plans at SHAPE (Supreme Headquarters of the Allied Powers in Europe), NATO's military headquarters located just outside Mons, Belgium. In peacetime SHAPE has a role in planning and preparations for all NATO forces, while in wartime it assumes direct command of all NATO forces, including the German, Italian, Belgian, and Dutch pilots who are tasked to fly the U.S. nuclear weapons based at Büchel, Ghedi Torre, Kleine Brogel and Volkel.

SACEUR (Supreme Commander Allied Powers Europe) is head of NATO forces in Europe. This office is always held by a U.S. general who is at the same time the supreme commander of U.S. troops in Europe. In peacetime he controls U.S. nuclear weapons in Europe, and the U.S. support troops such as the MUNSS squadrons.

However useful this policy of NATO nuclear sharing may be in fostering a sense of solidarity in an Alliance that has lost its enemy, it is facing a fractious future, prompted by doubts about U.S. unilateralism and serious legal questions.

In 1996, the International Court of Justice issued an advisory opinion which stated that the threat or use of nuclear weapons would generally be contrary to the rules of international law, and that the rules of international humanitarian law would apply to the use of nuclear weapons. It is clear that due to their yield and their proposed method of delivery the B61 nuclear weapons based in Europe could never be used lawfully. In particular, they could not distinguish in their effects between combatants and civilians, and they would contaminate countries not party to the conflict. Even before their actual use, merely threatening to use these weapons against countries which jeopardize the interests of the United States and its allies runs into conflict with the U.N. Charter. The ICJ made it clear that the U.N. Charter forbids the threat with an illegal use of force, even in self-defense.

In addition to those general principles of international law breached by the U.S. nuclear weapons in Europe, Article I of the Nuclear Non-Proliferation Treaty (NPT) states: "Each nuclear-weapon State Party to the Treaty undertakes not to transfer to any recipient whatsoever nuclear weapons ... directly, or indirectly; and not in any way to assist, encourage, or induce any non-nuclear-weapon State to manufacture or otherwise acquire nuclear weapons." Article II forbids non-nuclear states from receiving nuclear weapons. Under the terms of the NPT, the United States (and Britain) are nuclear-weapon states, while the remaining NATO nuclear-sharing countries are non-nuclear-weapon states. As the NPT has been signed and ratified by all of the NATO allies, and is therefore legally binding on them, it is likely that the policy of nuclear sharing is in violation of the spirit of the treaty.

However, the United States and NATO have argued that the treaty does not explicitly forbid the *deployment* of nuclear warheads in countries that are non-nuclear-weapon states (despite the fact that at least in some of the nuclear-sharing countries, the purpose of this deployment is to eventually turn over control of these weapons to the non-nuclear-weapon states). In addition, NATO argues that the conditions of the treaty do not apply in times of war (despite the statement made at the third review conference of the NPT in 1985 that Articles I and II should be respected in "any circumstances").[11]

Secrecy of nuclear weapons

Pentagon officials have standard answers to public questions about the location or disposition of nuclear weapons. It is DoD policy:

> 4.7. ... to respond to any public requests about the location of nuclear weapons as follows: "It is U.S. policy to neither confirm nor deny the presence or absence of nuclear weapons at any general or specific location." This response shall be provided even when such location is thought to be known or obvious.

> 4.8. That if asked why the United States has a "Neither Confirm Nor Deny" policy, the response should be as follows: "The basis for the security requirement inherent in the U.S. policy of neither confirming nor denying the presence or absence of nuclear weapons is to deny militarily useful information to potential or actual enemies, to enhance the effectiveness of nuclear deterrence, and contribute to the security of nuclear weapons, especially against the threats of sabotage and terrorism."[12]

The rationale for not discussing information on security grounds is understandable. However, it is clear that much of this information is already in the public domain, and the policy simply inhibits any public or political debate on the presence of nuclear weapons in any particular location. The lack of detail in the responses to parliamentary questions on the subject in many NATO nuclear-sharing countries has made this secrecy a problem as well for elected representatives.

NATO and the Belgian prime minister hatched a plan that would hopefully satisfy the demand for information regarding the nuclear weapons based at Kleine Brogel while complying with the official NATO policy of silence. The leaders of each of the democratic parties in the Belgian parliament, or a person that they nominated, could be informed about these matters. However, these people first had to receive NATO security clearance to make sure that they could be trusted with the information. This is parliamentary scrutiny turned upside down: NATO checks the parliament, so that they can decide who they are regulated by.

Faced with official silence regarding the presence of nuclear weapons, activists have obtained information through freedom-of-information requests and by physically entering or monitoring bases. "Citizens Weapons Inspections" have been carried out by anti-nuclear activists at many sites related to the development and deployment of weapons of mass destruction, including the U.S. nuclear weapon bases of Kleine Brogel, Volkel, Büchel, and Lakenheath.[13] These inspections, undertaken by concerned citizens, including prominent members of the community and elected representatives, paralleled the UNSCOM inspection in Iraq. The inspection actions have varied from the street theatre and the symbolic questioning of officials outside military bases to the mass trespasses of many thousands of people into bases used to store nuclear weapons. In many countries, inspection actions have played a central part in building campaigns against these bases, raising public awareness as a result of media reports and increasing the political pressure as governments are forced to admit that the presence of nuclear weapons is an issue. The results of the inspections were presented by a member of the Belgian Senate during the Non-Proliferation Treaty PrepCom meeting in 2004.[14] The following information is based on the results of these inspection actions, as well as other sources, including official government documents and activist/campaign materials.

Lakenheath

Although it is technically a Royal Air Force base, Lakenheath is home to the 48th Tactical Fighter Wing (also known as the "Liberty Wing") of the U.S. Air Force in Europe. Today, RAF Lakenheath hosts three squadrons of F-15 aircraft, including "dual capable" F-15E Strike Eagles, designed to carry both conventional and nuclear weapons. It is estimated that up to 110 B61 nuclear weapons are based at Lakenheath. Since it was allocated by the RAF for U.S. use in 1948, the base has played an important and ignominious role as a tactical bombing base, and since the 1950s as a site for the deployment of U.S. nuclear weapons.

The base was involved in one of the first significant accidents involving nuclear weapons. Shortly after nuclear weapons arrived at the base, on 27th July 1956, a U.S. bomber crashed into one of the concrete "igloos" used to store three nuclear bombs. Although the bombs were damaged in the fire that was caused by the crash, their conventional explosive triggers were not ignited.[15] The base also hosted the long-range F-111 fighter bomber aircraft that were used to attack Libya in 1986, as well as the first F-111 fighter unit to deploy to the Gulf during Operation Desert Shield/Desert Storm in 1991.

The 1958 Mutual Defense Agreement (MDA) provides the basis for the extensive nuclear collaboration between the United States and Britain. Under the agreement, the two nuclear-weapon states exchange classified information with the objective of improving each party's "atomic weapon design, development, and fabrication capability." The agreement allows cooperation on defense planning, delivery systems, training, some intelligence sharing, and development of military nuclear reactors. It also provides for the transfer of special nuclear material (plutonium or highly enriched uranium), components, and equipment between the two countries. The cooperation between the United States and Britain under the MDA is not limited to the basing of nuclear weapons at Lakenheath. Britain's supposedly "independent" Trident nuclear weapons system, based onboard nuclear submarines, is highly dependent on cooperation with the United States – the missiles are not owned by Britain, but are leased from a common pool of U.S. missiles, and the satellites that form an integral part of the guidance system are controlled by the United States. There is also an ongoing cooperation between the United States and Britain over the development of the nuclear warheads themselves.

The Mutual Defense Agreement was recently extended for a further ten years until the end of 2014, following secret negotiations between the U.S. and British governments (Butler 2004). According to the legal advice obtained from the respected legal practice Matrix Chambers, "it is strongly arguable that the renewal of the Mutual Defense Agreement is in breach of the nuclear Non-Proliferation Treaty."[16] There was no significant parliamentary debate on the renewal of this agreement.

Approximately 5,000 U.S. military personnel and 2,000 British and U.S. civilian staff are assigned to the base. However, the impact of having such a concentration of U.S. troops in what is a relatively sparsely populated area is limited by the fact that the base is largely self-contained, with the U.S. personnel and their families being housed, fed, and entertained predominantly on the base itself.

Weapon Inspection Team attempting search for WMD at USAF Lakenheath, England, 2003 (Friends of the Earth Flanders and Brussels).

The isolation of the base has intensified in recent years, especially following the terrorist attacks of September 11, 2001, as security measures have been stepped up around the base. These measures have included increased security patrols, and the construction of extra security infrastructure such as fences and cameras. Security in place before September 11 seemed to be aimed at dealing with the "threat" of anti-nuclear activists as much as terrorists.

A public footpath that ran across part of the base was closed in 1999, after concerns about security were expressed by U.S. forces. Bylaws covering Lakenheath and other U.S. bases in Britain were introduced in the 1980s to prohibit certain activities, including flying kites over the base, attaching items to the fence, or entering the base without permission.

These military-land bylaws, and similar bylaws at other military bases, have been the subject of legal challenges, and regular infringement, by anti-nuclear activists. The Campaign for Accountability of American Bases (CAAB) has long disputed the validity of the bylaws covering Lakenheath and other U.S. military bases around Britain. This is on the grounds that they have not been brought into force using the proper procedures outlined under the Military Lands Act 1892, or that they are inadequately precise in their definition of the area covered by the bylaws. The Ministry of Defence Police, who are responsible for policing military land in Britain, have been instructed not to arrest people under these bylaws, in order to prevent further legal challenges. The British government is currently engaged in a process of reviewing military-land bylaws, including many of those that cover the U.S. military bases in Britain.[17] The Serious Organised Crime and Police Act, which passed into British law in 2005, was ostensibly designed to give the police "the tools they need to reduce crime and keep ... communities safe."[18] As well as giving the police increased powers to obtain evidence and search premises, it also criminalizes trespass at a number of U.S. military installations.

CAAB and the Lakenheath Action Group (LAG) both draw attention to the fact that this remains a largely secretive and unaccountable base. They claim that by playing a role in U.S. war plans and extending the reach of U.S. militarism around the world, the base exists to enforce the economic and political interests of the United States, rather than those of Britain or the local community around the base. Lakenheath and other U.S. military bases occupy large areas of land in Britain, and as with Greenham Common this is land that has previously been open to members of the public for recreation or subsistence. This has introduced a land-rights aspect to the campaign. Many groups have answered the call to "reclaim the bases," opposing not only nuclear weapons and militarism, but also the exclusion of members of the public from large areas of land in Britain over which they previously had rights of access.[19]

Kleine Brogel

Since 1963, Kleine Brogel Airbase in Belgium has been used to store U.S. nuclear weapons, though the base has remained under Belgian Air Force control and U.S. planes have never been based there. Kleine Brogel plays an important role in NATO; in 1999 the 10th Tactical Wing based there flew bombing and other missions over Bosnia, Serbia, and Kosovo.

With no housing on the base, the 110 U.S. soldiers who work there live in the local area. The base currently hosts one nuclear-certified squadron of F-16 aircraft, and up to an estimated 20 B61 nuclear weapons. The use of U.S. nuclear weapons by Belgium is governed politically under a 1962 bilateral agreement as one of the Programs of Cooperation (POCs) established between the United States and its NATO allies.[20]

In common with the arrangements at Lakenheath, the nuclear weapons are stored in WS3 vaults in the floor of Protective Aircraft Shelters. The U.S. MUNSS and the Belgian air force both train in the raising and lowering of the nuclear weapons from their underground vaults, and practice loading these weapons onto Belgian F-16s. However, custody of the weapons remains with the 110-strong USAF Munitions Support Squadron until the time that they are ready to be used by the Belgian Air force.[21] The use of these weapons is controlled physically by the Permissive Action Link (PAL) locking system, which ensures that the weapon cannot be launched without the authorization of both the United States and the host nation. PAL links were introduced to nuclear weapons under the control of host nations during the 1960s after security worries were expressed by the United States (Stein and Feaver 1987). In theory, both the Belgian and U.S. governments would have to agree to a decision to use the nuclear weapons.

In practice, if Belgium were to forbid the use of the nuclear weapons based at Kleine Brogel, the United States could transfer the weapons to its own air force, or use nuclear weapons based elsewhere in Europe.

The secret bilateral agreements between the United States and Belgium which established the system of NATO nuclear sharing have been subject to criticism by parliamentarians. Bilateral agreements were also used to justify the transport of U.S. military equipment across Belgium in the build-up to the war on Iraq in 2002 and 2003, despite the official opposition of the Belgian government to the attack. The material was transported from bases in Germany to the port of Antwerp by rail. Civil transport planes with military goods also used Belgian airspace, and landed for refuelling at various airports.

Since 1997, the Bombspotting campaign has demanded greater openness about the nuclear weapons based at Kleine Brogel, as a first step towards the removal of the weapons. One key demand of the campaign is to "Bring Nuclear Weapons to Court," and acts of civil disobedience have been used to force the courts to debate the legality of nuclear weapons. The legal strategy depends on the fact that the crime of entering a military base can be justified in the context of an attempt to prevent a greater crime – the planning for the use of nuclear weapons, which would be a crime under international humanitarian law. Over the duration of the campaign, many thousands of people have been arrested for actions mainly involving the crossing of the one-meter-high perimeter fence around the base. In the largest of these actions, in October 2002, over 1,100 people were arrested either entering the base or attempting to enter the base. However, a quirk in the Belgian legal system means that none of these "Bombspotters" was prosecuted. The crime of entering a military base is judged to be a "political crime" under Belgian law. As such, it must be tried before a court with a jury. The fact that this would draw a large amount of press and public attention, and would risk the activists being acquitted, has convinced the public prosecutor not to begin the prosecution proceedings. An attempt to prosecute a token group of three Belgian members of parliament in a lower court ended with the court declaring itself incompetent to hear a trial for a political crime.

Despite the fact that it has never achieved a trial, the campaign has managed to mobilize massive public support. Actions have included the "complaint day," when members of the public were encouraged to go to their local police stations to make official complaints about the presence of nuclear weapons in Belgium and the complicity of the Belgian government in plans for their use. The campaign has also broadened its focus in recent years to draw attention to NATO headquarters in Brussels and SHAPE (the NATO military headquarters) near Mons. In 2006, ten different sites around Belgium related to the deployment, decision making, and support of nuclear weapons were targeted, in order to show how widespread the involvement in the nuclear policy is.

The Bombspotting campaign, and other anti-nuclear groups in Belgium, have built political support for their anti-nuclear demands. The Belgian Senate and House of Representatives both voted during 2005 for the withdrawal of nuclear weapons from Belgium and an end to NATO's nuclear-weapon policy. But NATO policy proves to be the outer limit for the foreign policy of its smaller member states, as the Belgian government does not dare to raise the issue inside NATO.

A similar conclusion could be drawn from the discussion during the invasion of Iraq in 2003. U.S. troops based in Germany shipped their material through Belgium to the Persian Gulf. These transports were legitimated by NATO agreements, even when they were used for a unilateral intervention to which the Belgian government was strongly opposed. As a result, the Bombspotting campaign transformed slowly into a general anti-NATO campaign, in which the themes of nuclear weapons, military interventions, and missile defense are linked as consequences of NATO membership. Two weeks before the Bucharest summit in April 2008, the "NATO – Game Over" action took place. About 1,000 activists from 17 European countries attempted to enter and close NATO Headquarters in Brussels. This represents an evolution in which anti-base activism, motivated by anti-nuclear campaigning, gets broadened and linked to campaigning against military intervention, and can be seen elsewhere in Europe as well. It follows the evolution of NATO from an organization in which nuclear weapons were an essential link between member states in the 1990s to one linked more by common participation in military operations such as those in Afghanistan. Anti-militarist activism followed the same track, especially when in 2003 the Iraq war made clear how war started from Europe even when the bombs were falling several thousands of kilometers away.

The Future Role for U.S. Tactical Nuclear Weapons in Europe

Although the U.S. seems prepared to maintain nuclear weapons in Europe until at least 2018, on two recent occasions it has seemed poised to withdraw the weapons. In 1999, Agence France-Presse stated that NATO was preparing to announce the withdrawal of all U.S. nuclear weapons from Europe. At the NATO defense ministers' meeting held the following month, these rumors were decisively quashed.[22]

A more recent discussion on the withdrawal of nuclear weapons took place in the context of the United States' decision in 2003 to review its military forces based in Europe.[23] Attention has focused on the proposed shift away from large permanent bases, situated in Germany, and towards more temporary bases, located in "New Europe," North and West Africa, Asia, and the Gulf (Johnson 2004). These new "lily pad" bases (of which Camp Bondsteel in Kosovo is the archetype) will enable the United States to intervene more quickly and flexibly against what they perceive as a new range of threats posed by terrorism, drug smuggling, and international criminal networks.

Comments made by General Jones in the Belgian Senate on March 9, 2004, and reported by *La Libre Belgique* indicated that a reduction in nuclear weapons based in Europe would be part of the review.[24] Subsequent parliamentary questions regarding this statement in both Belgium and the Netherlands have been met with the same blanket refusal to either confirm or deny the presence of nuclear weapons in those countries, and the further refusal to comment on the likely outcome of the review. Members of parliament attempting to enter the debate on the presence (and possible removal) of these nuclear weapons are met with a wall of official secrecy.

This restructuring round in the end had no impact on the nuclear-weapons policy. The review of U.S. forces in Europe led to the withdrawal of U.S. troops from Keflavik Airbase in Iceland,[25] as well as from many installations across the continent. In general this base restructuring was meant to improve the military intervention posture of the U.S. military in Europe and had most impact on the U.S. Army. Heavy U.S. Army brigades based in Germany would go back to the United States, while a new and lighter Stryker brigade replaces them. This replacement took place, but more troops than originally announced will stay in Germany, although it is not yet decided if this will be permanent or not. The remaining presence in Germany will be concentrated in fewer but larger bases. The U.S. military presence partly moves south to Vicenza in Italy, where the existing presence would be doubled with the construction of a new base. In Bulgaria and Romania, new bases are planned with a rotating presence. For the U.S. Air Force the main change was the closure of the Rhein-Main airport.

It now appears that the next chance for a debate on the withdrawal of nuclear weapons from Europe could be as part of the review of the NATO Strategic Concept document, which outlines NATO military policy. The NATO transformation process of which this is a part means transforming European militaries into intervention armies, constructing a new political consensus on how these forces will be used, and articulating the political aims of NATO. The new strategic concept will also give the rationale for the remaining nuclear weapons. As finding such consensus proves difficult, the start of the official review process gets delayed. Planning now is that the 60th anniversary summit in 2009 will start up such a review.

In late 2007, Germany and Norway started an initiative inside NATO to take stock of the possibilities for nuclear disarmament as part of a broader non-proliferation policy.[26] The NATO bureaucracy is arguing for a new role for the remaining nuclear weapons and a continuing deterrence policy aimed against Iran. NATO diplomat Michael Rühle stated: "As NATO gets ready for a new Strategic Concept sometime after 2009, one would hope that the language on the continued need for extended deterrence will be clear and unapologetic, and not hidden under arms control verbiage."[27] This view got very public with the report by five former NATO generals on the future of NATO strategy.[28] The political battle on the future of the U.S. nuclear weapons has started, but the result is still unpredictable.

Missile Defense as Part of the Nuclear Complex

Of the 26 NATO member states, only six (Belgium, Germany, Italy, Netherlands, Britain, and Turkey) are currently hosting U.S. nuclear weapons. However, all NATO member states with the exception of France are involved in the political and military planning for the use of the U.S. nuclear weapons based in Europe. Even if nuclear weapons are not actually present on their territory, NATO members can also be involved in practical support for U.S. (nuclear)-war-fighting plans, through the hosting of other U.S. bases on their territory. Thule, on the Danish island of Greenland, and Vardø in Norway, both play an important role in U.S. nuclear-weapon strategy, although Norway and Denmark both joined NATO on the condition that nuclear weapons would not be based on their territory. The planned missile defense installations in the Czech Republic and Poland are the newest parts of the U.S. nuclear complex in Europe.

Like many parts of the United States military infrastructure, the Ballistic Missile Defense program is shrouded in newspeak. It is portrayed as a defensive "shield," but in reality it is designed to facilitate a nuclear "first strike" by the United States. By removing the threat of "mutually assured destruction" through the ability to destroy incoming nuclear missiles, any reprisal against a United States first strike could be thwarted.

The construction of missile defense also risks provoking a new arms race. There is a danger that China will simply construct more strategic nuclear missiles capable of reaching the United States, in order to have the capacity to overwhelm the missile defense system. This in turn risks creating a regional arms race in Asia.

In Europe this risk is already turning into reality. Russia threatens to develop new missiles and to target the new missile defense installations. It has put on hold the CFE treaty, which limits conventional forces in Europe, and threatens to withdraw as well from the INF treaty, which abolished middle-range land-based nuclear missiles.

Thule

Thule Airbase in the self-governed Danish territory of Greenland has been used by the U.S. Air Force since 1941. In 1953, the indigenous residents of Thule (Uummannaq) were forcibly relocated from land that they had used for living and hunting. It took until 1999 for the 53 surviving former residents of Thule, known as the Hingitaq, or Dispossessed 53, to obtain a High Court ruling establishing that their territory had been expropriated without proper legislation and compensation as required by the Danish constitution.[29] The ruling did not agree with the claim of the Hingitaq 53 that they had the right to return to the land. The verdict was appealed to the Danish Supreme Court, which broadly supported the decisions of the original ruling.[30]

Declassified and leaked documents have revealed that the United States stationed four massive thermonuclear weapons at the base for several months in 1958 (Norris, Arkin, and Burr 1999). A further 48 nuclear missiles were located at the base between 1959 and 1965.[31] It has also been revealed that the United States regularly flew nuclear-armed B-52 bombers over Greenland. One of these planes crashed in 1968, with the destruction of four nuclear weapons on board and the death of one crew member.[32] Despite attempts to clean up after the accident, somewhere between 500g and 1.8kg of plutonium remains spread across a wide area. The seabed near the crash site shows high levels of plutonium contamination, with levels in shellfish up to 1,000 times higher than before the crash.[33] The local indigenous Inuit population claim that this plutonium, combined with pollution from the base, has caused an increase in birth defects amongst the animals in the area.[34]

The base has hosted early warning radar since 1961. Its location high above the Arctic Circle puts it in an ideal location to track the launch of strategic missiles from submarines in the Arctic and North Atlantic oceans, as well as parts of Russia. As the first warning of an incoming nuclear attack, the radar would act, in effect, as the trigger for a nuclear retaliation by the United States. Today, Thule Airbase provides missile warning and space surveillance information to North American Aerospace Defense (NORAD) command centers located at Cheyenne Mountain, Colorado. The base is set to play a leading role in the nuclear-war-fighting plans of the United States, as a host for an X-Band radar that makes up part of the Ballistic Missile Defense system.

During the Cold War, the Anti-Ballistic Missile (ABM) Treaty limited the size and scope of anti-ballistic missile systems employed by the United States and the Soviet Union and ensured that any nuclear strike could be met with an overwhelming response and "mutually assured destruction." The United States announced its intention to withdraw from the ABM treaty in 2001, in order to begin the deployment of Ballistic Missile Defense systems. Ballistic Missile Defense plays a vital role in the Pentagon's plans for "Full Spectrum Dominance": the "ability to conduct prompt, sustained, and synchronized operations with combinations of forces tailored to specific situations, and with access to and freedom to operate in all domains – space, sea, land, air, and information."[35]

The radar at Thule, as well as similar radar at RAF Fylingdales in England, is designed to detect the path of launched missiles. Based on the information received from these radar installations, interceptor missiles will be launched to destroy the weapons. This feat has been compared to "shooting a bullet with a bullet." Despite the huge cost of the scheme, serious doubts remain around the technical feasibility of the plans, after the failure of several tests of interceptor technology.

The Danish and Greenland Home Rule governments have given permission for the radar upgrading at Thule to form an important part of the Ballistic Missile Defense. The signing of the deal in 2004 was portrayed by the Greenland government as a step forward for the independence of Greenland, as the territory was given a direct voice in the decision making over the base. The previous agreement governing Thule was made in 1951 between the United States and Denmark, at a time when Greenland was a Danish colony. The agreement does not, however, give the Greenland government the right to veto further developments at the base, and only obliges the United States to "consult" with Denmark and Greenland. The Inuit Hingitaq 53, and their supporters including the Inuit Circumpolar Conference, continue to oppose the expansion of the base.[36] The $114.1 million contract for upgrading the Thule radar was awarded to Raytheon in 2006.[37]

Vardø

Norway, like Denmark, joined NATO on the understanding that nuclear weapons would not be stationed on its territory. It is, however, hosting a number of U.S. bases involved in Star Wars plans. Vardø is a Norwegian military intelligence base located 50 miles from the Russian border, in the far northeastern tip of Europe. Since the 1960s, the base has been home to the Globus radar system, used to track Russian submarine- and ground-launched missile tests. The population of Vardø, currently around 2,300, has decreased by over 20 percent in the past 10 years due to the collapse of the local fishing industry which followed Norway's decision not to join the European Union. This has left the base as a very important player in the local economy.[38]

In 1998 it was revealed that the United States was planning to move the 27-meter HAVE STARE radar dish to Vardø. The X-band radar had originally been constructed at Vandenberg Airbase in California, as part of the tests for the National Missile Defense system. Once in Norway, the radar became known as Globus II, and was given an official role in tracking space debris. The sophisticated radar can generate an exact radar "fingerprint" of nuclear missiles, including how they maneuver, and the decoys and counter-measures they deploy. This kind of precise information is vital to missile defense plans, as it allows the sensors to distinguish incoming warheads from decoys and other objects (Sellevåg 2000).

Since the plans to move HAVE STARE/Globus II to Norway were revealed by a Norwegian journalist, the precise role of the radar has been the subject of debate. The official Norwegian position is that the radar is used to track space debris; however, it has been claimed that much of the relevant debris cannot be observed from this latitude (Postol 2000). In fact, the radar is much better placed to track the test launches of Russian nuclear missiles from submarines in the Barents Sea as well as ground-based test launches from Plesetsk, Russia's main missile test facility (Sellevåg 2000). Evidence to back up this position came in 2000, when a storm removed the protective Teflon "golf-ball" protecting the radar dish, and revealed that it was pointing directly at Russia.[39]

Further questions remain regarding the cooperation between Norway and the United States in operating the radar and handling the data received from Globus II. Although there are no U.S. personnel stationed permanently at Vardø, it is clear that the information gathered by the radar is shared with the U.S. Space Command. The argument that there is no "real time" link between Vardø and U.S. Space Command headquarters in Cheyenne Mountain has been dismissed as misleading by the author of one report, who states that all satellite or radar monitoring has a built-in delay of some seconds while the information is being processed and transmitted, before the data is received by Space Command (Postol 2000).

Missile Defense Sites in the Czech Republic and Poland

The United States has been trying for some time to convince NATO to participate in its missile defense plans, but most European countries have buried the proposals by ordering studies about them. After the Riga summit in 2006 the United States became impatient and started formal negotiations separately with Poland and the Czech Republic. This strategy successfully put the European countries under pressure to accept missile defense sites in Europe. At a 2008 Bucharest summit, NATO accepted the U.S. missile defense plans. The only remaining debate inside NATO is how to embed this system within its broader structure. The governments of Poland and the Czech Republic have made the principal decision to host these installations.

Brdy in the Czech Republic will be the host of a radar installation, tasked with identifying and tracking the missile warhead and with guiding the intercepting missiles to it. The planned radar is X-band radar, to be moved from its current location at Kwajalein Atoll in the Marshall Islands.

A defunct airbase in Redzikowo in Poland will become a missile site with ten interceptor missiles. This site will work in connection with two U.S. sites with interceptor missiles in Alaska and California. All installations are slated to be complete in 2013. These installations will be augmented by a mobile, forward-deployed land-based X-band radar system, for which the Caucasus is often mentioned as a possible location.

Opinion polls in both Poland and the Czech Republic continue to show that a large majority is very much against the missile defense installations, contrary to their governments. In the Czech Republic, a broad coalition of movements started the No Bases or Ne Základnám initiative in 2006 and began campaigning for a national referendum.[40] This initiative organized several demonstrations with thousands of participants and grew into a country-wide movement. They were able to mobilize the villages near the planned installation where local referenda resulted in a clear No result. Local mayors began to speak out together. Given the history of the 1968 Russian invasion and occupation, the Czech people are very much against hosting foreign troops in their country. Although the Czech government continues to defend the planned installations, it clearly had not expected such strong resistance. The government coalition, composed of the center-right ODS Party, the Christian Democrat Party, and the Greens, has exactly half of the seats in parliament and cannot miss a single vote. The Czech Greens accepted the missile defense plans, but only if they had NATO approval. This was obtained in April 2008. Negotiations with the United States are expected to end in an agreement soon.

Polls in 2007 indicated that a majority of Czechs opposed building a proposed U.S. anti-missile base. The "No to Military Bases" alliance organized demonstrations in Prague (above) and other cities (Tomás˘ Adamec).

The population of Poland is as strongly opposed to the missile defense sites as the Czechs, although the movements against it have not been able to gather the same strength. One of the main movements is the "Stop the War" campaign or Inicjatywa "Stop Wojnie"[41]. This campaign started up as a campaign against the Iraq war, especially when Poland started to participate in the military occupation, and has now also taken up the missile defense issue. Once the planned site of the missile defense installation was more or less clear, the first local protest was organized on March 29, 2008 by the Polish Campaign Against Militarism and attracted 700 people.[42]

The missile defense plans were an issue during the recent elections and were partly responsible for the victory of the liberal opposition over the conservative government. But the new government only made stronger demands in return for the hosting of the missile defense sites, not a rejection of the bases altogether.

Although the prospects are not good, the struggle is not over yet. Both in the Czech Republic and Poland the struggle against the missile defense sites has helped to grow peoples' movements.

In both countries the struggle is seen less as a struggle against nuclear weapons, as these have in former Warsaw Pact countries a completely different history than in Western Europe; the struggle is seen as a struggle against participating in a new big-power war policy – specifically the United States' – and against the docile policy of the two countries' own governments.

This leads to broader identifications between movements. Across Europe, we see perspectives merging and links being made between the 'older' movements against nuclear weapons and 'newer' movements against the interventions in Iraq or Afghanistan. As the military policies are changing, new bases are needed and new sites of resistance are created. An important example of the 'newer' movements is the movement against a new military base in Vicenza, Italy. Vicenza already hosts the 173rd Airborne Brigade, which made a combat jump in northern Iraq in 2003 and which is one of the main U.S. combat forces in Europe. The new base will host the extra forces which are drawn from Germany and concentrated in Vicenza. Their point of departure in case of a military operation is Aviano, which is also a storage place of U.S. nuclear weapons.

Although Vicenza already hosted a U.S. military base, the local people objected to the expansion. A strong resistance movement started and became a focal point of the Italian peace movement.[43] On February 15, 2007, almost 200,000 people marched against the new base. This strengthened some left-wing parliamentarians enough for them to refuse to vote for a new budget for further Italian participation in the Afghanistan war, and the Prodi government lost its majority for the first time. Although the government in the end survived, it showed that peace issues could not be ignored. In December again more than 70,000 people demonstrated. Across Europe we see these movements linking up and merging their local perspectives into a common voice against the war policies of their governments.

Conclusion

We still have a long way to travel before we see all nuclear weapons and related infrastructure removed from Europe, and all the military bases reclaimed for use by local communities. However, the movement against nuclear weapons in Europe, and against U.S. bases more generally, has been successful in piercing the secrecy that shrouds these bases, an important first step in any informed debate on these issues.

If it were left up to military planners and governments, the debate on the role of Europe as a storage location for nuclear weapons would be stopped with a dogmatic refusal to either confirm or deny that role. The movement has managed to break down this defense by persistently drawing attention to the actual physical location of nuclear weapons of mass destruction in Europe, and the military infrastructure needed to support them. In many cases this has involved bringing protest and resistance to bases controlled by the United States or host nations.

This movement has also been at the forefront of the struggle against the use of many of these bases, and others, in assisting U.S./NATO-led wars of aggression. This has widened the struggle of many anti-nuclear groups to also include bases used in the U.S./U.K.-led war against Iraq. Anti-nuclear activists succeeded in disarming planes and support equipment at Leuchars in Scotland and Fairford in England that were being used in the war against Iraq.[44]

The practical skills and networks that were developed by "Cruisewatch" to track cruise missiles as they traveled around the English countryside have been instrumental in monitoring the transport of U.S. military equipment through Britain, as well as the secret flights involved in the transport of prisoners for "extraordinary rendition," and the transport of U.S. weapons to Israel before the war in Lebanon. In Belgium, the same groups who organized the Bombspotting actions against nuclear weapons at Kleine Brogel led the movement of direct action to prevent the transport of U.S. military equipment through the port of Antwerp for use in Iraq.

The awareness that preparations for war crimes have physical locations – where protests can be held and resistance can be exerted – has come in large part from the history of struggle against nuclear weapons. There is a strong feeling amongst many people in Europe that the continent is being used as an aircraft carrier, or staging post, in a U.S. plan for global hegemony. This brings little in the way of benefit to the people of the region, either financially or strategically. Yet it carries with it a perceived risk of being a target for terrorist or military attack. These are all issues that have been raised for many years by the anti-nuclear movement. It is a sad truth that it has taken the war against terror to renew public interest in these important issues.

Apart from their roles in directly challenging militarism and imperialism, the anti-nuclear and anti-bases movements across Europe have provided a very important training ground for people who have gone on to become involved in a wide range of social and environmental struggles. Many of the spectacular convergences of activists around Europe in recent years, on issues as diverse as resistance to G8 summits, the transport of nuclear waste, and the construction of environmentally destructive infrastructure, have been made possible by the practical skills, personal contacts, and models of organization that were developed in the anti-nuclear movement – and in particular in the struggle against nuclear-weapons bases. In turn, the European anti-bases movement is learning and developing as it makes links with anti-globalization, anti-capitalist, and environmental movements.

NOTES

1. By 1987 the USSR had deployed 654 SS-20 missiles in Europe (Harahan 1994).
2. Although the bylaws covering Greenham Common have been lifted, many of the other bylaws brought into force at this time, or their successors, are still in force.

3. Greenham Common Trust, "The history of Greenham Common," available online at www.greenham-common-trust.co.uk/history.htm. Date last accessed October 14, 2007.

4. Hans Kristensen, "United States Removes Nuclear Weapons from German Base, Documents Indicate," available online at www.fas. org/blog/ssp/2007/07/united_states_removes_nuclear.php.

5. The document was obtained under the Freedom of Information Act by Joshua Handler, Princeton University: "WS3 Sustainment Program," USAF Electronic Systems Center, Cryptologic Systems Group, Hanford Airforce Base, 2000, available online at www. nukestrat.com/us/afn/ESC_030300.pdf. Date last accessed October 14, 2007.

6. Forum voor Vredesactie, "Modernisering opslag kernwapens in Kleine Brogel ondanks aangekondigde terugtrekking Amerikaanse troepen uit Europa," 2004, available online at www.vredesactie. be/view.php?lang=nl&artikel=289. Date last accessed October 14, 2007.

7. Forum voor Vredesactie, "Kernwapens in Kleine Brogel tot 2018," 2001, available online at www.vredesactie.be/view. php?lang=nl&artikel=76. Date last accessed October 14, 2007.

8. Otfried Nassauer, "NATO's Nuclear Posture Review: Should Europe end nuclear sharing?" BITS, April 2002, available online at www. bits.de/public/policynote/pn02-1.htm. Date last accessed October 14, 2007.

9. A summary of the other U.S. nuclear weapon bases in Europe can be found in Arkin, Norris, and Handler (1998).

10. NATO, "The Alliance's Strategic Concept," April 24, 1999, available online at www.nato.int/docu/pr/1999/p99-065e.htm. Date last accessed October 14, 2007.

11. For a discussion on the legal issues raised by NATO nuclear sharing, see Nassauer (2001).

12. Department of Defense, "Directive Number 5230.16," December 20, 1993, available online at www.dtic.mil/whs/directives/corres/ pdf/523016p.pdf. Date last accessed October 14, 2007.

13. For Mother Earth, "Overview of Citizens' Weapons Inspection actions: The story so far ... ," 2004, available online at www. motherearth.org/inspection/inspection1.php. Date last accessed October 14, 2007.

14. David Heller (ed.) "Secret U.S. Nuclear Weapons in Europe: Citizens' Weapons Inspection Report," 2004, For Mother Earth, available online at www.motherearth.org/inspection/reportNPT2004.pdf. Date last accessed October 14, 2007.

15. Nuclear Age Peace Foundation, "Significant Nuclear Accidents," available online at www.nuclearfiles.org/menu/key-issues/nuclear-

weapons/issues/accidents/significant-nuclear-accidents.htm. Date last accessed October 14, 2007.

16. BASIC, the Acronym Institute for Disarmament Diplomacy and Peacerights, "Mutual Defence Agreement and the Nuclear Non-Proliferation Treaty," 2004, available online at www.basicint.org/nuclear/MDAlegal.htm. Date last accessed October 14, 2007.

17. See the CAAB website, www.caab.org.uk.

18. Home Office Press Office, "New Powers for Police," December 28, 2005, available online at http://press.homeoffice.gov.uk/press-releases/new-powers-for-police?version=1. Date last accessed October 14, 2007.

19. Website of Reclaim the Bases, www.reclaimthebases.org.uk/. Date last accessed October 14, 2007.

20. PENN Project on European Nuclear Non-proliferation, "NATO Nuclear Sharing and the NPT: Questions to be Answered," 1997, available online at www.basicint.org/nuclear/NATO/PENNnote2-nuclearsharing-1997.htm#22. Date last accessed October 14, 2007.

21. The lesson plan for the 717th MUNSS, based at Volkel in the Netherlands, was found by activists carrying out a "citizens weapons inspection" of the base.

22. NATO Notes, "NATO Ministers Meet: Denial of tactical nuclear weapon withdrawal and arguments over role for Europe," 1999, Centre for European Security and Disarmament.

23. Otfried Nassauer, "NATO's Nuclear Posture Review: Should Europe End Nuclear Sharing?" BITS Policy Note 02.1, April 2002, available online at www.bits.de/public/policynote/pn02-1.htm. Date last accessed October 14, 2007.

24. Online at www.globalsecurity.org/military/library/news/2004/03/mil-040310-shape02.htm. Date last accessed October 14, 2007.

25. American Forces Press Service, March 16, 2006, available online at www.defenselink.mil/news/newsarticle.aspx?id=15147.

26. Press release by the German Ministry of Foreign Affairs, available online at www.auswaertiges-amt.de/diplo/en/Infoservice/Presse/Meldungen/2007/071207-DtlNorAbruestungNATO.html.

27. Michael Rühle, "A Nuclear Iran: Implications for the non-proliferation regime, NATO's nuclear policy, and missile defence," available online at www.nato-pa.int/Docdownload.asp?ID=5124D5F6E702000D73.

28. Klaus Naumann, John Shalikashvili, Lord Inge, Jacques Lanxade, Henk van den Breemen, "Towards a Grand Strategy for an Uncertain World: Renewing the transatlantic partnership," available online at www.csis.org/media/csis/events/080110_grand_strategy.pdf.

29. Kory Cappoza and Stacey Fritz, "Thule: Greenland's role in missile defence," No Nukes North, 2005, available online at www.nonukesnorth.net/thule.html. Date last accessed October 14, 2007.

30. Inuit Circumpolar Conference, "Temporary Statement Regarding the Supreme Court of Denmark's Ruling of November 28th 2003 in the Thule case," 2002, available online at www.inuit.org/index.asp?lang=eng&num=218. Date last accessed October 14, 2007.

31. Greenpeace Nordic, "Star Wars and Thule Bringing the Cold War back to Greenland," July 2001, available online at www.stopstarwars.org/html/thulebrief.pdf. Date last accessed October 14, 2007.

32. Jaya Tiwari and Cleve J. Gray, "U.S. Nuclear Weapons Accidents," available online at www.cdi.org/Issues/NukeAccidents/accidents.htm. Date last accessed October 14, 2007.

33. Cappoza and Fritz, "Thule."

34. *Independent*, August 7, 2001.

35. William S. Cohen, "Annual Report to the President and Congress," Department of Defense, 2001, available online at www.defenselink.mil/execsec/adr2001/Chapter11.pdf. Date last accessed October 14, 2007.

36. Inuit Circumpolar Conference, "A Loud No to Agreement," 2004, available online at www.inuit.org/index.asp?lang=eng&num=256. Date last accessed October 14, 2007.

37. Defense Industry Daily, "$114.1m to Upgrade BMEWS Thule," 2006, available online at www.defenseindustrydaily.com/2006/04/1141m-to-upgrade-bmews-thule/index.php. Date last accessed October 14, 2007.

38. Vardø community website, www.vardo.kommune.no. Date last accessed October 14, 2007.

39. *Wall Street Journal*, June 6, 2000.

40. Website Ne Zakladnam, www.nezakladnam.cz.

41. Website Inicjatywa "Stop Wojnie," http://stopwojnie.webd.pl.

42. See the report online at http://m29.bzzz.net/content/view/148/43/lang,polish/.

43. Website No Dal Molin, http://nodalmolin.it.

44. See "Trident Ploughshares and the War in Iraq," available online at www.tridentploughshares.org/article1010; and the Reclaim the Bases website, available online at www.reclaimthebases.org.uk. Date both last accessed October 14, 2007.

REFERENCES

Arkin, William M., Norris, Robert S., and Handler, Joshua (1998) *Taking Stock: Worldwide Nuclear Deployments 1998* (Washington, D.C.: NRDC).

Butler, Nicola (2004) "U.S.–U.K. Mutual Defence Agreement," *Disarmament Diplomacy*, Issue No. 77. Available online at www. acronym.org.uk/dd/dd77/77mda.htm. Date last accessed October 8, 2007.

Cresswell, Tim (1996) *In Place/Out of Place: Geography, Ideology, and Transgression* (Minnesota: University of Minnesota Press).

Emberley, Julia and Landry, Donna (1989) "Coverage of Greenham and Greenham as Coverage," *Feminist Studies*, Vol.15, No. 3, pp. 485–498.

Harahan, Joseph P. (1994) *On-Site Inspections Under the INF Treaty: A History of the On-Site Inspection Agency and Treaty Implementation, 1988–1991* (Darby PA: Diane Publishing Co).

Haraway, Donna (1991) *Simians, Cyborgs and Women: The Reinvention of Nature* (New York: Routledge).

Johnson, Chalmers (2004) *The Sorrows of Empire: Militarism, Secrecy, and the End of the Republic* (New York: Metropolitan).

Nassauer, Otfried (2001) "Nuclear Sharing in NATO: Is it Legal?" *Science for Democratic Action*, Vol. 9, No. 3. Available online at www.ieer.org/sdafiles/vol_9/9-3/nato.html. Date last accessed October 8, 2007.

Norris, Robert S. and Arkin, William M. (1995) "U.S. nuclear weapon locations, 1995," *Bulletin of the Atomic Scientists,* Vol. 51, No. 6, pp. 74–75.

—— and Burr, William (1999) "Where They Were," *Bulletin of the Atomic Scientists*, Vol. 55, No. 6, pp. 26–35.

Postol, Theodore A. (2000) "The Target Is Russia," *Bulletin of the Atomic Scientists*, Vol. 56, No. 2, pp. 30–35.

Sellevåg, Inge (2000) "Uncovering Vardø," *Bulletin of the Atomic Scientists*, Vol. 56, No. 2, pp. 26–29.

Stein, Peter and Feaver, Peter (1987) *Assuring Control of Nuclear Weapons: The Evolution of Permissive Action Links* (New York: University Press of America).

4

IRAQ AS A PENTAGON CONSTRUCTION SITE[1]

Tom Engelhardt

Back in April 2003, just after Baghdad fell to American troops, Thom Shanker and Eric Schmitt reported on the front page of the *New York Times* that the Pentagon had launched its invasion the previous month with plans for four "permanent bases" in out of the way parts of Iraq already on the drawing board. Since then, the Pentagon has indeed sunk billions of dollars into building those "mega-bases" (with a couple of extra ones thrown in) at or near the places mentioned by Shanker and Schmitt.

When questioned by reporters at the time about whether such "permanent bases" were in the works, Secretary of Defense Donald Rumsfeld insisted that the United States was "unlikely to seek any permanent or 'long-term' bases in Iraq" – and that was that. The *Times* piece essentially went down the mainstream-media memory hole. On this subject, the official position of the Bush administration has never changed. In November 2007, for instance, General Lute slipped up, in response to a question at his press gaggle. The exchange went like this:

Q: And permanent bases?
GENERAL LUTE: Likewise. That's another dimension of continuing U.S. support to the government of Iraq, and will certainly be a key item for negotiation next year.

White House spokesperson Dana Perino quickly issued a denial, saying: "We do not seek permanent bases in Iraq."

Back in 2003, Pentagon officials, already seeking to avoid that potentially explosive "permanent" tag, plucked "enduring" out of the military lexicon and began referring to such bases, charmingly enough, as "enduring camps." And the word remains with us – connected to bases and occupations anywhere. For instance, of a planned expansion of Bagram Air Base in Afghanistan, a Col. Jonathan Ives told an AP reporter:

> We've grown in our commitment to Afghanistan by putting another brigade (of troops) here, and with that we know that we're going to have an enduring presence. So this is going to become a long-term base for us, whether that means five years, ten years – we don't know.

Still, whatever they were called, the bases went up on an impressive scale, massively fortified, sometimes 15–20 square miles in area, housing up to tens of thousands of troops and private contractors, with multiple bus routes, traffic lights, fast-food restaurants, shopping, and other amenities of home, and reeking of the kind of investment that practically shouts out for, minimally, a relationship of a distinctly "enduring" nature.

A full contingent of 2,000 non-Iraqi construction workers (admittedly, impoverished Third Worlders, evidently stowed away under less than lovely conditions) are in Baghdad to finish work on the mother of all embassies. We're talking about a U.S. embassy compound under construction these last years that's meant to hold 1,000 diplomats, spies, and military types (as well as untold numbers of private security guards, service workers, and heaven knows who else). It will operate in the Iraqi capital's heavily fortified Green Zone as if it were our first lunar colony. According to William Langewiesche, writing in *Vanity Fair*, it will contain "its own power generators, water wells, drinking-water treatment plant, sewage plant, fire station, irrigation system, Internet uplink, secure intranet, telephone center (Virginia area code), cell-phone network (New York area code), mail service, fuel depot, food and supply warehouses, vehicle-repair garage, and workshops."

As yet, the 21-building, nearly Vatican-sized "embassy" remains unfinished and significantly behind schedule. That's what happens, of course, when you insist on redesigning your food court to serve not just lunch, but three meals a day, and – oh, yes – to be bomb-, mortar-, and missile-proof, at the cost of an extra $27.9 million. Some of the embassy's wiring systems have already blown a fuse; its 252 guard trailers have filled with formaldehyde fumes, and "during a recent test of the embassy sprinkler system, 'everything blew up.'" (A bit worrisome, should a well-aimed mortar start a fire.) And to add insult to injury, the project is now $144 million over the nearly $600 million budget Congress granted it (and, when fully operational, is expected to cost another $1.2 billion a year to run). A State Department spokesman, Sean McCormack, rejecting charges of inadequate oversight, offered the following clarification of the embassy's present financial situation: "It is not a cost overrun. It is an additional contract requirement." It's true, as well, that the construction contract was long ago farmed out to local Middle Eastern talent – First Kuwaiti General Trading and Contracting was made prime contractor.

When, in the future, you read in the papers about administration plans to withdraw American forces to bases "outside of Iraqi urban areas," note that there will continue to be a major base in the heart of the Iraqi capital for who knows how long to come. As the *Washington Post*'s Glenn Kessler put it, the 21-building compound "is viewed by some officials as a key element of building a sustainable, long-term diplomatic presence in Baghdad." Presence, yes, but diplomatic?

National Public Radio's Defense Correspondent Guy Raz spent some time at Balad Air Base about 70 kilometers north of Baghdad. As Thomas Ricks of the *Washington Post* reported, back in 2006, Balad is essentially an "American small town," so big that it has neighborhoods and bus routes – and its air traffic rivals Chicago's O'Hare International Airport. According to Raz, the base now houses 30,000 American troops as well as perhaps another 10,000 private contractors. It has well-fortified Pizza Hut, Burger King, and Subway fast-food outlets, two PXs that are as big as K-Marts, and actual sidewalks (each of which someone had to build and profit from). Billions of dollars have reportedly gone into Balad, one of at least five mega-bases the Bush administration has built in that country (not counting the embassy, which is functionally another base) – and, Raz tells us, "billions of dollars are being spent on upgrades."

Of Balad, Raz writes:

> The base is one giant construction project, with new roads, sidewalks, and structures going up across this 16-square-mile fortress in the center of Iraq, all with an eye toward the next few decades ... At the base, the sounds of construction and the hum of generators seem to follow visitors everywhere. Seen from the sky at night, the base resembles Las Vegas: While the surrounding Iraqi villages get about 10 hours of electricity a day, the lights never go out at Balad Air Base.

Former Centcom Commander General John Abizaid, the man who dubbed the president's global war on terror the "Long War," suggested that American troops could well be stationed in the Middle East half a century from now. ("[W]e shouldn't assume for even a minute that in the next 25 to 50 years the American military might be able to come home, relax and take it easy.")

Balad is not the only other major construction site in Iraq. Consider, for instance, al Asad Air Base, another of our billion-dollar mega-bases. This one's off in Iraq's western desert. When the president "visited" Iraq in early September, this was where he landed – and a bevy of journalists hit the base with him (a base, mind you, that is supposed to have a 19-mile perimeter!) and managed to describe next to nothing about it to the rest of us. Fortunately, a corporal in the U.S. Marine Reserves (and sometime writer for the *Weekly Standard* and *National Review*), Matt Sanchez, has been traveling Iraq, embedded with U.S. troops, and recently offered a rare, vivid description.

Al Asad, he tells us, is known among Americans as "Camp Cupcake" ("a military base where you can have all the ice cream you want, swim in an air-conditioned indoor pool, drink caffè lattes at 3 a.m. and even take yoga courses in the gym.") At present, according to Sanchez, it holds 17,000 people ("most of whom don't even work for the military") and evidently has its own Starbucks. Arriving there from rougher lodgings, he found it a disorienting experience.

With sidewalks, clean paved roads and working street lamps (a combination not common in Iraqi cities), there are times when I felt I was in a small city in Arizona instead of the Sunni Triangle. Al Asad is the only place I know of in Anbar province where drivers get speeding tickets and vehicles are towed for bad parking.

And don't forget the traditional "steak and lobster" Thursday meals at the mess hall or the "Ugandans" – African private security personnel – who generally man checkpoints around the base. And building hasn't stopped yet.

Bases are springing up in Iraq all the time. Consider, for instance, the delightfully named "Combat Outpost Shocker." It's only seven provocative kilometers from the Iranian border and

New U.S. "enduring bases" in Iraq
Source: globalsecurity.org

it's a nothing, really. A mere bagatelle of a forward base, meant to block what the Bush administration claims is a flow of deadly Iranian weaponry. It went up almost overnight for chump change on a $5 million contract. And it's such a modest "camp," – sized for just 100 troops from the Republic of Georgia (on loan to the ever-shrinking "coalition of the willing"), about 70 American soldiers, and a few U.S. Border Patrol agents (who, it seems, can be assigned to any border on the planet, not just our two official territorial demarcation lines). It's so small it doesn't even have an airstrip for fixed-wing aircraft, a requisite for any larger base.

When news of Combat Outpost Shocker suddenly came out in the *Wall Street Journal* in 2007, it caused a tiny media ripple (though a blink and you would have missed it). After all, it seemed like one more in-your-face gesture at the Iranians on the noble road to preventing "World War III." Far more noteworthy, though, is something no one in the United States ever discusses: the Pentagon can evidently build bases just about anywhere it pleases. It seems not to have bothered even to consult Iraqi government officials before announcing that Combat Outpost Shocker was well under way – or perhaps Congress either. But that's pretty much the latitude you get when you're the "defense department" for most of a planet; when you already have 737 or 850 or even 1,000 bases and installations of one sort or another outside the United States; when your global properties stretch from Germany, Romania, the island of Diego Garcia, and Kyrgyzstan to South Korea, Guam, and Australia and you're still eyeing the few blank spots on that map like, say, Africa.

Keep an eye on Africa, by the way. It could be the next boom continent for base construction. The Bush administration just recently set up Africom, a new global command to cover that land mass. It may be the last such command formed – unless, someday, Russiacom and Chinacom prove to be available. The Pentagon is now reportedly searching Africa for spots to position what they like to call "lily pads," which are basically small, relatively spartan bases that won't be so noticeable (or generate local ill will and resistance so readily). Right now, about all the United

States has is a "lily pad" at Djibouti on the Horn of Africa. But stay tuned.

Things are going really, really badly in Afghanistan – which means that U.S. troop strength just keeps rising. It's now at 25,000 and, of course, we have to put them somewhere. As a result, the old Soviet base we took over in 2001, Bagram Air Base, is about to grow by a third. Where there were once only 3,000 American troops on the base, there are now 13,000, and more to come. So new runways, new barracks, you name it. It's going to be like a construction horn of plenty.

The Iraq bases were part of what should be considered the facts on the ground there, though, between April 2003 and the present, they were rarely reported on or debated in the mainstream in the United States. But if you place those mega-bases (not to speak of the more than 100 smaller ones built at one point or another) in the context of early Bush administration plans for the Iraqi military, things quickly begin to make more sense.

Remember, Iraq is essentially the hot seat at the center of the Middle East. It had, in the previous two-plus decades, fought an eight-year war with neighboring Iran, invaded neighboring Kuwait, and been invaded itself. And yet, the new Coalition Provisional Authority, run by the president's personal envoy, L. Paul Bremer III, promptly disbanded the Iraqi military. This is now accepted as a goof of the first order when it came to sparking an insurgency. But, in terms of Bush administration planning, it was no mistake at all.

At the time, the Pentagon made it quite clear that its plan for a future Iraqi military was for a force of 40,000 lightly armed troops – meant to do little more than patrol the country's borders. (Saddam Hussein's army had been something like a 600,000-man force.) It was, in other words, to be a "military lite" – and there was essentially to be no Iraqi air force. In other words, in one of the more heavily armed and tension-ridden regions of the planet, Iraq was to become a Middle Eastern Costa Rica – if, that is, you didn't assume that the U.S. Armed Forces, from those four "enduring camps" somewhere outside Iraq's major cities, including that giant air base at Balad, and with the back-up help of U.S. Naval forces in the Persian Gulf, were to serve as the real Iraqi military for the foreseeable future.

Again, it's necessary to put these facts on the ground in a larger – in this case, pre-invasion – geopolitical context. From the first Gulf War on, Saudi Arabia, the largest producer of energy on the planet, was being groomed as the American military bastion in the heart of the Middle East. But the Saudis grew uncomfortable – think here, the claims of Osama bin Laden and Co. that U.S. troops were defiling the kingdom and its holy places – with the Pentagon's elaborate enduring camps on its territory. Something had to give – and it wasn't going to be the American military presence in the Middle East. The answer undoubtedly seemed clear enough to top Bush administration officials. As an anonymous American diplomat told the *Sunday Herald* of Scotland back in October 2002, "A rehabilitated Iraq is the only sound long-term strategic alternative to Saudi Arabia. It's not just a case of swopping horses in mid-stream, the impending U.S. regime change in Baghdad is a strategic necessity."

As those officials imagined it – and as Deputy Secretary of Defense Paul Wolfowitz predicted – by the fall of 2003, major American military operations in the region would have been reorganized around Iraq, even as American forces there would be drawn down to perhaps 30,000–40,000 troops stationed eternally at those "enduring camps." In addition, a group of Iraqi secular exiles, friendly to the United States, would be in power in Baghdad, backed by the occupation and ready to open up the Iraqi economy, especially its oil industry, to Western (particularly American) multinationals. Americans and their allies and private contractors would, quite literally, have a free run of the country – the equivalent of nineteenth-century colonial extraterritorial-ity (something "legally" institutionalized in June 2004, thanks to Order 17, issued by the Coalition Provisional Authority, just before it officially turned over "sovereignty" to the Iraqis). And, sooner or later, a Status of Forces Agreement or SOFA would be "negotiated" that would define the rights of American troops garrisoned in that country.

At that point, the United States would have successfully repositioned itself militarily in relation to the oil heartlands of the planet. It would also (once you included the numerous new U.S. bases that had been built and were being expanded in occupied Afghanistan as part of the ongoing war against the Taliban) have essentially encircled a second member of the "axis of evil," Iran. It would be triumphant and dominant and, with its Israeli ally, militarily beyond challenge in the region. The cowing of, collapse of, or destruction of the Syrian and Iranian regimes would surely follow in short order.

Of course, much of this never came about as planned. But among the most tenacious and enduring Bush administration facts on the ground are those giant bases, still largely ignored – with honorable exceptions – by the mainstream media. Thom Shanker and Cara Buckley of the *New York Times*, to give but one example, managed to write that paper's major piece about the joint "declaration" without mentioning the word "base," no less "permanent," and only General Lute's slip made the permanence of bases a minor note in other mainstream reports. And yet it's not just that the building of bases *did* go on – and on a remarkable scale – but that it continues today.

Whatever the descriptive labels, the Pentagon, throughout this whole period, has continued to create, base by base, the sort of "facts" that any negotiations, no matter who engages in them, will need to take into account. And the ramping up of the already gigantic mega-bases in Iraq proceeds apace. Reports in late 2007 indicate that the Pentagon will call on Congress to pony up another billion dollars soon enough for further upgrades and "improvements."

Reports have emerged on the latest U.S. base under construction, uniquely being built on a key oil-exporting platform in the waters off the southern Iraqi port of Basra and meant for the U.S. Navy and allies. Such a base gives meaning to this passage in the Bush–Maliki declaration: "Providing security assurances and commitments to the Republic of Iraq to deter foreign aggression against Iraq that violates its sovereignty and integrity of its territories, *waters*, or airspace."

As the British *Telegraph* described this multi-million dollar project: "The U.S.-led coalition is building a permanent security base on Iraq's oil pumping platforms in the Gulf to act as the 'nerve centre' of efforts to protect the country's most vital strategic asset." Chip Cummins of the *Wall Street Journal* summed up the project this way in a piece headlined "U.S. Digs in to Guard Iraq Oil Exports – Long-Term Presence Planned at Persian Gulf Terminals Viewed as Vulnerable": "[T]he new construction suggests that one footprint of U.S. military power in Iraq isn't shrinking anytime soon: American officials are girding for an open-ended commitment to protect the country's oil industry."

Though you'd never know it from mainstream reporting, the single enduring fact of the Iraq War may be this constant building and upgrading of U.S. bases. Since the *Times* revealed those base-building plans back in the spring of 2003, Iraq has essentially been a vast construction site for the Pentagon. The American media did, in the end, come to focus on the civilian "reconstruction" of Iraq which, from the rebuilding of electricity-production facilities to the construction of a new police academy has proved a catastrophic mixture of crony capitalism, graft, corruption, theft, inefficiency, and sabotage. But there has been next to no focus on the construction success story of the Iraq War and occupation: those bases.

In this way, whatever the disasters of its misbegotten war, the Bush administration has, in a sense, itself "endured" in Iraq. Now, with only a year left, its officials clearly hope to write that endurance and those "enduring camps" into the genetic code of both countries – an "enduring relationship" meant to outlast January 2009 and to outflank any future administration. In fact, by some official projections, the bases are meant to be occupied for up to 50 to 60 years without ever becoming "permanent."

You can, of course, claim that the Iraqis "asked for" this new, "enduring relationship," as the declaration so politely suggests. It is certainly true that, as part of the bargain, the Bush administration is offering to defend its "boys" to the hilt against almost any conceivable eventuality, including the sort of internal coup that it has, these last years, been rumored to have considered launching itself.

In an attempt to make an end-run around Congress, administration officials continue to present what is to be negotiated as merely a typical SOFA-style agreement. "There are about 100 countries around the world with which we have [such] bilateral defense or security cooperation agreements," General Lute said reassuringly, indicating that this matter would be handled by the executive branch without significant input from Congress. The guarantees the Bush administration seems ready to offer the Maliki government, however, clearly rise to treaty level and, if we had even a faintly assertive Congress, would surely require the advice and consent of the Senate. Iraqi officials have already made clear that such an agreement will have to pass through their parliament – in a country where the idea of "enduring" U.S. bases in an "enduring" relationship is bound to be exceedingly unpopular.

Still, a formula for the future is obviously being put in place and, after years of frenzied construction, the housing for it, so to speak, is more than ready. As the *Washington Post* described the plan, "Iraqi officials said that under the proposed formula, Iraq would get full responsibility for internal security and U.S. troops would relocate to bases outside the cities. Iraqi officials foresee a long-term presence of about 50,000 U.S. troops."

No matter what comes out of the mouths of Iraqi officials, though, what's "enduring" in all this is deeply Pentagonish and has emerged from the Bush administration's earliest dreams about reshaping the Middle East and achieving global domination of an unprecedented sort.

Notes

1. Excerpted from "Iraq as a Pentagon Construction Site," TomDispatch. com, December 2, 2007 and "Advice to a Young Builder in Tough Times," TomDispatch.com, November 4, 2007.

Part II

Global Resistance

5

PEOPLE'S MOVEMENT RESPONSES TO EVOLVING U.S. MILITARY ACTIVITIES IN THE PHILIPPINES

Roland G. Simbulan

The Filipinos did not get the same message from God as U.S. President William McKinley's benevolent assimilation, and the Filipinos' resistance to U.S. military intervention began in 1899 in what has remained, up to the present time, organized efforts by Filipinos in opposition to U.S. interference.
—Howard Zinn, *A People's History of the United States*

In the past two decades, especially after the 1986 people power revolt against the Marcos dictatorship, the proliferation of people's organizations has become one of the most prominent features of Philippine political life. Over the years, these movements have been the people's response to the inadequacy of the government in providing for the welfare of the citizenry. They have also played a crucial role in advancing the people's demands toward genuine change. These movements articulate what social scientists call the possibility and desire for human security and genuine development through their common opposition to neoliberal globalization (Bello 1999; Pollard 2004). In fact, many civil society movements in the Philippines are now playing significant roles in building transnational solidarity alliances on debt relief, environmental protection, indigenous peoples, and women's issues. But the so-called "war on terror" campaign of the United States, on which certain states like the Philippines have been piggy-backing, threatens to label any form of dissent as terrorism and has, in fact, evolved into an attempt to destroy the capacity of people's movements to achieve social, economic, and political reforms.

Though historically people's movements are not strangers to the Philippine political environment, especially in the country's anti-colonial struggles (Ileto 1979), there is a movement among the grassroots in the Philippines and it is a movement fueled by the recognition that they have the right to participate in the affairs of their government, even on matters related to foreign policy and defense issues. This movement has been referred to as organized civil society or cause-oriented groups, and it is growing in *barangays* (villages) and municipalities all over the country, where more and more people have recognized it as necessary for the pursuit of social reform and survival. These local movements "struggle to integrate previously excluded groups and issues into local or national politics" (Foweraker 1995:63). But while these groups often posit themselves as being in clear opposition to government or to the socio-economic elite and their policies, they are equally dependent upon government to redress certain wrongs or bestow rights. Thus, their strategic interaction with the state brings these movements clearly into the realm of the political. As Foweraker concludes, "all social movements must be defined in some degree by their political projects, or their attempts to influence institutional and political change" (1995:69).

A distinct quality of the people's movement in the Philippines is its reflection of the Filipino people's vision for themselves, their society, and their future as institutionalized in the 1987 constitution, in terms of building a peaceful, prosperous, democratic, just, and humane society. The people's movement has a broad constituency that includes the peasant movement, the workers' movement, the women's movement, and so forth. Recent in-depth studies have shown that the Philippines has the most vibrant social movement in Southeast Asia, with organized popular forces intervening in the political and socio-economic affairs of society (Third World Studies Center 1997; Lindberg and Sverrisson 1997).

This chapter documents an aspect of this social movement related to peace and national sovereignty issues, especially in the aftermath of the September 11, 2001, attacks that made the Philippines the second front after Afghanistan in the "war on terror." There is no dearth of theories on social movements. This chapter therefore discusses the Philippine experience and lessons drawn from it.

The 1987 Philippine constitution institutionalizes people's participation in governance. The issues of the Bataan Nuclear Power Plant, the U.S. military bases, and Philippine military involvement in Iraq provide examples of participatory governance in foreign and security policies. The successful struggle and campaign of the Nuclear-Free Philippines Coalition (NFPC) is a case in point, in which a coalition built by a people's movement covers not just all political blocs but also local governments, civic organizations, and churches. Such a coalition stopped the operation of the controversial nuclear power plant that was built by the corrupt Marcos dictatorship. The NFPC also provided the experience and core to the expanded Anti-Treaty Movement that lobbied and put pressure on the Philippine Senate to reject the renewal of a military bases agreement in 1991. These experiences show that the gap between the government and the people can be bridged, by empowering the latter and by providing the opportunities for their voices to be heard.

Anti-nuclear Roots of the Contemporary Anti-bases Movement

The Nuclear-Free Philippines Coalition was initially a "desk" under the Citizens' Alliance for Consumer Protection (CACP). During the Marcos dictatorship, the CACP dealt with consumer issues that involved pharmaceutical drugs, oil companies, sale of soft drinks, safety of toys, etc. It represented a full range of consumerist concerns, eventually touching upon the issue of energy because of warnings by Marcos that the country would soon be having problems with power shortage. At that time, there was a strong campaign for the peaceful uses of nuclear power. On the other hand, there was resistance to nuclear technology, particularly the development of nuclear weapons. To win public acceptance of nuclear energy as a source of power, the government told the public that nuclear energy has two uses: one that is destructive and is therefore being rejected, and the other, peaceful, which should be acceptable because it harnesses nuclear energy supposedly for the public good. These peaceful uses include the use of nuclear power to preserve food by subjecting it to low-dosage radiation and for x-rays to detect disorders in the human body. One more peaceful use of nuclear power, the government said, is its ability to produce electricity through a nuclear power plant. It was a claim that the CACP questioned, and soon this issue became the subject of a national campaign. The desk on nuclear concerns at the CACP then began to have a life of its own.

On January 26, 1981, the Nuclear-Free Philippine Coalition (NFPC) was established. As the nuclear-plant issue became an increasingly serious concern, the NFPC evolved into a campaign-oriented coalition of 129 national and sectoral organizations of professionals, teachers, youth and students, farmers, women, health professionals, churches, labor, urban poor, science and technology organizations, and human rights advocates nationwide. To the surprise of political observers, and perhaps its own members, the campaign against the power plant succeeded. Following the unrelenting opposition of the coalition and bolstered by testimonies of nuclear-energy experts, the Bataan nuclear power plant was mothballed permanently.

In 1988, after the permanent mothballing of the nuclear power plant by the Cory Aquino government, the NFPC found itself focusing on a second cause: nuclear weapons and the U.S. military bases. With the Military Bases Agreement scheduled to end in 1991, the U.S. and Philippine governments needed to sign a new treaty that would allow for the extension of the stay of the bases. But a groundswell of opposition to the bases was building up, led by people's organizations which remember the role of the military bases in propping up the Marcos dictatorship. Because of the broad and strong opposition from the people's organizations, the Senate in the newly restored democracy decided to reject the new treaty, this despite strong U.S. pressure exerted on then president Corazón Aquino who, in turn, had tried in vain to persuade the senators to renew the treaty. As a result, U.S. troops and facilities were withdrawn from the Philippines in 1991. The next task for the NFPC was the formation of the People's Task Force for the Bases' Clean-up (PTFBC), an offshoot of the organization's belief that toxic and hazardous wastes may have been dumped and contaminated the vast territories of the U.S. bases. From 1993 to 1996, the NFPC functioned as the secretariat, culminating in the holding of the First International Forum on Military Toxic and Bases Clean-up in November 1996. Today, the People's Task Force on Bases Clean-up stands as an independent group that is focused on issues related to military toxic wastes. As a result of its efforts, litigation is pending in both Philippine and U.S. courts concerning the deaths and illnesses of people believed to have been harmed by the toxic wastes (Chanbonpin 2003).

Providing educational and information services to its member organizations and to the general public, the NFPC has become the national center for the anti-nuclear, anti-foreign military-access and bases-conversion issues. It gives advice on nuclear and bases issues to city councils, as well as provincial and municipal boards, many of which have passed resolutions declaring their localities as bases-free, nuclear-free territories.

The efforts are in line with the NFPC's objectives: (1) to inculcate a consciousness of freedom from nuclear power and weapons among Filipinos by launching educational campaigns; (2) to broaden the anti-nuclear movement by mobilizing existing national and local organizations, schools, and communities nationwide; and (3) to generate strong international support for the nuclear-free Philippines movement and contribute to the realization of a nuclear-free and independent Pacific by fostering solidarity relations with international, regional, and national anti-nuclear, anti-bases, and peace movements.

The NFPC (1) served as the national coordinating and resource center on information concerning nuclear power, U.S. military access and bases conversion; (2) conducted education drives and led mobilizations against nuclear weapons and military bases nationwide; (3) lobbied the executive and legislative bodies of the Philippine government for polices supportive of the peace and anti-nuclear provisions of the Philippine constitution; and (4) served as the national campaign center for the abolition of nuclear weapons and opposition to nuclear testing in the Asia Pacific region, and as coordinating center for the No-Nukes Asia Forum–Philippines, and the Nuclear-Free and Independent Pacific Movement/Pacific Campaign for Disarmament and Security (PCDS).

To oppose the nuclear option, NFPC used different forms of resistance. It used these to inform the public about the effects of the nuclear power plant and to influence the decisions of the government with regards to the use of nuclear power. The NFPC campaign had three phases. First, there was a major campaign during the Marcos dictatorship that lasted up to the time of Corazón Aquino. During the Marcos era, the coalition sought to stop the construction of the nuclear power plant by lobbying in the executive and legislative branches, even though these were then mere rubber stamps of the dictatorship. The coalition also appealed before the courts: a petition was filed with the Philippine Supreme Court against Westinghouse Corporation, the builder of the nuclear power plant. Simultaneously, an educational campaign was conducted to make the public aware of the safety aspect of the nuclear issue, the connection between nuclear power plants and nuclear weapons, as well as with weapons and bases, and the problems and risks that accompany the operation of nuclear power plants. Images of Hiroshima and Nagasaki were shown in slide shows, films, and exhibits in schools and communities. The campaign's environmental appeal that also struck a chord with all those concerned with people's safety and "natural security" gave it an almost universal appeal that cut across all sectors of Philippine society. The idea was to create a constituency that would say no to the government that insisted on adopting the nuclear option to solve its energy problem, and linking this with the risks entailed in storing and transiting nuclear weapons in the U.S. bases.

A campaign in the local areas was also developed, specifically in Bataan province, where the nuclear plant was being constructed, and in Central Luzon, the site of the two largest U.S. bases in the country. Together with the coalition, the local people in these areas made up the strongest opposition to the nuclear power plant, nuclear weapons, and also the U.S. bases. It was at this point that the NFPC organized the Nuclear-Free Bataan Movement (NFBM) and the Central Luzon Alliance for a Sovereign Philippines (CLASP). There were discussions at the *barangay* level, with residents expressing their views. Organizing efforts were also made at the municipal level. Town and municipal councils came up with their positions on the nuclear issue and these were raised before the provincial boards. In Bataan, where the nuclear plant was being built, most of the province's ten towns, including the capital town Balanga, submitted resolutions against the plant's operation.

The second phase of the campaign began in 1985 when the Marcos dictatorship tried to open and operate the nuclear power plant. With the construction completed, a clearance for its operation was already under way. The uranium needed was ready to be loaded. Despite the many safety questions raised by experts as well as the public, the government was bent on using the plant. The NFPC countered by waging a *welga ng bayan* (a people's strike), which was participated in by allied organizations and even local governments. The strike effectively paralyzed transportation and operations in the entire province of Bataan.

Despite the success of the people's movement in blocking the operation of the nuclear power plant during the Marcos regime, its work was far from over when the Aquino administration came to power. When Corazón Aquino was campaigning for president, she promised never to allow the operation of the power plant. With this platform, the NFPC supported her candidacy. When she became president, Aquino appointed a Constitutional Commission to replace the constitution that had been in effect since political independence in 1946. This provided the coalition the opportunity to make its victories in the anti-bases and anti-nuclear struggles permanent by including provisions in the new constitution that would make the ban permanent. The Commission decided on a compromise: it would ban nuclear weapons from Philippine territory, but not the option of using nuclear energy in the future. It was a good enough decision. By adopting a provision prohibiting nuclear weapons in Philippine territory in 1987, the Commission made it a state policy.

Institutionalizing Advocacy Objectives

Among the countries in the Asia Pacific, the Philippines has historically had the longest security relations and alliance with the United States, giving it the image of being a stable U.S. stronghold in the Asia Pacific region. In recent years, however, the Philippines has also become the Achilles heel of U.S. military forces in the Asia Pacific. There are two important reasons for this and these are related to the institutionalization of certain aspects of the demands and objectives of the people's movement for sovereignty in the Philippines.

One reason is the 1987 Philippine constitution, which incorporates explicit pro-peace and anti-nuclear weapons provisions. Section 2, Article II of the constitution's Declaration of Principles states:

> The Philippines renounces war as an instrument of national policy, adopts the generally accepted principles of international law as part of the law of the land and adheres to the policy of peace, equality, justice, freedom, cooperation and amity with all nations.

Furthermore, the state policies enunciated in the same constitution include the following:

> The State shall pursue an independent foreign policy. In its relations with other states, the paramount consideration shall be national sovereignty, territorial integrity, national interest and the right to self-determination. (Section 7, Article II)

and:

> The Philippines, consistent with the national interest, adopts and pursues a policy of freedom from nuclear weapons in its territory. (Section 8, Article II)

The other reason is the institutionalization of organized people's power through the pertinent provisions of the 1987 constitution, to wit:

> The State shall respect the role of independent people's organizations to enable the people to pursue and protect, within the democratic framework, their legitimate and collective interests and aspirations through peaceful and lawful means. People's organizations are bona fide associations of citizens with demonstrated capacity to promote the public interest and with identifiable leadership, membership and structure. (Section 15, Article XIII: Social Justice and Human Rights – The Role and Rights of People's Organizations)

and

> The right of the people and their organizations to effective and reasonable participation at all levels of social, political and economic decision-making shall not be abridged. The State shall, by law, facilitate the establishment of adequate consultation mechanisms. (Section 16, Article XIII)

At first, not all anti-nuclear-weapons advocates inside or outside the government were against U.S. bases. But it was the Americans who unwittingly reconciled the two, thus making anti-nuclear pacifists into fierce anti-bases advocates (Simbulan 1998, 2004).

Everyone assumed then that the U.S. Navy regularly transited and always had on "standby storage" tactical nuclear weapons in their bases on Philippine territory. U.S. authorities made this clear when they threatened to give up the bases if the constitutional ban on nuclear weapons was enforced. Moreover, the U.S. insistence on its policy of neither confirming nor denying the presence of nuclear weapons on the bases naturally led Filipinos to link nuclear weapons with the bases, and consequently to call for the removal of all U.S. bases and facilities.[1]

It must be emphasized that the real moving spirit behind the vote of the Philippine Senate on September 16, 1991, to dismantle U.S. military bases was the broad and unified people's movement outside the Senate. In the end, it was the power of the people that ended the most visible symbols of colonial legacy and the Cold War in the Philippines. It ended 470 years of Spanish and U.S. military bases on foreign soil.

The Anti-Treaty Movement was forged with the broadest unity possible among organized forces and individuals. Because of this, academics, economists, and scientists, as well as other personalities involved with the movement, were able to influence the preparation of the government's base-conversion development plan that was commissioned from 1988 to 1990.[2]

The growth of the resistance against the bases mobilized under the broad umbrella of the Anti-Treaty Movement is reflected in the fact that on September 10, 1991, six days before the historic Senate rejection of the treaty, about 50,000 people marched against the bases. But on September 16, the day of the vote, the number of protesters outside the Senate building had swelled to 170,000, despite a heavy downpour.[3]

The anti-nuclear and anti-bases movement grew into a broad but visibly strong organization because of the consciousness and commitment inculcated in the minds of the public. The purpose for which the NFPC was set up had been achieved. The Bataan nuclear power plant was closed down and was never operated by the government. The U.S. military bases and the nuclear weapons believed to be stored there were dismantled in the early 1990s. With these successes, the NFPC redirected its campaign thrusts. It became involved in campaigns aimed at converting the use of the bases to peaceful purposes. It also worked for the cleanup and removal of toxic wastes from the former military facilities. And in the face of efforts by the U.S. and Philippine governments to revive military ties through new "access agreements" forged during the post-bases era (such as the Visiting Forces Agreement and the Mutual Logistics Support Agreement), the coalition has vigilantly taken part in exposing and addressing this emerging issue.

With the success of the NFPC, Foweraker's (2001) observation has proven true: "Successful social movements inevitably lose their reason for being." With the changes in government policy and political circumstances in the post-bases era – changes that the NFPC itself had an important hand in bringing about – the coalition adopted new forms of organizational alliances and shifted gears.

In the post-bases era, various configurations of people's power have tried to replicate the models presented by the NFPC and the Anti-Treaty Movement: from the post-9/11 Gathering for Peace

(GFP) to the Peace Camp and to the Junk the VFA (Visiting Forces Agreement) Movement. The latter movements were formed in October 2001 after key leaders of the 1991 anti-bases campaign met to discuss the effects and implications on the Philippines of the September 11, 2001, attacks and the U.S. war against terrorism.

The Gathering for Peace began as a coalition of 51 non-government organizations, people's organizations, political blocs, and individuals promoting peace, tolerance, and national sovereignty, and opposing U.S. military intervention in the Philippines (Gathering for Peace 2002). Launched on February 12, 2002, in the heart of Manila, the national launching was attended by representatives of various sectors and classes of society. This included academe, government units, the entertainment industry, national politicians, leaders of the different religious faiths, workers, students, women, business, farmers and peasants, and the urban poor.

The GFP is a loose, broad, but centrally coordinated activist campaign center involved in issues concerning peace. It advocates the principles of sovereignty and self-determination as basic rights of people, and seeks to uphold these rights in the face of U.S. military operations and other forms of intervention. In pursuit of these objectives and principles, GFP engages in various activities to promote understanding and awareness on U.S. intervention in the Philippines, particularly in conflict-torn Mindanao. This organization undertakes material development, media campaigns, training, discussions, and occasionally mass actions.

It was also established to respond to the new situation of a less visible U.S. military presence: there are no more U.S. bases, but there are still year-round joint military exercises, U.S. naval ship visits, and deployment of U.S. Special Operations Forces in conflict areas, taking place under the legal framework of the Philippine–U.S. Visiting Forces Agreement and the Mutual Logistics and Support Agreement. In addition to the highly-publicized Balikatan exercises, year-round joint military exercises are now held in practically any part of the country. They include small- and large-scale military exercises such as "Carat," "Masurvex," "Palah," "Teak Piston," "Balance Piston," "Handa Series," "Flash Piston,"

"EODX," and "Salvex," in which U.S. Special Operations Forces units all the way from Okinawa and the Pacific Command in Hawai'i are involved for "combat training, surveillance and reconnaissance training" and, ostensibly, to improve the two countries' "interoperability."[4]

One incident shows the continuing ability of the Philippine social movement to influence government foreign policy. In 2004, a Filipino truck driver named Angelo de la Cruz was held by Iraqi resistance forces, who demanded the withdrawal of the small Filipino military contingent in Iraq. Having placed the Philippines in the U.S.-led "coalition of the willing," President Gloria Macapagal Arroyo was faced with a quandary: to follow the U.S. policy of refusing the demands of the Iraqi resistance or to heed the call of the Filipino people for the safe and immediate return of de la Cruz. On the one hand was strong U.S. pressure, made visible by the public pronouncements of its diplomats in Manila; on the other were the mounting demonstrations by organized as well as unorganized forces, whose growing numbers were a grim reminder of a similar outpouring of grief and outrage that followed the execution of a Filipino domestic helper in Singapore a few years back. The death of the domestic helper triggered a crisis that nearly consumed the Ramos administration at that time. In a country in which every family has a member working abroad, the plight of one overseas worker is the plight of all. It was an incident that Arroyo had no wish to see repeated. In a move that startled U.S. officials, she ordered the withdrawal of the Filipino troops from Iraq. Even then, she had to publicly explain her decision, albeit for the benefit of the United States:

Why then did I bring our Filipino troops back home from Iraq? I trust that our allies will come to understand that the Philippines is in a special circumstance, that unlike the U.S. or Australia or Bulgaria or other countries, eight million Filipinos also live and work abroad: 1.5 million Filipinos live in the Middle East; 4,000 Filipinos are working in Iraq today ... There are perhaps more meaningful ways to strengthen our strategic relationship with the United States. We shall always work to keep the relationship firm in propelling the common commitment to fight terrorism, domestically, regionally and worldwide. My highest priority to our country is economic growth and job creation. That drives our foreign policy. (Presidential News Desk, August 6, 2004)

A Burgeoning People's Movement

Success may have cost one coalition its reason for being, but it has also encouraged the formation of other groups with advocacies of their own. Because of the U.S. war on terror that is perceived to be infringing on the Philippines' hard-won commitment to peace, many other organizations have emerged. These include OUT NOW! (Out U.S. Troops Now), Junk the VFA Movement, and the Kilusan Laban sa VFA (Movement Against the VFA), which are identified with the leftist party, the Bagong Alyansang Makabayan (Bayan). The Justice No War Coalition was also formed with retired navy Captain Danilo P. Vizmanos as convenor. There is also the regional Peace, Disarmament and Symbiosis in Asia Pacific and the Magulang at Paslit Laban sa Digmaan at Karahasan (Parents and Children Against War and Violence), which co-hosted a regional consultation on the International Criminal Tribunal for Iraq in Manila on October 16, 2004.

Worthwhile noting is the campaign on women and children's issues related to the U.S. military involvement in the Philippines. Foremost among these is GABRIELA, which stands for General Assembly Binding Women for Reform, Integrity, Equality, Leadership, and Action. The group was named after one of the first and fiercest women generals in the Philippines, Gabriela Silang, who led the longest series of successful revolts against the eighteenth-century Spanish colonizers. GABRIELA figures prominently in the international arena as well, with chapters in the United States and Canada. It is among the women's groups struggling against the return of U.S. military forces, because of the prostitution and sexual abuse of women and children that inevitably follow such presence.

Notable also is the Coalition Against Trafficking of Women–Asia Pacific (CATW-AP), formed in 1988, whose regional office is based in the Philippines. Specifically, the CATW-AP has been active in "campaigns on issues of military prostitution in the Asia Pacific region" and according to a CATW-AP brochure it gives strong "support for the Women's International War Crimes Tribunal towards a just resolution for the victims of Japanese Military Sexual Slavery." The Asia Pacific CATW is composed of representatives from eight countries. In the Philippines, the CATW is composed of the following women's groups: Alternative Network of Bicol Women, BIDLISIW, BUKAL, Buklod Center, Center for Overseas Workers, Conspectus Foundation Inc., DAWN Foundation, Development of People's Foundation, DSWP, EBGAN, Freedom from Debt Coalition–Women's Desk, IMA Foundation, ISSA, KAKAMMPI, Kalayaan, Lawig Bubai, Lihok-Pilipina, Nagkakaisang Kababaihan ng Angeles City, Saligan, Samaritana, Talikala, TW-MAE-W, WEDPRO, Women's Crisis Center, Woman Health Philippines, and WomenLEAD.

Sectoral organizations with comprehensive political and economic programs like the Bayan Muna (People First) Party, Suara, Anakpawis, GABRIELA, Philippine International Forum (PIF), Promotion for Church People's Response (PCPR), May 1 Labor Movement (KMU), Peasant Movement of the Philippines (KMP), Migrante International (an international organization of migrant Filipinos), Anakbayan (a youth association), PAMALAKAYA (a national alliance of fisher-folk organizations), Health Alliance for Democracy (HEAD), Alliance of Concerned Teachers (ACT), COURAGE (a national federation of government employees' associations), KALIKASAN (a people's network for the environment), KARAPATAN, KAMP (a national council for indigenous peoples' organizations), and the Ecumenical Movement for Justice and Peace (EMJP).

In the local regions, the formation of broad sectoral alliances can be cited. One good example is the region south of Manila, the Southern Tagalog region, where a local multi-sectoral alliance against U.S. intervention was organized. This was the SAKAY or Samahan ng Kanayunan ng Timog Katagalugan Laban sa Giyerang Agresyon ng Estados Unidos (Rural Association of Southern Tagalog Against the United States' War of Aggression). The alliance is named after Macario Sakay, a Tagalog revolutionary leader who fought U.S. occupation from 1902 until he was captured in 1906 and sentenced to death by hanging by the colonial authorities. The regional alliance SAKAY condemned increasing U.S. military presence in the region, citing as example an incident in February 2005 when military trucks carrying more than 700 heavily armed U.S. soldiers accompanied by troops of the Philippine Army were sighted in three towns of Quezon province as well as in the upland areas of Laguna and Rizal provinces. The group claimed that the "U.S. military even plays upon issues of disaster relief, infrastructure development and anti-narcotics to conceal its real intentions in Southern Tagalog region." SAKAY has also reported that U.S. troops have regularly conducted "site assessments" with psy-war units of the region's military command in the provinces of Camarines Sur, Sorsogon, and Masbate, which are known to have very active New People's Army (NPA) guerrilla activity.

The Peace Camp, a campaign for peace with justice, is a coalition of more than 50 interfaith groups and individuals against war and state terrorism. Peace Camp's main thrust is against the U.S. war of racist aggression against the world's oppressed and poor majority, conducted under the cover of the war on terrorism, which aims to ultimately re-establish U.S. hegemony over the international economic, political, military, and socio-cultural system. Peace Camp is also campaigning against the Philippine government's intensifying war against liberation movements in the country and its participation in the U.S.-led coalition against terrorism. The local war has put many civilians in "war camps," thereby endangering lives and communities in the process.

The No to War Coalition–Philippines, or NO TO WAR, is a multi-sectoral coalition of organizations and individuals calling for peace and an end to the occupation of Iraq. NO TO WAR conducts workshops, trainings, discussions, and film screenings to help the public achieve a deeper understanding of peace issues. The coalition also organizes press conferences, public actions, and other events as part of its advocacy for peace and genuine human security. It is part of the global anti-war movement to end foreign occupation in Iraq.

An interesting feature of these movements against U.S. military presence, both in the past and the present, is that they are not single-issue movements, but are involved in other sectoral or national economic and political concerns. Thus, for instance, they consider themselves part of the anti-corporate globalization movement as well. People's organizations in the Philippines which are involved in anti-war and disarmament campaigns regard security agreements such as the Visiting Forces Agreement and the Mutual Logistics and Support Agreement with the United States as the military aspect of U.S.-led globalization efforts. In their view, globalization is not just about the free movement of U.S. capital, but also its armed components that will assure the protection of international capital.

Shifting the Focus to Mindanao

Since 2001, there has been a remarkable emphasis on U.S. military presence in Mindanao. For instance, 15 of the 23 projected U.S.–Philippine military exercises for 2005 were scheduled to take place in Mindanao, particularly in the Muslim-dominated areas.[5] The joint military exercises, code-named Balikatan (Shoulder-to-Shoulder), have come to include predominantly Muslim provinces like Basilan, Sulu, Zamboanga, Sultan Kudarat, and Cotabato. Military exercises in such areas would bring U.S. Special Operations Forces closer to actual combat operations in these conflict-ridden provinces.[6] U.S. soldiers landed in Sulu in 2004 at the height of hostilities between the Armed Forces of the Philippines (AFP) and the resurgent Moro National Liberation Front (MNLF) of Nur Misuari, the Moro leader who is languishing in jail.

Under the guise of fighting terrorism, U.S. military presence has indeed increased in the southern Philippine island of Mindanao.[7] Thousands of U.S. troops have taken part in Balikatan war exercises and special operations training. In many instances, actual combat missions have been reported in which U.S. forces fought side by side with elite units of the Philippine Army in hunting down Abu Sayyaf bandits and other erstwhile terrorist groups.[8] This presence has caused tension among communities such as those in Basilan, where a U.S. soldier, Sergeant Reggie Lane, killed a civilian, Buyong-Buyong Isnijal, in 2002. Sgt. Lane was not prosecuted in any Philippine court, but instead hurriedly shipped out, because of criminal immunity of U.S. forces under the terms of the Visiting Forces Agreement. American soldiers have also caused alarm in communities in Carmen, North Cotabato, and in Palembang town in Sultan Kudarat province, where a U.S. drone plane, or Unarmed Aerial Vehicle (UAV) surveillance plane, crashed.

After September 11, 2001, the Philippine government suddenly became involved in a conflict with Jemaah Islamiya and Al-Qaeda terrorists in Mindanao, rather than the Muslim secessionist groups they had previously focused on.[9] The death of an American missionary who, along with his wife and several Filipinos, was kidnapped by the bandit group, the Abu Sayyaf, as well as the beheading of another American, became the convenient excuse for the special attention being given to this island. Outgoing U.S. Ambassador to the Philippines Francis Ricciardone has even described Mindanao as the "doormat of international terrorists" in Southeast Asia. But is this the real reason for the special attention now being given to Mindanao?

Mindanao, one of the world's largest islands, is the Philippines' mining capital. It is known for its gold, silver, copper, nickel, cobalt, limestone, iron, aluminum ore, and coal reserves. Mindanao is the source of almost 50 percent of the Philippines' gold deposits and 65 percent of its nickel reserves. American plantations owned by Dole, Del Monte, United Fruit, and Firestone have long operated in the area.[10] Weyerhauser Corporation obtained 72,000 hectares of forest lands in concession.

But the strong interest being taken by the Pentagon in Mindanao appears to go beyond economic interests. Stratfor, a U.S.-based think tank of former diplomats and intelligence personnel, has observed that Mindanao is being eyed for "facilities that would serve as an operations and logistics base and would be a springboard for U.S. military power in Asia." Stratfor cites on its website the construction, made through funding by the U.S. Agency for International Development (USAID), of the airfield and port facilities in Sarangani Bay near General Santos City in Southern Cotabato province. It states in its report that the United States "is preparing to widen its footprint in conflict-torn Mindanao." A base in southern Mindanao would be an ideal fulcrum for U.S. operations not only on that island, but also for future counter-terrorism strikes in Southeast Asian countries, particularly in the predominantly Islamic Indonesia and Malaysia (Radics 2004).

This development has not gone unnoticed among the people of Mindanao. Grassroots Muslim peace groups have emerged, such as the Moro–Christian People's Alliance (MCPA), Silaturrahim Peace and Unity Task Force, the Muslim Women Peace Advocates, Jolo Federation of Peace Advocates, and the Philippine Council for Islam and Democracy. There are also the Assalam Party, Salam Women's Group, Islamic Directorate of the Philippines, Lanao Youth for Peace and Development, Insan Islamic Assembly, Al Mujadillah Development Foundation, Ranao Media, Maradeca, Muslim Youth National Assembly, and the Bangsamoro People's Consultative Congress.

The Sulu Civil Society Organization counts among its constituents those who are concerned with the conditions of the most vulnerable groups in conflict zones, such as children, women, and the elderly. It is composed of civil-society and elected local officials led by Sulu Governor Benjamin T. Loong, who is insisting on the urgency of a ceasefire because of the increasing loss of human lives and hundreds of millions of pesos going into military expenditures rather than economic development.

In recent years, more Muslim civil society groups in Mindanao have responded to the increasing attention being given by U.S. Special Operations Forces in the island's conflict areas. With many Muslim and Christian civilians getting caught in the crossfire, calls have been raised for mediation by the international community, such as the Organization of the Islamic Conference and the United Nations. The concentration of military operations in Mindanao involves the use of brigade-strength units and several battalions of ground troops, missile strikes from the air, battle tanks and artillery on land, and naval shelling from the sea. In general,

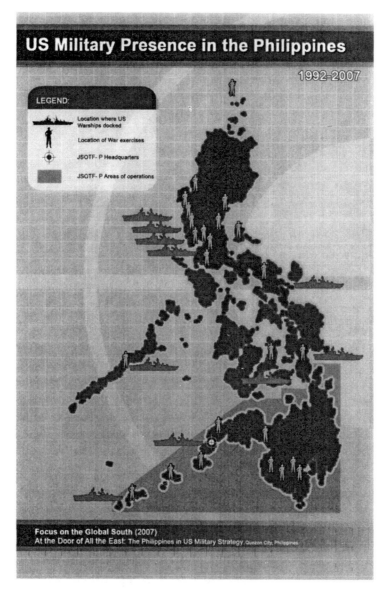

US military presence in the Philippines, 1992–2007, from Herbert Docena, 'At the Door of All the East': The Philippines in United States Military Strategy (Focus on the Global South, 2007).

the people's response to U.S. military presence in Mindanao has taken the form of consensus building, strengthening local movements in the communities, exposing human rights violations and militarism, resisting the plunder of their natural resources and ancestral lands by U.S. and other foreign companies, but more importantly, fighting Islamophobia through issues-based Muslim–Christian solidarity. A good example of this is the Muslim–Christian People's Alliance (MCPA).

Pressure politics from people's organizations and NGOs have made various local governments in Mindanao take a stand on the issue of U.S. military exercises in the Philippines. In Davao City, the premier city in Mindanao and considered the largest city in the world in terms of land area, the mayor led his legislative council and local officials in passing a resolution disallowing U.S.-Philippine Balikatan military exercises in any part of the city. Despite this official resolution, the U.S. forces and the Philippine Armed Forces and National Police held their "Balance-Piston Anti-Narcoterrorism Training" in Davao City in early 2005. In 2002, the Basilan Province Provincial Board of the Autonomous Region for Muslim Mindanao had passed a resolution strongly opposing the exercises.[11] This government resolution was also ignored by both the AFP and the U.S. Special Operations Forces which have conducted not only training exercises but also actual combat operations in the island province of Basilan. Invoking the Visiting Forces Agreement (VFA), the Joint Special Operations Task Force–Philippines (JSOTF-P) consisting of between 160 and 350 U.S. troops from the Special Operations Forces have been deployed in Basilan from 2002 to the present.[12]

To highlight the human rights, social, economic, and human security aspects of the intensified militarization in Mindanao, human rights groups such as Karapatan and Task Force Detainees have organized and sent fact-finding missions to investigate reports of abuses and violations. One of these missions led to the issuance of "Basilan Under Siege," a report on human rights violations by a relief and medical mission to Basilan province from September 9 to 16, 2001. Another report, by the Sulu Fact-Finding and

Medical Mission to Sulu province from April 18 to 23, 2002, is titled "The Hidden War."

The Role of Women in Demilitarization and Bases Conversion

Women's organizations and support groups were key in bringing justice to the case of a Filipina who was raped in November 2005 by a group of U.S. marines on "liberty leave" at the former U.S. base at Subic. A Task Force Subic Rape (TFSR) was organized by mostly women's organizations to provide legal, financial, psychological, and public support for the rape victim, who bravely confronted the might and power of the United States government. A feminist law firm called Women's Legal Bureau (WLB), headed by attorney Evalyn Ursua, volunteered to prosecute the case, which was considered a landmark test for the Visiting Forces Agreement. This is not the first time that women's groups have significantly contributed to the struggle for peace and demilitarization in the Philippines.

During the crucial anti-bases campaign in the late 1980s, groups like the Women's Education, Development, Productivity, and Research Organization (WEDPRO) contributed actively in the formulation of the official comprehensive bases-conversion program on the alternative uses of the U.S. military bases commissioned by the Philippine government. WEDPRO was among the "consulting firms" tapped by the Philippine government to help prepare the official Comprehensive Base Conversion Program. Its studies on prostituted women in the base economies were considered significant inputs for base-conversion plans (Lee and WEDPRO, 1992; Miralao et al., 1990). WEDPRO proposed a government-supported program for prostituted women, which included services for "transition, relocation, education, training in entrepreneurship, livelihood and support services," among others.[13] In Angeles City and Olongapo City, the sites of Clark Air Base and Subic Naval Base respectively, women's groups in the 1980s organized many prostituted women and bar girls needing assistance against violence and for their empowerment. A case in point is the Buklod Center in Olongapo City which was organized in 1987 as a drop-in center for prostituted women in Olongapo. Buklod has sought to raise their consciousness and promote solidarity among bar women based in Subic and Olongapo City, while seeking to promote the welfare of Amerasian children. Buklod, together with the local multi-sectoral organization KASARINLAN (Sovereignty), based in Olongapo City, lobbied and campaigned in the late 1980s and early 1990s for alternative livelihood and training programs, as part of a people-oriented base-conversion framework that is pro-poor, pro-Filipino, and environment-friendly. This was to smooth the path of the economic and social conversion of U.S. military bases, especially for those who would be affected and displaced by the transition.

The Churches Take a Stand

A significantly strong and influential ally of the people's movement against U.S. military presence and intervention is the church. More than 80 percent of the Philippine population is Catholic, and about 10 percent Protestant. The Catholic Bishops Conference of the Philippines (CBCP) and the Association of Major Religious Superiors of the Philippines (AMRSP) have both taken a stand against the U.S. bases and any restoration of U.S. military presence through the Visiting Forces Agreement. Likewise, the country's largest Protestant group, the National Council of Churches of the Philippines (NCCP), which is composed of ten mainstream churches with an estimated 13 million members, criticized the increasing U.S. military presence in the country during their 2004 General Convention. The NCCP stated that the United States "has secured its interventionist presence in the country, particularly in Mindanao, through unequal arrangements such as the U.S.–R.P. Balikatan Exercises, the Visiting Forces Agreement and the Mutual Logistics and Support Agreement." Both the Catholic and Protestant churches have called for the abrogation of the unequal treaties and agreements (Philippine International Forum, 2004). Both churches believe that foreign military presence in the country exposes the people to the danger of getting caught in the crossfire, of being displaced from their homes, and of seeing their property destroyed. The social costs to women and children are also clear to the civilian population. In August 2003, the Catholic and Protestant churches in the Philippines jointly hosted the "International Ecumenical Conference on Terrorism in a Globalized World," an event participated in by churches from 28 countries. The conference issued a highly publicized statement opposing U.S. domination in the world and U.S. military presence in the Philippines.

The Risks to Advocacy

An alarming phenomenon happening in the country today is the proliferation of "Operation Phoenix"-type assassinations against leaders and members of people's movements in the country. It will be recalled that during the Vietnam War, the Central Intelligence Agency (CIA) engaged in a massive operation to liquidate the political infrastructure of the National Liberation Front of South Vietnam (NLF-SV) in the late 1960s. The clandestine killing operation, codenamed "Operation Phoenix," took the lives of at least 30,000 suspected members and sympathizers of the NLF-SV in mass organizations and local governments that the CIA listed as part of the legal political infrastructure of the NLF. It appears that the same type of operation is now taking place in the Philippines. From March 2001 to June 2007, selective liquidations of members of the leftist party, Bayan Muna, took place in Mindoro and Southern Tagalog, in a pattern that was strikingly similar to that of Operation Phoenix. This has now escalated nationwide, targeting social movements and NGOs, with 869 cases of extrajudicial killings and 180 cases of enforced disappearances.[14] It was announced by then U.S. Ambassador Francis Ricciardone in a *Washington Post* interview that a strategic support branch of U.S. intelligence had been formed in the Philippines, with 70 U.S. spies working with the Philippine Southern Command "to bring intelligence for the AFP and law enforcement disposal as part of our ongoing cooperation against terrorism."

The reported recent deployment in the Philippines of a U.S. Department of Defense Strategic Support Branch, similar to the MACV-SOG (Military Advisory Composite Vietnam–Studies and Observation Group) of the Vietnam era, only lends credence to fears that a version of Operation Phoenix has been launched in the Philippines. Barton Gellman of the *Washington Post* reported on January 24, 2005, that this new clandestine operations unit, which was under the control of U.S. Defense Secretary Donald Rumsfeld, included the "Philippines, Yemen, Somalia, Indonesia and Georgia as the emerging target countries in the global war versus terrorism." In the past, it has been normal practice for the DoD's Defense Intelligence Agency (DIA) to simply assign its Defense Human Intelligence Service as military attachés in U.S. embassies abroad. Admission of espionage and covert operations sometimes come unwittingly straight from the horse's mouth, as when then U.S. Ambassador Ricciardone denied a report quoting him as saying that U.S. spies were sent to Mindanao. In an interview with the local newspaper Mindanews, the American ambassador said:

I never said that ... I'm not saying that (they are U.S. military spies). What I am saying is we have about 70 soldiers temporarily in Zamboanga. Sometimes they venture out ... but their main mission is OPS-INTEL Fusion. OPS-INTEL Fusion is not spying. It is working in a rural area linking up computers, linking up data from the U.S., from outside, money laundering, profile of bad groups, identities, fingerprints, photos, locally available ... putting it together and making it available ...

Counter-insurgency strategies by the AFP and the Philippine National Police have historically been designed at Pentagon drawing boards with the help of U.S. military advisers like the Joint U.S. Military Advisory Group (JUSMAG). From the time of the involvement of CIA operative Colonel Edward Lansdale and JUSMAG chief Major General Leland Hobbs in directing the Philippine anti-insurgency campaign against the Huk peasant rebellion in the 1950s to the current counter-insurgency strategies like "Katatagan" (1981), "Mamamayan" (1986), "Lambat Bitag" (1988), and the "Special Operations Team" (SOT) strategy of the 1990s, U.S. advisory influence and technical direction of the Philippine armed forces has not really been reduced, but in fact has undergone significant refinement and resurgence in recent years. And the role of the United States is apparently not lost on local insurgents who ambushed Colonel James Rowe, JUSMAG military adviser, in Manila in 1989. Rowe was chief of the army division of the JUSMAG, providing counter-insurgency training for the Philippine military, and was described by a colleague as having "worked closely with the CIA ... in its nearly decade-long program to penetrate the New People's Army and its parent Communist Party in conjunction with Philippine intelligence organizations."[15]

In recent years, the Pentagon has been influencing the direction of the security policies of the country through the Philippine–U.S. Joint Defense Assessment (JDA), which was initiated in late 2001 and updated in 2004. The JDA assists the Philippine Department of National Defense (the mother agency of the Philippine armed forces) in "developing a comprehensive defense program and plan for prioritized Philippine defense capabilities." U.S. military advisers compose the 25-member JDA Planning and Implementation Group, which allows American officials access to classified Philippine national security information, including operational and training capabilities.

The people's movement in the Philippines that is struggling for the country's sovereignty against foreign military intervention is becoming the target of widespread systematic and vicious attacks by U.S.-trained and -armed Philippine military and police agencies. Killings of political activists, peasant and trade union leaders, human rights workers, and lawyers and church people run unabated. Then there are the unresolved killings of crusading and hard-hitting media practitioners. According to the human rights watchdog, *Karapatan*, from January to March 2005 alone, 39 activists were executed, 24 of whom were local leaders of people's organizations. Since September 11, 2001, and up to May 2005, 59 local coordinators of the Bayan Muna party, and 19 from the Anakpawis (Toiling Masses) party have also been killed, all this in furtherance of the supposed campaign against global and domestic terrorism (Ocampo 2002).

In addition, many civilian communities and non-combatants are being subjected to collective punishment and grievous human rights violations in the name of "counter-terrorism." Legal organizations and individuals are uniformly tagged as "enemies of the state," "terrorists," or "destabilizers" by the AFP. Finally, there is the challenge posed by the government's plan to enforce a National Identification System and enact an Anti-Terrorism Bill in which draconian measures are to be introduced to clamp down on critical and dissenting voices and curtail civil liberties and democratic rights.

Meanwhile, the Philippine president Gloria Macapagal Arroyo's pronouncements have only contributed to the tensions:

> We will continue waging this fight against terror to clean up our shores of terrorists and, alongside our neighbors, to sweep the region of their clandestine cells. We will do our best to bring the battle against terror forward, and we will continue to be a strong link in the global chain of constricting terrorism. (*Philippine Tribune* 2004)

Issues against U.S. Military Presence

From the mid 1960s up to the present, the people's movement in the Philippines has raised a number of issues against U.S. military presence:

1. Infringement of territorial sovereignty by visiting foreign forces under the Visiting Forces Agreement, where U.S. troops visiting the Philippines cannot be legally prosecuted in Philippine courts even if they violate Philippine laws.
2. Violation of the constitution, since foreign facilities and bases and foreign troops are "not allowed" on Philippine territory except by a treaty ratified by two-thirds of all the members of the Senate.
3. Toxic and hazardous waste contamination of former bases, for which the U.S. government refuses to take responsi-

bility despite the death of more than 50 Filipinos, mostly children.

4. Environmental destruction during military exercises, during which U.S. forces use live bullets, artillery shells, and ammunition.

5. The violation of the rights and dignity of women and children who become victims of a military economy.

6. The abandonment of Amerasian children by visiting American military servicemen who fathered them.

7. Economic dependence and distortion of the economy by the year-round activities of U.S. military forces on Philippine soil.

8. The jeopardizing of efforts to convert bases into non-military uses, as U.S. military forces distort the economic conversion of the former military facilities.

9. The stifling of the Philippine government's attempts to modernize its armed forces, which are again becoming dependent on a foreign army for its strategic doctrine, weapons systems, and training.

10. Internationalization of an internal conflict with the intervention of foreign military forces. What is seen as continued U.S. intervention in counter-insurgency operations (now dubbed counter-terrorism) through the deployment of Special Operations Forces trainers could explode into a full-scale conflict considering that the Philippines still has a very active national insurgency led by the Communist Party of the Philippines and its military wing, the New People's Army, and an armed secessionist movement, the Moro Islamic Liberation Front (MILF).

11. Continued control of the AFP by the United States in the guise of military assistance, joint war exercises, training, and indoctrination of senior and junior military officers – all of which are made possible through outdated security agreements such as the Mutual Defense Treaty of 1951 and the Military Assistance Agreement of 1947, which, in turn, created JUSMAG, the permanent U.S. military advisory group in the Philippines.

12. Under the cover of the VFA, espionage and covert operations by the CIA and other Pentagon intelligence units and agencies fronting for these intelligence units, such as the National Endowment for Democracy, the USAID, and the controversial USAID-funded "Agile" project in key Philippine sectors, which involved manipulating the country's economic and political policies to be consistent with Washington and the Pentagon's viewpoint. To portray themselves as humanitarians, some of the toughest units in the U.S. military are conducting psychological operations in the guise of "civic action," "relief and disaster missions," and "medical missions," especially in Central Luzon, Southern Tagalog and Mindanao regions.

Resistance to U.S. military presence in the Philippines includes protest actions in front of the U.S. Embassy or the JUSMAG office. A few years ago, a cargo container containing toxic wastes from the former military bases was left parked in front of the U.S. embassy in Manila to dramatize the U.S. government's environmental irresponsibility in leaving behind toxic and hazardous wastes in their former military facilities.

International Solidarity

The globalization of resistance to militarism is one of the answers to the globalization of oppression, exploitation, and militarism. International solidarity against a common militaristic hegemony is crucial. Related to this, international peace missions to the Philippines have been quite useful in countering the news blackout on events in the militarized local areas and in making the issues known not only to the Philippine public but also internationally.

International peace or solidarity missions are important in national campaigns. An example is the International Peace Mission (IPM) to Basilan in March 2002, which included representatives from eight countries and an Australian member of Parliament; its report was titled "Basilan: The Next Afghanistan." Another example is the International Solidarity Mission (ISM) against U.S. Armed Intervention in the Philippines in July 2002, in Basilan and Zamboanga, whose report was titled "Behind the Second Front."

A significant aspect of international solidarity work in the previous campaign against U.S. military bases and against current U.S. military presence and intervention was the formation of international support groups in the United States, Australia, New Zealand, Japan, and in at least eight European countries. In the United States, an anti-intervention movement developed under the leadership of the Friends of the Filipino People, in the tradition of the Anti-Imperialist League of Mark Twain in 1899, which sought to block the annexation and colonization of the Philippines by the United States.[16] At its peak, there were at least ten chapters around the United States that actively campaigned against the U.S. bases in the Philippines. Invited to speak before these support groups, Filipino advocates and leaders shared their experiences and insights into the Philippine people's movement, especially its harnessing of people's power in bringing down two despotic presidents and waging a successful campaign against the bases. These were particularly useful in strengthening international linkages with countries hosting U.S. bases or facilities, such as Japan, Australia, and South Korea.

Philippine groups involved in peace and disarmament issues have long had strong bilateral and multilateral linkages with international peace networks (Simbulan 1988). As early as the mid 1980s, the Nuclear-Free Philippines Coalition had opened links with the European Nuclear Disarmament, and was invited to its conference in the Netherlands and to other parts of Western Europe. In the Pacific, Philippine groups are actively involved with the Nuclear-Free and Independent Pacific Movement (NFIP). At present, the NFPC secretary-general heads the NFIP's Pacific Resource Center and steering committee. Groups like the No-Nukes Asia Forum, Peace, Disarmament, and Symbiosis in Asia Pacific (PDSAP) and the Pacific Campaign to Disarm the Seas (PCDS) are some of the active Asia Pacific networks with strong ties to Philippine-based anti-nuclear, anti-base movements. In 2002, the Gathering for Peace and other Philippine organizations, in coordination with the Asian Regional Exchange for New Alternatives (ARENA), hosted the formation in Manila of the Asian Peace Alliance (APA), where more than 100 peace advocates from at least 18 countries in Asia came together to formalize the region's first broad coalition against war and U.S. aggression after the September 11, 2001, attacks.

Resistance within the Philippine Government

In recent years, since the bases withdrawal, the U.S. and Philippine governments have tried to forge an Access and Cross-Servicing Agreement (ACSA), but this was met with strong opposition both from the social movement and the legislative body. Then, in 1999, the Visiting Forces Agreement was forged and ratified by the Senate. This was followed by the Mutual Logistics and Support Agreement that was signed on November 21, 2002, by the AFP and the Pacific Command, ostensibly as a "low-level executive agreement" in which the Philippines was once again made into a logistics hub (Colmenares 2003).

This is not to say that certain Philippine officials have accepted this restoration of U.S. military presence in the Philippines without any resistance. Philippine Vice President Teofisto Guingona, who was President Gloria Macapagal Arroyo's foreign secretary, was forced to leave his post because of his outspoken criticism of the Balikatan war exercises and the Visiting Forces Agreement (VFA). So was the foreign undersecretary and VFA commissioner Amado Valdez, who was reprimanded and then sacked for reporting U.S. troop violations of the VFA to the media. Valdez also reported a drunken-driving incident involving U.S. soldiers in Zamboanga City, and an incident in Cebu City in which a local cab driver was beaten up by visiting U.S. servicemen.

The clout of U.S. embassy officials exerted on Philippine foreign policy is also very much evident in the 2001 case of Elmer Cato, the director of the VFA Commission, which was precisely tasked to monitor violations in the implementation of the Visiting Forces Agreement. Cato was demoted to a regional consular office after he submitted a report to the president regarding "the deviation of the visiting U.S. Forces." In 2001, he had a disagreement with a senior U.S. embassy official in Manila for refusing, based on Philippine policy, to allow the flight of a U.S. Marine F-18 jet from Clark to Cebu City unless accompanied by a Philippine aircraft. What often insults the dignity of Philippine officials is the insistence of U.S. government and embassy officials on violating the 1987 Philippine constitution, particularly its prohibition against nuclear weapons as well as the transitory provisions pertaining to foreign troops and facilities.

Now It Can Be Told

During the post-bases period from 1993–1994, Philippine Department of Foreign Affairs officials secretly invited and consulted the author as well as key leaders of the anti-nuclear, anti-bases movement regarding the Philippine position on the draft of the Southeast Asia Nuclear Weapons-Free Zone (SEA-NWFZ) Treaty which was then being finalized by the Association of Southeast Asian Nations (ASEAN) secretariat. At that time, the United States was vehemently opposed to this anti-nuclear-weapons treaty for Southeast Asia, for it perceived this as restricting, if not challenging, the unhampered operations, especially of the U.S. Seventh Fleet. Despite this, the SEA-NWFZ Treaty was later collectively signed by ASEAN members on December 15, 1995 as a "concrete action which will contribute to the process towards general and complete disarmament of nuclear weapons" in Southeast Asia. From the perspective of the peace movement in the Philippines, this was a major victory towards demilitarizing and de-nuclearizing the seas and oceans in the region. It is also seen as an important step in denying the United States its infra-structure in the region, or in weakening it, since the United States uses its "access" and bases in Southeast Asia as a springboard for aggression and destabilization against the Middle East and Asia itself.

Some key officials in the executive and legislative branches of the Philippine government, including those in the defense establishment, share the popular view that Filipinos should live out the spirit of the 1998 centennial of Philippine independence – that after the dismantling of the U.S. bases, all foreign military forces visiting the country should be coming here on our terms and abiding by our rules and laws, as befits a truly sovereign nation.

Conclusion

The Nuclear-Free Philippines Coalition (NFPC) remains a good model for latter-day people's organizations and NGOs in the Philippines that oppose the restoration of U.S. military bases and the presence of military forces.

To be successful, it is necessary for the members of an organization to totally understand its purposes, identify its goals, and appreciate the depth of the issues at hand. The best lesson that can be derived from the NFPC experience is the importance of continuing education of the public, the country's decision makers, and the members, as well as in espousing the issues and concerns of the organization. To develop the consciousness of the people, it is important for them to fully understand the issues and problems, so that in the end they would be able to make a stand or even take action necessary for their welfare. Continuous education is an important tool in consolidating mass actions and in strengthening the campaigns. It is easier to organize and mobilize people if they fully understand the problems and the need to act on these problems.

An advocacy organization has to have members or staff who are always there to maintain continuity of the work. There is a need for reliable people who can be delegated with tasks and are able to assume responsibilities to do extra duties. Aside from the "all-around staff," it is best for an organization to have people with the specialized skills needed for the more technical aspects of campaigns and mass actions. In the case of the NFPC, it had the assistance of volunteer experts, scientists, doctors, lawyers, economists, the academe, and other professionals who share their specialized knowledge of the issues.

In all campaigns, it is also important to maximize the strengths of an organization in order to exert the greatest impact on a broad population. Coalescing with other organizations and networks – even including local governments – is needed to widen the base of resistance. In this light, strategic planning must take place, in order that strengths and limitations may be known, as well as the options and the various possibilities and consequences of the actions to be taken. Planning smooths the direction an organization will take. Likewise, campaigns that will appeal to the public and to decision makers should be carefully determined and assessed to maximize results and minimize waste of resources as well as the possible failure of an action.

Most importantly, the members of the organization should have commitment and dedication to the cause of the organization. They must be able to participate in its programs and activities. An advocacy organization that is composed of weak and uncommitted members will have difficulty attaining results. In the Philippines, strong commitment is especially imperative in the light of the potentially violent consequences of advocacy work. It is only when members themselves believe in the cause of the organization that the people will believe too and join their cause.

This chapter utilizes the Foweraker model to highlight an arena where decisions can be made with the active political input and intervention of organized civil society. It discusses the venues that have been newly opened for mass participation in governance, especially areas related to evolving military infrastructures for global intervention and destabilization. And it describes the role played by people's movements and NGOs in empowering citizens to struggle against U.S. military intervention in the Philippines. It is hoped that it will encourage further studies into the dynamics and tensions in the engagement of social movements with each other and with the state.

Notes

1. Roland G. Simbulan, "How the Battle of the Bases Was Won," keynote speech, Pacific People's Forum towards a Century Free of

Overseas Bases, Yokohama, Japan, May 3–4, 1992. Available online in the Sentenaryo section of www.boondocksnet.com website. Date last accessed October 14, 2007.

2. Legislative–Executive Bases Council, "KUMBERSYON (Comprehensive Conversion Program): Alternative Uses of the Military Baselands and the Military Camps in Metro Manila," Government of the Philippines, 1990.

3. Ronald G. Simbulan "The Day the Senate Said No to Uncle Sam," U.P. Forum, Community Publication of the University of the Philippines, September 2, 2002.

4. Commodore Carlos Agustin, Philippine Navy (retired) "Military Exercises in the Context of Philippine Security Requirements," unpublished paper presented in a forum entitled "The Return of GI Joe: U.S. Troops in Mindanao," University of the Philippines Third World Studies Center, February 7, 2002.

5. Beverly Selim-Musni, "U.S. Intervention and the Implications to Peace in Mindanao," unpublished paper presented to the Pilgrims for Peace Forum, University of the Philippines, Diliman, Quezon City, May 12, 2005.

6. San Francisco Chronicle, February 21, 2003.

7. Presidential News Desk, "Primer on Balikatan: Joint R.P.–U.S. Military Training Exercises," Office of the President Secretariat Operations Center, Manila, February 2002.

8. See Colmenares 2003; Selim-Musni, "U.S. Intervention."

9. See Ocampo 2002.

10. Selim-Musni, "U.S. Intervention."

11. Sangguniang Panlalawigan ng Basilan, "A resolution strongly opposing the Balikatan exercise of the joint U.S. military troops and the Armed Forces of the Philippines to be conducted in the province of Basilan," Resolution No. 02-025, unpublished, February 6, 2002.

12. Focus on the Global South, "Unconventional Warfare: Are U.S. Special Forces Engaged in an 'Offensive War' in the Philippines?" Quezon City, 2007.

13. Legislative–Executive Bases Council, "KUMBERSYON."

14. Dr. Edelina De la Paz, presentation as chairperson of the human rights organization KARAPATAN, National Consultative Summit on Extrajudicial Killings and Enforced Disappearances, unpublished. Organized by the Supreme Court of the Philippines, Manila, July 16–17, 2007.

15. The U.S. Veteran News and Report, available online at www. pownetwork.org. Date last accessed October 14, 2007.

16. Daniel B. Schirmer, "The Movement Against U.S. Intervention in the Philippines: A Sketch," based on a talk given March 4, 1989, in New York City, at a conference called by the Campaign to End U.S. Intervention in the Philippines. Available online in the Sentenaryo section of www.boondocksnet.com website. Date last accessed October 14, 2007.

References

Bello, Walden (1999) *People and Power in the Pacific: The Struggle for the Post-Cold War Order*, second edition (Amsterdam/London: Pluto Press).

Chanbonpin, Kim David (2003) "Holding the U.S. Accountable for Environmental Damages Caused by the U.S. Military in the Philippines: A Plan for the Future," *Asia–Pacific Law and Policy Journal*, Vol. 4, No. 2, Summer.

Colmenares, Neri Javier (2003) "U.S. Military Operations in the Philippines: A Threat to Peace and Democracy," available online at www.carbonequity.info/vicpeace/images/Phillipines.doc. Date last accessed October 14, 2007.

Foweraker, J. (1995) *Theorizing Social Movements* (London: Pluto Press).

—— (2001) *Grassroots Movements, Political Activism and Social Development in Latin America: A Comparison of Chile and Brazil* (Geneva: UNRISD).

Gathering for Peace (2002) *Philippine Reader on the U.S. Bases* (Gathering for Peace Secretariat).

Ileto, Reynaldo (1979) *Pasyon and Revolution: Popular Movements in the Philippines, 1840–1910* (Quezon City: Ateneo University Press).

Lee, Lyn and WEDPRO (1992) *From Carriers to Communities: Alternative Employment, Economic Livelihood, and Human Resource Development for Women in the Entertainment Industry –The NGO Version of the Bases Conversion Program for Women* (Manila: WEDPRO).

Lindberg, S. and Sverrisson, Á. (eds.) (1997) *Social Movements in Development: The Challenge of Globalization and Democratization* (London: Macmillan).

Miralao, Virginia, et al. (1990) *Women Entertainers in Angeles and Olongapo: A Survey Report* (Manila: WEDPRO and Katipunan ng Kababaihan Para sa Kalayaan).

Ocampo, Satur (2002) "U.S. Armed Intervention in the Philippines and the People's Struggle for National Freedom," unpublished speech,

International Solidarity Mission Against U.S. Armed Intervention in the Philippines, July 28.

Philippine International Forum (2004) *U.S. "War on Terror" Ramifications for the Philippines* (Letter of Concern of Foreign Churches and Development Workers in the Philippines), booklet.

Philippine Tribune (2004) August 4, p. 3. Also available online at www. news.ops.gov.ph/archives2004/aug04.htm.

Pollard, Vincent Kelly (2004) *Globalization, Democratization and Asian Leadership* (Burlington, USA: Ashgate Publishing Ltd).

Radics, George Baylon (2004) "Terrorism in the Philippines and the United States War Against Terrorism," *Stanford Journal of East Asian Affairs*, Vol. 4, No. 2, Summer.

Simbulan, Roland G. (1988) "Militarization in Southeast Asia," in Yoshikazu Sakamoto (ed.) *Asia: Militarization and Regional Conflict* (Tokyo: United Nations University).

—— (1998) "Behind and Beyond the Bases Negotiations," *Public Policy Journal*, Vol. 2, No. 2, University of the Philippines Center for Integrative and Development Studies.

—— (2004) "U.S. Military Power and Interests in the Asia–Pacific: The Challenges to Human Security and Development," *Kasarinlan, Philippine Journal of Third World Studies*, Vol. 19, No. 1.

Third World Studies Center (1997) "Introduction," special issue on New Social Movements, *Kasarinlan, Journal of Third World Studies*, Vols. 12 and 13.

6

"GIVE US BACK DIEGO GARCIA": UNITY AND DIVISION AMONG ACTIVISTS IN THE INDIAN OCEAN

David Vine and Laura Jeffery

In the waning hours of the British Empire, as decolonization swept across Asia and Africa, the United States persuaded the United Kingdom to create its last colony. In 1960, U.S. government officials quietly approached their British counterparts about acquiring the tiny island of Diego Garcia in the middle of the Indian Ocean as a site for a military base. By 1964, the United Kingdom agreed to detach Diego Garcia and the rest of the surrounding Chagos Archipelago from colonial Mauritius and several island groups from colonial Seychelles to create a strategic military colony, the British Indian Ocean Territory (BIOT). The United Kingdom also agreed to remove the native inhabitants of Diego Garcia and Chagos, known as Chagossians.

The United States secretly paid $14 million toward the removals and the costs of silencing any objections to the detachment from Mauritius and Seychelles. By 1973, British agents had removed all of the approximately 2,000 Chagossians to Mauritius and Seychelles, 1,300 miles away. In the same year, the United States completed the nucleus of a base that would eventually become one of its most important foreign bases, growing more than any U.S. base since the Vietnam War.[1] Diego Garcia helped launch the recent wars in Afghanistan and Iraq, and has become the site for a secret detention facility for suspected terrorists.

In the years that followed the creation of the base, three major movements have emerged in reaction to Diego Garcia. First, for more than three decades, the displaced Chagossians have protested their expulsion, struggling to return to their homeland and gain reparations. There are more than 5,000 Chagos islanders and their descendants now living in exile, the vast majority in Mauritius. As a result of their protest, the group has twice secured small amounts of compensation from the British government. In recent years, the group has won major legal victories, including rulings in 2000 and 2006 by the British High Court that the expulsion and a subsequent ban on their return were illegal under U.K. law. In 2002, many won the right to full U.K. citizenship and passports.

Second, the post-independence Mauritian state, a small nation of about 1.3 million people in the Indian Ocean, has attempted to regain sovereignty over Diego Garcia and the rest of Chagos. Since the United Kingdom detached Chagos on the eve of Mauritian independence, Diego Garcia has been an emotionally charged political issue in the country, raising issues of neo-colonialism, militarism, and ethnic division. Opposition political parties and, since 1980, successive Mauritian governments have pursued a return of sovereignty primarily by seeking the support of non-aligned nations at international forums during the Cold War and, at times, through attempts at negotiation with the United Kingdom. Most recently, in 2004, the then Mauritian prime minister, Paul Bérenger, was unceremoniously denied a meeting with then British prime minister, Tony Blair, when he came to London to discuss a reversion of sovereignty. The official position of the United Kingdom is that it will cede Chagos when the islands are no longer needed for defense purposes.[2]

Third, the leftist Mauritian political party Lalit de Klas (The Class Struggle; known widely as Lalit), which represents an active but marginal remnant of a once mainstream socialist streak in Mauritian politics, has long campaigned to close the base. Unlike the other movements, Lalit argues that the three struggles (for the right to return, sovereignty, and closure of the U.S. base) are intertwined and must be pursued together. While the party has supported the Chagossians and the sovereignty claim, Lalit has focused much of its attention on rallying international campaigns to close the base as part of a broad anti-militarist, anti-imperialist, anti-capitalist agenda. The party has rallied some international support and has linked its efforts to the No U.S. Bases campaign.

For more than two decades, the movements have sporadically united their causes around the Mauritian Kreol phrase *Rann nu Diego!* (Give Us Back Diego!) Despite deep divisions, disagreements, and contradictions between them, the ambiguity of the Kreol has allowed members of each group to chant the slogan in unison. The phrase leaves various kinds of uncertainty – Does the *us* mean the Chagossians or does it mean Mauritius and the Mauritian people? Similarly, does *Rann nu* mean "give us back" or "return us to?" And does giving back Diego mean that the base must go, or perhaps just a reversion of control over the island with the base allowed to stay?

These and other questions raised by the rallying cry, about the right of return, sovereignty, anti-militarism, indigeneity, and overlapping legal systems, illustrate ideological, political, and strategic differences among and even within the movements that have repeatedly fractured unity among the groups and that, at times, have frustrated the efforts of each. This chapter discusses the complexities, contradictions, and challenges faced by the three movements. We begin with a brief history of life in Chagos, the development of the base, and the expulsion. The chapter then traces the history of each movement, examining moments of unity, the issues that have caused division, and how the U.S. and U.K. governments have wielded their economic and political power to frustrate the movements' aims. We return to the *Rann nu Diego* rallying cry to consider what lessons the movements, and their moments of unity and division, might offer other base campaigns, before concluding by considering the future of the movements and the base.

The History of an Archipelago and a People

Around 1783, a boatload of 22 enslaved people landed on Diego Garcia. Brought to the island by a Franco-Mauritian plantation owner to create a coconut estate, the group established the first permanent settlement in the Chagos Archipelago (Ly-Tio-Fane and Rajabalee 1986:91–92; Walker 1993:563; Scott 1976:20). More plantations followed on Diego Garcia, Peros Banhos, Salomon, and other islands in Chagos as the colonial government in Mauritius granted *jouissances* (land concessions) to Franco-Mauritian plantation owners. Each estate revolved around the use of enslaved labor, primarily from coastal southeast Africa and Madagascar, to turn coconuts into coconut oil. By 1808 there were 100 enslaved people working on the largest of four major plantations on Diego Garcia, and by 1813, a similar number in Peros Banhos (Walker 1993:563).

Located near the geographic center of the Indian Ocean, Chagos was originally a French dependency, along with the Seychelles archipelago. With the fall of Napoleon and the 1814 Treaty of Paris, France formally ceded Mauritius and most of its other islands in the ocean to Great Britain. Britain assumed control of Chagos, governing it, like the French before them, as one of the dependencies of Mauritius.

Life in Chagos changed little under the British. Slavery remained the defining feature of the settlements until its abolition in Mauritius in 1835. Around the time of emancipation, Franco-Mauritian plantation owners started importing indentured laborers from India. Over the course of the nineteenth and twentieth centuries, a diverse group of peoples developed into a community known initially as the *Ilois* (the islanders), with a distinct society, their own Chagos Kreol language, and what many referred to as a *culture des îles* (culture of the islands) (Ly-Tio-Fane and Rajabalee 1986:105). As a result of the isolation of the islands and the vast numerical superiority of the plantation laborers to the management staff of mostly French ancestry, Chagossians struck what, for a plantation society, was a relatively good work bargain. By the mid twentieth century, in exchange for their work on the plantations, the islanders enjoyed virtually guaranteed universal employment, regular if small salaries in cash and food, land and housing, education, pensions, vacations, health care, and other benefits.

The "Strategic Island Concept"

Around 1956, Stuart B. Barber, a civilian working for a long-range planning office in the U.S. Navy, began drawing up lists of islands in the Indian Ocean from every map, atlas, and nautical chart he could find. His list included Desroches, Farquhar, Aldabra, Cocos, Phuket, Masirah, and the Chagos Archipelago and Diego Garcia, among many others. "Barber's basic idea," explains former U.S. Navy officer Vytautas Bandjunis, "was that the United States should acquire base rights in certain strategically located islands, mostly in the southern hemisphere, and stockpile them for future use as potential refueling stations, air patrol bases, and communication sites" (Bandjunis 2001:2). Barber's Long-Range Objectives Group called the plan the "Strategic Island Concept" and identified as many as 60 such islands in the Indian Ocean and around the globe for U.S. acquisition (Bandjunis 2001:3).[3]

The group argued that as much of the colonial world was moving (for them, unpredictably) toward independence, the United States was likely to lose many of its existing overseas bases, which were encountering rising local opposition and calls for their closure. To prepare to replace these installations, the group recommended that the United States acquire and stockpile rights to develop new bases in as many strategically located and "sparsely populated" islands as possible.[4] Isolated and sparsely populated islands would be far easier to hold in the long term once they were removed from any soon-to-be-independent colonial government and held in U.S. or Western hands. As Bandjunis explains of navy thinking at the time, small islands would "be the easiest to acquire and would entail the least political headaches," shielded as they were from local protest and decolonization pressures (Bandjunis 2001:2). The navy was "buoyed by the fact that there were so many such islands in the Indian Ocean ... [and] did not see any real difficulty in persuading [the reigning colonial power] Great Britain to enter into such an agreement" (Bezboruah 1977:58).

Barber soon identified Diego Garcia as a key target for acquisition. Particularly attractive to navy planners were Diego's central location in the Indian Ocean, one of the world's great natural harbors in its protected lagoon, and enough land to build a large airstrip (Bezboruah 1977:58; Bandjunis 2001:2). Navy officials also noted that Diego Garcia's population was "measured only in the hundreds."[5]

In 1960, the navy initiated secret conversations with the British government about the island. Formal diplomatic negotiations between U.S. Secretary of Defense Robert McNamara and British Minister of Defence Peter Thorneycroft began in 1962.[6] The United States suggested that before Mauritius and Seychelles gained their independence the United Kingdom should detach Diego Garcia and the rest of Chagos from Mauritius and some outlying islands from Seychelles to create a new British colony for exclusive military use. Once the islands were fully in British hands, the plan was to remove all the local inhabitants. As U.S. officials put it, they wanted "exclusive control (without local inhabitants)" (U.S. Embassy London 1964a:1–2).

British officials agreed to the terms. Her Majesty's Government "should be responsible for acquiring land, resettlement of population and compensation at H.M.G.'s expense," while the United States would assume responsibility for construction and maintenance costs on the base (U.S. Embassy London 1964b:2–3). While agreeing to the plan, Labour Prime Minister Harold Wilson warned U.S. officials that Her Majesty's Government would "pay a price" at the U.N. for its actions (U.S. Department of State 1965). In 1960, the U.N. General Assembly had passed Declaration 1514 (XV) "on the Granting of Independence to Colonial Countries and Peoples." The declaration called for the complete independence of non-self governing territories like Mauritius and Seychelles without alteration of their borders, thrice demanding that states respect their "territorial integrity" during decolonization, and condemning "any attempt aimed at the partial or total disruption of the national unity and the territorial integrity of a country" (United Nations 1960: Section 6).

The British understood that they would have to pay Mauritius and Seychelles to silence their protests over the detachment: "If we do not settle quickly (which must mean generously) agitation in the colonies against 'dismemberment' and 'foreign bases' (fomented from outside) would have time to build up to serious proportions, particularly in Mauritius."[7] A British official was more blunt during face-to-face meetings, telling U.S. representatives that British officials could not proceed with detachment of the islands until they knew what "bribe" they could offer the Mauritian and Seychellois governments (U.S. Embassy London 1965). On June 14, 1965, Secretary of Defense McNamara agreed to contribute up to half – or $14 million – of British detachment and removal costs (Foreign Relations of the United States 2000:97).[8]

In June 1964, the U.K. government began to pressure Mauritius's pre-independence leader and future first prime minister, Dr. Seewoosagur Ramgoolam, to give up Chagos. Ramgoolam reacted favorably to the idea of a base but "expressed reservations" about the detachment for fear of losing future economic benefits in Chagos.[9] In exchange, he asked for a Mauritian immigration quota to the United States and a "huge U.S. sugar quota of 300–400,000 tons a year" for Mauritius's only significant source of economic activity at the time.[10] British representatives told Ramgoolam that they would speak with their U.S. counterparts but made no promises.

During final Mauritian independence negotiations the following year, British Prime Minister Wilson met with Ramgoolam for a private 40-minute meeting. Wilson offered Ramgoolam little choice: Accept the detachment of Chagos from Mauritius and £3 million or there would be no independence. Both British and Mauritian representatives knew that if Ramgoolam's Labour Party – originally a working-class party but increasingly based in the Indo-Mauritian Hindu community – returned to Mauritius without an independence agreement it risked losing power to its political rival on the right, the Mauritian Social Democratic Party

(PMSD), which argued against independence while mobilizing fears about Indo-Mauritian domination among so-called Creoles and Coloureds of primarily Franco-African and French ancestry (Boolell 1996:27; Selvon 2001:382–385). "A request was made to me," Ramgoolam later explained. "I had to see which was better – to cede out a portion of our territory of which very few people knew ... [or] independence. I thought that independence was much more primordial and more important than the excision of the island which is very far from [the island of Mauritius], and which we had never visited" (de l'Estrac 1983:22).

Ramgoolam chose independence and the money. In the negotiations, he again expressed hope that the United States might offer Mauritius a preferential price on its sugar exports and supply it with wheat and other commodities while using Mauritian labor and materials for construction of the base. The British government promised nothing more than to "do their best" with the Americans (de l'Estrac 1983:57). In exchange for its islands, Seychelles won construction of an international airport (worth well over £3 million) that transformed the Seychelles economy from one described as a "rundown plantation" (Benedict and Benedict 1982:161) based on negligible agricultural exports into a tourism-based economy that has become the wealthiest per capita in sub-Saharan Africa. Seychellois leaders later negotiated the return of their islands when Seychelles gained independence from the United Kingdom in 1976.

With the islands secured, on November 8, 1965, the British government used an archaic power of the queen to pass laws without parliamentary approval, called an order in council, to create the British Indian Ocean Territory. Weeks later, the U.N. General Assembly passed Resolution 2066 noting its "deep concern" over actions taken by the United Kingdom "to detach certain islands from the Territory of Mauritius for the purpose of establishing a military base." Citing the U.N. prohibition on disturbing the territorial integrity of non-self-governing territories, the General Assembly asked the United Kingdom "to take no action which would dismember the Territory of Mauritius and violate its territorial integrity" and instead to implement Declaration 1514 of 1960 fully (United Nations 1965).

The United Kingdom ignored the resolution and after further negotiations, on December 30, 1966, the U.S. and U.K. governments confirmed their arrangements for the base with an exchange of notes. (The exchange of notes allowed the governments to avoid signing a treaty, which would have required congressional and parliamentary oversight.) According to the published agreement, the United States would gain military use of the new colony "without charge." In secret agreements accompanying the notes, the United States agreed to the $14 million payment and the United Kingdom agreed to take "those administrative measures" necessary to remove the islands' inhabitants.[11]

The Expulsion

The administrative measures meant that beginning in 1968, Chagossians leaving Chagos for medical treatment or regular vacations in Mauritius were barred from returning and marooned 1,300 miles from their homes. Often they were stranded without family members and most of their possessions. The British soon began restricting supplies for Chagos and by the turn of the decade more Chagossians were leaving as food and medical supplies dwindled. British authorities, one of whom referred to the Chagossians as "Tarzans" and "men Fridays,"[12] designed a public relations plan for the international community aimed at, as one official put it, "maintaining the fiction" that the Chagossians were transient contract workers with no connection to the islands.[13]

By 1971, the navy began construction on Diego Garcia and ordered their British counterparts to complete the removal of the islanders. First, British agents and U.S. soldiers on Diego Garcia herded up the Chagossians' pet dogs and exterminated them en masse in front of their traumatized owners. Then, between 1971 and 1973, British agents forced the remaining Chagossians to board a series of overcrowded cargo ships and left them on the docks in Mauritius and, in smaller numbers, in Seychelles.

Chagossian children in Cassis, Mauritius, a slum outside the capital, Port Louis (David Vine).

On September 4, 1972, the U.K. government paid the newly independent and highly unstable government of now Prime Minister Seewoosagur Ramgoolam £650,000 to resettle the Chagossians. British officials realized that the sum was too little for an adequate resettlement but were happy to have struck such a deal. When asked by their superiors in Washington if they thought the resettlement plan would work, the U.S. Embassy in Port Louis noted, "We doubt it," given the already "disgraceful lassitude" in movement to compensate the Chagossians, the Mauritian government's then poor record of implementing national development projects, and a scheme to turn Chagossians into pig farmers, a profession for which few had expressed any interest.[14] The plan was never implemented and Chagossians effectively received no resettlement assistance. By 1975, a journalist from the *Washington Post* described Chagossians in Mauritius as living in "abject poverty."[15] A year later, a British official sent to Mauritius to consult on the still non-existent compensation found the group to be "living in deplorable conditions."[16] In the succeeding years, despite some improvement in their condition, most Chagossians have remained impoverished, as a marginalized underclass at the bottom of the socio-economic hierarchies in Mauritius and Seychelles (Walker 1986; Anyangwe 2001; Dræbel 1997; Vine, Sokolowski, and Harvey 2005).

The Chagossians' Struggle

In May 1973, after British agents deported the last 125 Chagossians from Peros Banhos on the BIOT cargo ship the M.V. *Nordvær*, the group refused to disembark upon arriving in Mauritius. They demanded that they be returned to Chagos or receive compensation and housing. For nearly a week the Chagossians remained on board in "deplorable" conditions before the Mauritian government convinced them to leave.[17] The government paid each around $1 (in 1973 U.S. dollars) and gave 19 families dilapidated apartments, amidst pigs, cows, and other farm animals, in the slums of Port Louis. Twelve other families found their own housing, crowding into the shacks of relatives or friends.[18]

A tradition of protest first began among the Chagossians in 1968 as soon as the first islanders were prevented from returning to their homes and stranded in Mauritius. In 1971, Chagossians protested against leaving "their 'own country,'" when the administrator of the BIOT announced that Diego Garcia would be closed and all its inhabitants displaced.[19] Protest continued after the last boatload ended their strike when Chagossians in Mauritius had still received none of their promised resettlement assistance.

"We, the inhabitants of Chagos Islands – Diego Garcia, Peros Banhos, Salomon, have been uprooted from those islands because the Mauritian government sold the islands to the British government to build a base," declared a 1975 petition to the U.K. government demanding action. "Our ancestors were slaves on those islands, but we know that we are the heirs of those islands," the signatories wrote. The petition cited failed promises of compensation made by British agents in Chagos. It detailed "at least 40 persons" who "died through sorrow, poverty and lack of food and care" in exile. The Chagossians asked the U.K. government to "urge" the Mauritian government to provide land, housing, and jobs, or to return them to their islands.[20]

The petition, along with numerous subsequent pleas to the governments of the United Kingdom, the United States, Mauritius, and Seychelles, went unheeded. Finally in 1978, after six years of protests and pressure, the government of Mauritius made compensation payments to some Chagossians from the £650,000 paid by the United Kingdom. Although a majority requested that the compensation come as housing, eligible Chagossians instead received cash payments of MRs7,590 for adults (around $1,225) and between MRs1,000 ($165) and MRs1,500 ($245) for children 18 and under (de l'Estrac 1983:3–5). Many families, including all the Chagossians in Seychelles, received no money.

Even for those who received the payments, the money proved "hopelessly inadequate" (Madeley 1985:7). It paid off some debts incurred since their arrival but generally was too little to purchase land or a house, let alone to provide full restitution. Six months later, a group of eight Chagossian women went on a hunger strike to protest their conditions. After living with their families under tarpaulin sheets for two months following the destruction of their rented shacks in a cyclone and their eviction from emergency accommodations by the Mauritian government, the protesters demanded proper housing. "Give us a house; if not, return us to our country, Diego," one of their flyers read.[21]

The hunger strike lasted 21 days in an office of the Mauritian Militant Party (MMM), a leftist working-class opposition party whose leaders, including future Prime Minister Paul Bérenger, had assisted the Chagossians' struggle since the first arrivals in 1968. Two leaders of Lalit, then a wing of the MMM, Lindsey Collen and Ragini Kistnasamy, also provided important support. Later that year, four Chagossians were jailed for resisting the police when Mauritian authorities tore down their shacks (Madeley 1985:7). Both protests yielded few concrete results but added to mounting political momentum for the group.

In 1979, again with MMM assistance, Chagossians engaged British lawyer Bernard Sheridan to negotiate with the U.K. government about providing additional compensation. Sheridan was already suing the United Kingdom on behalf of Michel Vincatassin, a Chagossian who charged that he had been forcibly removed from his and his ancestors' homeland. British officials reportedly offered an additional £1.25 million on the condition that Vincatassin drop his case and Chagossians sign deeds "in full and final settlement," waiving future suits and "all our claims and rights (if any) of whatsoever nature to return to the British Indian Ocean Territory" (Madeley 1985:6, 8, 15).

Sheridan came to Mauritius offering the money in exchange for the renunciation deeds. Initially many of the impoverished Chagossians signed them (more precisely, as most Chagossians were illiterate, the majority provided thumbprints on deeds written in English). When other Chagossian and MMM leaders heard the terms of the deal, they halted the process and sent Sheridan back to London. A support group of Chagossians and Mauritians (many linked to the MMM) wrote to Sheridan that the Chagossians who had signed the forms had done so without "alternative legal advice," and "as a mere formality" to obtain the compensation rather than out of agreement with its conditions. No money was disbursed.

Soon after, Chagossians demonstrated in the streets of Mauritius again, launching more hunger strikes and their largest protests yet in 1980 and 1981. Led by women who repeatedly faced police intimidation, violence, and arrest, hundreds of Chagossians marched on the British High Commission, protested in front of government offices, and slept aside the streets of the Mauritian capital. Chagossians again demanded the right to return to the Chagos Archipelago as well as immediate compensation, decent housing, and jobs. They also asked for recognition as refugees, a demand which was immediately rejected by the Mauritian government, which considered Chagossians to be Mauritians who technically could not be refugees on Mauritian soil. A broad coalition of Mauritian political groups and unions, including the MMM and Lalit leaders, supported the Chagossians under the *Rann nu Diego* rallying cry, uniting the Chagossians' struggle with the desire of some Mauritians to return Chagos to Mauritian sovereignty and close the base (Lalit 2002:113–117).[22]

After an 18-day hunger strike and violent clashes that included the arrest of six Chagossian women and Lalit members Collen and Kistnasamy, Mauritian Prime Minister Ramgoolam left for London to meet British Prime Minister Margaret Thatcher. The two governments agreed to hold talks including Chagossian representatives. After two rounds of negotiations in which the MMM's Bérenger played a prominent role, the British government agreed to provide £4 million in compensation,[23] with the Mauritian government contributing land it valued at £1 million. Money totaling around MRs55,000 for each adult (about $4,600 at the time), including land plots and houses, was distributed slowly between 1982 and 1985. Although housing conditions improved for many Chagossians, research shows that people again used much of the money for paying off debts and buying consumption items. Improvement for the community as a result of the compensation was slight (Madeley 1985:10–11; Vine, Sokolowski, and Harvey 2005).[24]

In the wake of the compensation agreement, many Chagossians felt that their interests had not been well represented by some of their Mauritian spokespeople. Several, including prominent Chagossian leaders (and former hunger strikers) Charlesia Alexis and Aurelie Lisette Talate, along with Louis Olivier Bancoult, the 18-year-old son of another leader, helped create the first solely Chagossian support organization, the Chagos Refugees Group (CRG). The group pressed for the right to return and additional compensation throughout the 1980s and 1990s but made little progress, gradually losing support within the community when they failed to show results.

Another Chagossian organization, the Chagossian Social Committee (CSC), created by Fernand Mandarin and his Mauritian barrister Hervé Lassemillante, eventually assumed a leadership role. The CSC considered lodging a case for compensation in a British court but concluded that such a suit would acknowledge U.K. sovereignty over Chagos, damaging Mauritius's claim to the islands. The group instead pursued out-of-court negotiations with the U.K., U.S., and Mauritian governments for compensation and the right to return. While the CSC had little success in pursuing negotiations, the group gained recognition for Chagossians as an indigenous people before the U.N. in 1997 (see Vine 2003).

Beginning in 1997, the CRG regained the initiative when, with the help of Mauritian attorney Sivakumaren Mardemootoo and British solicitor Richard Gifford, the group launched a suit against the British Crown challenging the legality of the expulsion. To the surprise and attention of people around the world, in November 2000, the British High Court found for the Chagossians, ruling their expulsion illegal under U.K. law (*Regina v. Secretary of State for the Foreign and Commonwealth Office, ex parte Bancoult* (2000) Q.B.). Almost immediately the British government announced that it would not appeal the judgment and changed the laws of the BIOT to allow Chagossians to return to all of Chagos except Diego Garcia. Lacking the means to charter boats to visit Chagos let alone to resettle and reconstruct their shattered societies, Chagossians filed a second suit against the Crown for compensation and money to finance a return and reconstruction. For the first time, they were joined in the suit by Chagossians in Seychelles, organized as the Chagos Social Committee (Seychelles).

Chagossian activists celebrating the 2000 British High Court ruling that the U.K. had unlawfully exiled them (David Vine).

In Washington, D.C., the groups enlisted the legal assistance of Michael Tigar, a highly regarded U.S. litigator known for bringing cases against Henry Kissinger and Augusto Pinochet (Dræbel 1997). In 2001, Tigar filed a class action lawsuit (*Bancoult et al. v. McNamara et al.*, 360 F.Supp. 2d (D.D.C. 2004)) in the Federal District Court for Washington, D.C., against the U.S. government, government officials who participated in the expulsion, such as Robert McNamara and Donald Rumsfeld, and companies that assisted in the base construction, including the Halliburton Corporation. The suit accused the defendants of harms including forced relocation, cruel, inhuman, and degrading treatment, and genocide. They asked the court to grant the right of return, award compensation, and order an end to employment discrimination preventing Chagossians from working on the base (non-Chagossian Mauritians, Filipinos, Singaporeans, and others have worked there since the early 1980s).

The case has highlighted divisions among Chagossians in their feelings about the base, although the issue has remained subsidiary to the right of return and compensation. During the 1980–1981 protests, under the *Rann nu Diego* slogan, Chagossians included the demand to close the base: many native Chagossians still oppose the base on the grounds that it was the cause of their expulsion. As a Chagossian from Diego Garcia explained, "I suffer because they took my country and made it into a base for war." Others oppose the base because they believe it would endanger resettlement. As a second-generation Chagossian said, they worry that "if America can bomb Iraq from Diego Garcia, then Iraq could bomb Diego Garcia" (Jeffery 2007).

Other Chagossians are more tolerant or even supportive of the base. While the CSC opposes the base, the CRG's position, despite its opposition to the current war in Iraq, is, according to Bancoult, that "we have no problem with the military base on Diego Garcia." Some are even proud of the role Diego Garcia plays militarily, including one young activist who said, "I firmly believe that the construction of this military base was a must for the world's protection against terrorism and any other mischievous enemy" (Ramdas 2003).

The Chagossians' positions on the base must be understood within the context of their struggle to return and gain compensation. Many (mostly men) have been interested in working on the base – and thus finding one way to return to their homeland – since the base began employing non-U.S. or -U.K. support personnel. Because discriminatory policies have barred Chagossians from working on the island[25] (Bowman and Lefebvre 1985:28), the CRG's U.S. suit has made an end to this discrimination one of its claims. Others see the base as essential to any resettlement effort, both as a source of employment and, given that it provides the only runways in the archipelago, as a regular air link with the outside world.

The intricacies of U.S. law seem also to have played a role in shaping Chagossians' feelings about the base. Because U.S. law broadly prohibits suits against the U.S. government that challenge the foreign policy-making power of the U.S. executive and legislative branches, the CRG and its lawyers had to distance themselves from any positions appearing to oppose the legitimacy of the base. Instead, they make clear that they are only challenging the legality of the removals. Lalit has criticized what party members describe as a resulting "chorus" from Chagossians repeating "again and again" in "unusually servile language" that they are "*not* against the military base."[26]

Others in Mauritius have accused the CRG and Chagossians of damaging Mauritius's sovereignty claim over Chagos by taking lawsuits to the British High Court and implicitly accepting U.K. jurisdiction over the islands.[27]

Some Mauritian commentators (and some Chagossians in the CSC) have been concerned that Chagossians' acceptance of U.K. citizenship and passports, granted for the first time in 2002, may further undermine Mauritius's sovereignty claim[28] (Lassemillante 2002:89). (Some Mauritians were particularly angered when CRG members publicly celebrated their new citizenship by waving the Union Jack and pictures of the Queen.) Bancoult and the CRG have remained noncommittal on the issue of sovereignty, refusing to say whether they would prefer resettlement of Chagos as a British Overseas Territory or as part of the Republic of Mauritius. Many Chagossians have angry or, at best, ambivalent feelings about Mauritius, a nation from which most have felt excluded since their arrival and which many feel won its independence at their expense (some Mauritians even acknowledge that independence was "bought with the blood of Chagossians" (Teelock 2001:415)).

Publicly, the Mauritian government has been equally noncommittal about the U.K. lawsuits and U.K. citizenship. At the same time, governing parties have offered various forms of high- and low-profile support to the islanders, including increasing government social assistance, renovating two government-built Chagossian community centers, building a commemorative monument to the expulsion, and awarding Bancoult the nation's second highest medal in recognition of his leadership in the CRG's legal victories.

On the other hand, the Mauritian government has strongly rejected recognition of the Chagossians as an indigenous people on several counts (Jeffery 2007). Both the CRG's Bancoult and the

CSC's Mandarin have represented Chagossians as an indigenous people before the U.N., aware of the rights to self-determination accorded to indigenous peoples under international law. The government and others are concerned that acknowledging Chagossians as indigenous would threaten Mauritius's sovereignty claim, especially if Chagossians were to resettle the islands. Mauritian politicians also insist that there has never been an indigenous population in Mauritius and its dependencies, since the islands were populated through slavery and indentured labor beginning in the seventeenth century. Envisioning Mauritian history in this way, as a nation of immigrants from Europe, Asia, and Africa, has been an important aspect of Mauritian popular mythology since independence. Acknowledging Chagossians' claim to indigeneity thus would not only challenge Mauritian sovereignty and give the group rights over the archipelago's future, but would also undermine part of the national myth and, potentially, peace between ethnic groups in the country.

Mauritian governments have similarly rejected claims by the Chagos Refugees Group and other Chagossians to being refugees, beginning with the protests of 1980–1981. In 2003, the CRG's London legal team approached the U.N. High Commissioner for Refugees (UNHCR) to inquire about Chagossians gaining recognition as refugees. To obtain refugee status, however, the government of the country of residence must support a group's application to the UNHCR. From the perspective of the Mauritian government, recognition as refugees would acknowledge that Chagossians had arrived in the island of Mauritius from outside the state, conceding U.K. sovereignty over Chagos and damaging Mauritius's sovereignty claim. Then Deputy Prime Minister Bérenger thus refused the CRG's request to support its UNHCR application because, from the perspective of the Mauritian government, Chagossians were internally displaced within the state of Mauritius. In both cases of Chagossians gaining recognition as indigenous and as refugees, and despite close ties between the group and government leaders, state-level politics surrounding the Mauritian sovereignty claim have restricted the community's access to the U.N.'s supranational legal frameworks (Jeffery 2007).

In October 2003, Chagossians faced another setback when the British High Court denied their claim for compensation in the new U.K. suit. In December 2004, a federal court dismissed the U.S. suit, finding no wrongdoing on the part of the government or its officials. Their appeal was struck down, and the U.S. Supreme Court recently declined to review the case. With another suit pending against the U.K. government in the European Court of Human Rights, in June 2004, the U.K. government made a stunning announcement. In the name of the Queen, the government enacted two new orders in council barring any return to Chagos. In effect, without parliamentary debate or consultation, the U.K. government again used the archaic power of royal decree to overturn the November 2000 court victory. Although the Chagossians and their lawyers announced that they would challenge the orders, legally speaking they were back where they started.

The Mauritian Struggle for Sovereignty

Within weeks of the United Kingdom's detachment of Chagos to create the BIOT, the leading opposition party at the time, the Mauritian Social Democratic Party (PMSD), attacked the governing Labour Party for agreeing to the detachment. The PMSD objected, however, not to the loss of the islands, but to the "terms and conditions" that gave away the islands so cheaply (de l'Estrac 1983; Teelock 2001:415). Since the detachment various opposition parties have attacked the long-ruling Labour Party for having "sold" Chagos and Diego Garcia. Following the PMSD, the MMM has had particular success in attacking Labour for selling part of the Mauritian state and for permitting Mauritian soil (an island nation with no enemies, no military, and only a small coast guard) to be used for the expansion of militarism in the Indian Ocean. Only weeks after Bérenger and the MMM helped secure the £4 million compensation deal from the British government in 1982, the party used the issues of sovereignty, the Chagossians, and the closure of the base, along with major economic difficulties, to sweep Ramgoolam's Labour Party out of office for the first time since independence. When the new Mauritian Parliament convened, it unanimously passed legislation declaring Diego Garcia and Chagos part of Mauritius (Madeley 1985:10).

Part of the resonance of the MMM's attacks on the Labour Party stems from ethnic divisions that have been prominent features of Mauritian politics for roughly 50 years (Selvon 2001). Although the Labour Party developed as a broad progressive working-class movement, by the 1960s the party generally represented Hindu Indo-Mauritians, who are about two-thirds of the population. Despite its beginnings as a radical working-class movement, the MMM has over time increasingly represented Afro-Mauritians (also called "Creoles"; about 30 percent of the population), as well as some Muslim Indo-Mauritians, Franco- and Sino-Mauritians, and some Hindu Indo-Mauritians. With roots in the Marxism of its leaders' experiences as students in 1960s Paris and with strong backing from Mauritian trade unions, the MMM has sought to position itself as the champion of the mostly Afro-Mauritian working class (Seegobin and Collen 1977). Supporting the Chagossians (who are seen as Afro-Mauritians) became a high-profile way for the MMM to show its support for its main constituency (especially in the party's stronghold, the capital, where most Chagossians and other Afro-Mauritians live).

MMM co-founder Dev Virahsawmy told the second author that in recent years, after finally coming into power, Bérenger (a rare Franco-Mauritian in Mauritian politics) and the MMM needed to demonstrate that they had not abandoned the Afro-Mauritian working class in favor of majority Indo-Mauritian or middle-class capitalist interests. This could be achieved relatively cheaply, easily, and in a high profile way by supporting the Chagossians, who are mostly dark-skinned people of African descent. This relationship has also been mutually beneficial for the Chagossians, including by allowing Bancoult and the CRG to demonstrate loyalty to Mauritius through ties with Bérenger and the MMM. (The close relationship has not been uncontroversial among Chagossians, some of whom feel that they have been manipulated by politicians, including Bérenger, in the past.)

As a result of the MMM's attacks, Labour and MMM governments since 1980 have repeatedly pressed the nation's sovereignty claim and its opposition to the base at the U.N. and other international forums. During the Cold War, Mauritius elicited statements supporting its sovereignty over Chagos from the Organisation of African Unity (now the African Union) and the Non-Aligned Movement (de l'Estrac 1983:29,51,71). Many in Mauritius believe that reclaiming Chagos would mark the completion of the decolonization process. In response to Mauritius's claims, the U.K. government has consistently responded by asserting its sovereignty, while assuring the Mauritian government that it will "cede the territory to Mauritius when it is no longer required for defence purposes" (Foreign and Commonwealth Office 1999:51). The British have offered no indication of when that might be.

There are signs that even if Mauritius is no closer to regaining Chagos, some of the government's calls for sovereignty may have been useful in sustaining the economic livelihood of the nation. Jean-Claude de l'Estrac, who served in coalition governments as MMM foreign minister in 1982–1983 and 1990–1991, told the second author that the MMM's position on the base changed dramatically during the 1980s. By the time B-52s were launched from Diego Garcia during the 1991 Gulf War, MMM leaders no longer officially opposed the U.S. base (Anyangwe 2001:48). De l'Estrac and others have suggested that Mauritian governments led by the MMM and all the major parties have traded economic benefits for the sugar and textile industries (which along with tourism now form the heart of a relatively healthy, if tenuous, Mauritian economy) in exchange for silence on sovereignty and the U.S. base (Lalit 2002:65).[29]

Sir Satcam Boolell, a former leader of the Labour Party, confirmed that in May 1990, the Mauritian government withdrew a plan to place Chagos on the U.N. agenda as a result of threats from the U.K. and U.S. governments against Mauritian sugar and textile export quotas in the United States. He explained that "it was necessary to choose between the future of [the textile] industry and Chagos," adding that

> the debate around the return of Chagos to Mauritius was academic in the sense that even if a majority at the United Nations condemned Great Britain and the United States, which they had already done in the past, it was nearly certain that neither the English nor the Americans were going to leave Chagos.[30]

Lalit activists have made similar claims about the effects of the African Growth and Opportunity Act (AGOA) trade agreements between African states and the United States.[31] Beginning in the 1990s, AGOA awarded African textile companies trade benefits and larger quotas for exports to the United States provided that African governments met conditions that included guarantees not to "undermine United States national security or foreign policy interests" (Lalit 2002:62). Lalit points out that since passage of the act, the MSM–MMM government (2000–2005) dropped its opposition to the base, supported the U.S. war on terrorism, and voiced no opposition to the wars in Afghanistan and Iraq[32] (Lallah 2002:62,65).

Following September 11, 2001, Bérenger and others in Mauritius seem to have understood that the increased military prominence of Diego Garcia in the U.S. wars has complicated the Mauritian government's efforts to regain sovereignty and close the base.[33] In 2002, Bérenger hinted that Mauritius would drop its opposition to the base in exchange for recognition of its sovereignty, noting Mauritius's intention to assist the United States in its declared war on terrorism.[34] Some suggest that the MSM–MMM government's changing position on the base stemmed from its interest in claiming rent from the United States if Mauritius were to regain sovereignty (Anyangwe 2001:47–48). In 2004, after Bérenger became prime minister, the government made its boldest moves yet to regain sovereignty but said nothing about the base. Bérenger sent a letter to Tony Blair informing him of Mauritius's intention to press its claim. The government expressed interest in claiming rent from the United States, as well as in exploiting the archipelago's fishing and tourist potential and assisting in the

Chagossians' resettlement.[35] When Bérenger flew to London to discuss the sovereignty issue with Blair, the British prime minister canceled their meeting, citing "other commitments."[36]

Lalit's Struggle to Close the Base

"We want to close this base down," Lindsey Collen wrote for Lalit in an open letter to the people of the United Kingdom and the United States, days after the United States began bombing Afghanistan from Diego Garcia. "We want the terrible emptiness of the tarmac runways out! And the concrete docks out! We want the emptiness of all the military hardware out, too" (Collen 2002:224–229).

Having played an active role in the Chagossians' strikes of 1978 and 1981–1982, Lalit portrays Diego Garcia as emblematic of its campaigns for decolonization, demilitarization, and human rights.[37] On these and other issues, including the maintenance of the Mauritian social welfare system, workers' and women's rights, and education for the poor, the party has been a consistent (if relatively marginalized) leftist voice in Mauritian politics for three decades. Since the strikes of the early 1980s, there has been occasional collaboration between Lalit and Chagossians (the CRG in particular), with the party actively supporting the right of return and reparations (Lalit 2002). Lalit has long campaigned for the closure of the base and the return of Chagos to Mauritian control (Lalit 1986:4,15; Lalit 1987:8,19; Lalit 2002:9; Lallah 2002:64–65; Subron 2002).

In 1998, Lalit and the CRG jointly initiated the Rann Nu Diego Committee, aimed at unifying their struggles under a single platform. Notably, the platform was shaped largely by Lalit and other Mauritian organizations and prioritized closing the base and regaining sovereignty ahead of Chagossians' claims. The platform's description of Chagossians as "Mauritians of Chagossian origin" likewise represents a refusal to recognize them as an indigenous people, instead defining them as, first and foremost, Mauritians who happen to have been born in Chagos.

Tensions between Lalit and Chagossians have become more overt at times because of their divergent stances on Mauritian sovereignty and the base (Jeffery 2006; Jeffery 2007). In early 2003, Lalit mobilized Mauritian organizations opposed to the invasion of Iraq for an anti-war demonstration and invited the CRG to participate. Relations soured when the CRG declined, having decided that it was neither anti-American nor opposed to the U.S. base. The CRG increasingly distanced itself from Lalit's opposition to the base, and began to stress instead its claims for an end to employment discrimination there. It insisted that, in the event of resettlement, the base should remain as an important source of employment and logistical support.

By 2004, each side was independently trying to organize a boat trip to Diego Garcia.[38] Lacking a boat but joined by small yacht owners and peace groups, Lalit concentrated its efforts on a campaign, supported by the No U.S. Bases network, to send a "Peace Flotilla" to the base, only to have the U.K. government's orders in council halt the trip. As declared in a recent press release, Lalit's struggle "working on all three fronts" remains ongoing, "now united with the overall struggle to abolish all foreign military bases."[39] Collaboration with the CRG is sporadic.

For its part, the CRG began negotiating with British officials about organizing and funding a short visit to the islands. On March 30, 2006, British authorities finally allowed more than 100 Chagossians to travel to Chagos for a 10-day visit, and to tend to their ancestors' graves. The trip was made possible in part because a new Mauritian government withdrew the Bérenger government's prior objections to using a Mauritian boat on the voyage. The trip, the first-ever to Chagos since the expulsion,[40] generated media attention internationally and was widely seen as a concession by British officials.[41]

Upon arriving back in Mauritius, Bancoult and a delegation of 24 Chagossians from the CRG rushed to London's High Court of Justice, where they had challenged the Queen's 2004 orders in council that reinstated their expulsion. For the second time, the court ruled that their expulsion and the ban on their return had been illegal. The orders were overturned. "The suggestion," two judges wrote, "that a minister can, through the means of an order in council, exile a whole population from a British Overseas Territory and claim that he is doing so [as was done] for the 'peace, order and good government' of the territory is, to us, repugnant."

In May 2007, two judges struck down a government appeal, calling the 2004 orders in council an "abuse of power." After a second appeal, the case is now headed to the Law Lords of the House of Lords, the highest court in the United Kingdom, and a final legal showdown over the right of return.

Rann Nu Diego

Give us back Diego. A simple, straightforward demand, but one that has obscured numerous controversies, divisions, and disagreements between the three movements. Each of the words in the slogan has multiple meanings and connotations. Understanding the complexity of the phrase highlights some of the divisive issues that remain at play.

Most troubling is the first-person plural pronoun *nu*, meaning *we* or *us*. The *we* can mean either, "we, the Chagossians" or, "we, Mauritius and the Mauritian people." The phrase can thus be read as either, "Give the Chagossians Back Diego," or "Give Mauritius and the Mauritian people Back Diego." Although the two could be combined, questions would still remain over whether the Chagossians' or the Mauritian claim would be prioritized and where ultimate sovereignty would reside if the United Kingdom were to give up the island. So, too, Chagossians have found it difficult to say "we, the Mauritian people," living in a nation that sold their homeland for independence, where most have felt like homeless outsiders (Vine, Sokolowski, and Harvey 2005).

The word *Diego* is similarly ambiguous – does it mean the island or the base? – revealing cleavages in activists' positions on closing the base. For members of Lalit, the word clearly means both the island and the military installation as part of its unified struggle to return the island to Mauritian sovereignty and close the base. While many Mauritians and Chagossians are opposed to the base and share Lalit's meaning, "Give us back the island and the base," others do not demand the base's closure, having an interest in claiming rent from the United States or gaining employment and other benefits from the base. These Mauritians and Chagossians make the more limited claim, in effect, "Give us back the island, but let us keep the benefits of the base."

Finally, the word *rann* can be translated as *give back*, as *return*, or as *return back*. While non-Chagossian Mauritians generally mean, "Give us back Diego," or "Return Diego to us," Chagossians can say "Return us to Diego." CRG leader Bancoult explained, "for us, Diego is our native land, but they [Lalit members and other Mauritians] believe that Diego belongs to Mauritius." Whereas Lalit, the Mauritian government, and other Mauritians interpret *Rann nu Diego* to mean "Return Diego to Mauritian sovereignty," for most Chagossians, the phrase means, "Return the Chagossians to Diego" (Collen and Kistnasamy 2002:112; Jeffery 2007). Which raises the underlying question posed by Bancoult: To whom does Diego Garcia really belong?

Though the challenges facing three interrelated movements are particularly difficult, the movements confronting Diego Garcia illustrate some of the constraints common to anti-base movements around the globe and most social movements. The challenges are particularly extreme for movements led by formerly colonized peoples and governments that are small in number and in political and economic power and that must confront the power of governments like the United States and the United Kingdom. Small nations like Mauritius may be in some ways the most constrained, given their deep dependence on economic agreements with the major powers for their economic survival (Houbert 2000). The history of Diego Garcia is also yet another example of how the actions of the powerful, by design or otherwise, can generate dynamics that pit the less powerful against one another (as Lalit charges, it is likely that some of the divisions between the movements are the result of efforts by the U.S. and U.K. governments to drive a "wedge" between the Chagossians and the others).[42]

The power of the United States and the United Kingdom has clearly shaped the history of Diego Garcia and the environment in which the movements have operated. The idea for creating a base on Diego Garcia developed out of growing concerns in the U.S. government in the 1950s and 1960s about the problems that local opposition was causing bases on foreign territory. Diego Garcia and strategic island bases like it were envisioned as a way to minimize any such political complications by removing islands from the sovereignty of "third world" governments, leaving them in the hands of the United States or its closest Western allies, and forcibly displacing any local peoples who might protest or eventually demand the removal of a base. Despite the crude methods to which the U.S. and U.K. governments resorted, they have to a great extent successfully averted any serious political backlash against Diego Garcia (with the only real exceptions being some parliamentary opposition, a few days of congressional questioning in the mid 1970s, a few largely rhetorical international declarations, and lawsuits that in the United Kingdom may never compel the government to return the Chagossians and that in the United States may never come to trial).

If the U.K. government has faced relatively more opposition internationally and domestically, this too was by design. The joint U.S.–U.K. plan for Diego Garcia and the BIOT was for the United Kingdom to retain sovereignty and do the dirty work of setting up the territory, removing the population, and taking any political heat, while the United States would focus on building the base. When both governments have faced any significant opposition, the history of Diego Garcia also illustrates the ability of the powerful to silence protest by changing laws to their liking (witness the orders in council and changing the rules of the Commonwealth) or by buying off opposition with what for them are relatively small trade benefits (witness sugar and textile quotas for Mauritius) or direct monetary payments (witness the "bribes" paid to Mauritius and Seychelles to set up the BIOT).

Despite the power of the United States and the United Kingdom, the story of Diego Garcia also demonstrates the power of a small people and small governments and political parties to oppose major powers. Amid the conflicts and divisions that have arisen among the movements, each has enjoyed some measure of success.

Chagossians have won two small allotments of compensation and in recent years significant court victories, full U.K. citizenship, and broad international support, all of which have threatened U.S. and U.K. control of the base. The Mauritian government has for two decades successfully maintained a significant degree of international attention and support for its sovereignty claim and has likely used the issue to leverage economic concessions from both governments (Lallah 2002). Lalit has led a movement, linked to anti-base and anti-military struggles globally, that has gained international recognition and placed increasing pressure on the base. Lalit rightly describes the three struggles as interrelated. As we have shown, however, the three movements have distinct and potentially contradictory aims, and their strategies have at times been incompatible with or detrimental to each other's goals. Many of the underlying conflicts that have arisen among and between the movements – about sovereignty, refugee status, and the military base in particular – arose as a result of the complex legal, diplomatic, and strategic issues involved.

While it may be advantageous for Lalit to link its anti-base struggle to the other two movements, Chagossians in particular have reason to be wary of aligning their struggle too closely to the struggles of Mauritians whose interests have at times conflicted with their own. This is not to say that the movements cannot be pursued simultaneously and in conjunction with one another. On the contrary, since one would expect to find divisions even within a single social movement pursuing a single aim, ideological and strategic uniformity is unlikely within a coalition pursuing three goals. Strategically, it may be most advantageous for such interrelated movements at times to find simple points of agreement around which to rally publicly and at other times to allow partners to offer silent, less public forms of support and assistance when public declarations would be counterproductive.

Conclusion: The Future for the "Footprint of Freedom"

Nicknamed the "Footprint of Freedom," the base on Diego Garcia has expanded dramatically since the final deportations.[43] Most of the expansion occurred after the 1979 revolution in Iran, when Diego Garcia saw the "most dramatic build-up of any location since the Vietnam War," with more than $500 million invested by 1986.[44] Diego Garcia's lagoon is home to an armada of "pre-positioned" ships lying in wait for wartime, with enough tanks, weaponry, ammunition, and fuel to equip an expeditionary force of tens of thousands of U.S. troops for 30 days. The harbor has enough room to host an aircraft carrier taskforce, including tens of navy surface vessels and nuclear submarines. Two parallel runways over two miles long are home to billions of dollars worth of B-1, B-2, and B-52 bombers, reconnaissance, cargo, and in-air refueling planes. The island also hosts a range of high-technology intelligence and communications equipment, including NASA facilities, an electro-optical deep space surveillance system, satellite navigation monitoring antenna, a HF–UHF–SHF satellite transmission ground station, and (probably) a sub-surface oceanic intelligence station (Hayes, Zarsky, and Bello 1986:439–446). Nuclear weapons are likely stored on the base.

Since September 11, 2001, the base has grown even more important to the military, which sent additional troops to the island, stationed on a new facility called "Camp Justice." Bombers flying from Diego Garcia dropped more ordnance on Afghanistan than any other squadron in the 2001 war.[45] The (once) secret 2002 "Downing Street" memorandum shows that U.S. war planners considered basing access on Diego Garcia "critical" to the invasion of Iraq.[46] Leading up to the invasion, weaponry and supplies pre-positioned on Diego Garcia were among the first to arrive at staging areas near Iraq's borders, with bombers from the island again playing a key role in overthrowing the Hussein regime. The Council of Europe confirmed that, along with sites in Poland and Romania, the atoll has been a secret CIA detention center for captured terrorist suspects.[47] Now the base appears to be a model for the U.S. military's expansion across Africa, with talk of "another Diego Garcia" on São Tomé and Príncipe, off the oil-rich west coast, and bases considered or already established in Algeria, Djibouti, Gabon, Ghana, Kenya, Mali, Nigeria, Senegal, and Uganda (Cooley 2005; Foster 2006).

"It's the single most important military facility we've got," military expert John Pike told the first author in a telephone interview. Pike, who runs the military analysis website GlobalSecurity.org, explained, "It's the base from which we control half of Africa and the southern side of Asia, the southern side of Eurasia." Diego Garcia is "the facility that at the end of the day gives us some say-so in the Persian Gulf region. If it didn't exist, it would have to be invented." The military's goal, Pike said, is that "we'll be able to run the planet from Guam and Diego Garcia by 2015, even if the entire Eastern Hemisphere has drop-kicked us" from bases on their territory. In the words of the Bush administration, "Diego Garcia is a vital and indispensable platform for global military operations" (*Regina (on the application of Bancoult) v. Secretary of State for the Foreign and Commonwealth Office* (2006) EWHC 1038 Admin. 4093, para. 96).

While the prospect that the United States would leave or be evicted by Britain from the island appears dim in the short term, the Chagossians' recent court victories, their visit to Diego Garcia, and growing media attention appear to signal new momentum that could lead to longer-term successes for each of the three movements. With the British High Court three times having found in their favor since 2000, the Chagossians are seemingly in a good position to increase pressure on British officials not only to allow the Chagossians' return but to finance some kind of rehabilitation of their society on the islands, possibly as part of a wider reparations package.

If Chagossians were to return even in small numbers to some of Chagos's outer islands, the financial and political costs of maintaining the BIOT as a militarized territory will certainly increase for both governments. The presence of a non-self-governing population in Chagos may force the U.N. to give renewed attention to the Chagossians and the conditions under which the BIOT was created. Even without a return, pressure is likely to mount on the U.S. government to, at the very least, accommodate Chagossians' demands to work on the base as awareness of the case grows in the United States.

The initial U.S.–U.K. agreement for Diego Garcia ends in 2016. While exercising an optional 20-year extension written into the agreement once appeared automatic, growing momentum for the three movements coupled with an all-but-inevitable retrenchment of the failing Anglo-American military project in the Middle East and reductions in extraterritorial U.S. military deployments worldwide make the future of the base and the three movements anything but certain.

Notes

NARA = National Archives and Records Administration II, College Park, MD, USA.

NHC = Naval Historical Center, Operations Archives Branch, Navy Yard, Washington, D.C.

PRO = National Archives, Public Records Office, Kew Gardens, England.

1. Diego Garcia "Camp Justice." Available online at www.globalsecurity. org/military/facility/diego-garcia.htm. Date last accessed October 14, 2007.
2. Ministry of Foreign Affairs, "Statement by the Hon. Prime Minister on Recent British Action involving the Chagos Archipelago," speech to Parliament, June 16, 2004. Available online at http://foreign.gov. mu/speech/chagos.htm. Date last accessed July 24, 2004.
3. The history in this section stems from Vine (2009) and Vine (2006).
4. Coordinating Office (NSC and Collateral Activities), U.S. Overseas Bases, memorandum, NARA, ASD ISA Decimal File 1961, Box 27, 680.1, 1961; Horacio Rivero, "Assuring a Future Base Structure in the African-Indian Ocean Area," memorandum to Chief of Naval Operations, July 11, 1960, enclosure, NHC, 00 Files, 1960, Box 8, 5710.
5. Roy L. Johnson, "Memorandum for Deputy Chief of Naval Operations (Plans and Policy)," July 21, 1958, NHC, 00 Files, 1958, Box 4, A4-2 Status of Shore Stations, p. 3
6. Talks continued into 1964, when U.S. officials made plain the roots of their interest in the Indian Ocean: they were concerned about "threats to the stability and security of the area" from "massive communist military power" to the north, and local disturbances that might offer the Soviets and Chinese opportunities to intervene in the region. "This, coupled with the fact that the Persian Gulf

area is the largest source of petroleum available to the West on financially acceptable terms," policy makers wrote, "makes the [Arabian] Peninsula a key area" around which to have U.S. military power available for rapid intervention from strategically positioned island bases (Foreign Relations of the United States 2000:83–86).

7. E. H. Peck, "Defence Facilities in the Indian Ocean," May 7, 1965, PRO.

8. Jeffrey C. Kitchen, "Letter to the Secretary of State," October 8, 1965, NARA, Subject–Numeric Files 1964–1966, 59/250/6/23/3–4, Box 1638, pp. 1–3.

9. Ramgoolam later professed, falsely as documents show, not to have known about the detachment until final independence negotiations (de l'Estrac 1983). See also David K. E. Bruce, "Letter to Secretary of State," Washington, D.C., July 6, 1964, NHC, 00 Files, 1964, Box 20, 11000/1B.

10. Kitchen, "Letter to the Secretary of State," p. 3

11. Chalfont, "Letter to David K. E. Bruce," December 30, 1966. NARA, RG 59/150/64–65, Subject–Numeric Files 1964–1966, Box 1552.

12. D. A. Greenhill, "Handwritten notes on letter from P. R. H. Wright," August 24, 1966, PRO.

13. A. I. Aust, "Letter to Mr. Knight," January 16, 1970, PRO.

14. Precht [U.S. Embassy Port Louis], "Airgram to Department of State," May 2, 1972. NARA, RG 59/150/67/1/5, Subject–Numeric Files 1970–1973, Box 1715.

15. Washington Post, September 9, 1975.

16. A. R. G. Prosser, "Visit to Mauritius, from 24 January to 2 February: Mauritius-Resettlement of Persons Transferred from Chagos Archipelago," report, Port Louis, Mauritius, September 1976, p. 6.

17. Le Mauricien, May 4, 1973.

18. L'Express, May 10, 1973.

19. John Todd, "Letter to Allan F. Knight," February 17, 1971, PRO, T317/1625.

20. Rosemond Saminaden, Fleury Vencatassen, and Christian Ramdass, "Petition to British Government," English translation, Port Louis, Mauritius, 1975.

21. Le Mauricien, September 21, 1978.

22. Le Mauricien, March 17, 1981.

23. In exchange, Chagossians signed or thumb-printed "renunciation forms" to protect the U.K. government from further claims for compensation or the right to return. Many Chagossians have later disputed the legality of these forms and their knowledge of their contents (again written in English).

24. Eric Newsom, "Letter to Richard D. Wilkinson," June 21, 2000, Documents of Michael Tigar, Washington College of Law, American University, Washington, D.C.
25. *New York Times*, December 14, 1982.
26. Lindsey Collen and Ragini Kistnasamy, "Diego Garcia Visit after Life-time Banishment Due to Base," press release, March 25, 2006, Lalit, Port Louis, Mauritius.
27. *Week-end*, August 6, 2000; *Le Mauricien*, November 15, 2000; *Le Mauricien*, February 27, 2001.
28. *Le Mauricien*, February 27, 2001; *Weekend*, December 22, 2002; *Le Mauricien*, November 15, 2000; *Le Mauricien*, November 12, 2000.
29. Beginning in the 1970s, Mauritius has enjoyed quotas and high prices for its sugar and textile exports into the United States and the European Community (Bowman 1991:122–140; Teelock 2001:404).
30. *Week-end*, January 25, 1998; *Week-end*, April 6, 2003.
31. *Week-end*, March 23, 2003
32. *Week-end*, March 30, 2003.
33. *Le Mauricien*, November 24, 2001.
34. *Economic Times*, April 13, 2002.
35. *BBC News*, March 30, 2004.
36. *L'Express*, July 13, 2004.
37. Lindsey Collen, "U.S. Military Base on Diego Garcia: The Intersection of So Many Struggles," background paper, 2004, Lalit, Port Louis, Mauritius.
38. *Le Mauricien*, January 9, 2004.
39. Collen and Kistnasamy, "Diego Garcia."
40. In 2000, the U.K. government allowed Olivier Bancoult and two other Chagossian leaders to visit the islands briefly.
41. *Times Online*, March 25, 2006.
42. Collen and Kistnasamy, "Diego Garcia."
43. Parts of this conclusion stem from Vine (2006).
44. Available online at www.globalsecurity.org. Date last accessed October 14, 2007.
45. www.globalsecurity.org, ibid.
46. *Times Online*, 2005.
47. *Toronto Star*, July 2, 2005.

References

Anyangwe, Carl (2001) *Question of the Chagos Archipelago: Report on the Fact-Finding Mission to Mauritius* (Port Louis: SAHRINGON).

Bandjunis, Vytautas Blaise (2001) *Diego Garcia: Creation of the Indian Ocean Base* (San José: Writer's Showcase).

Benedict, Marion, and Benedict, Burton (1982) *Men, Women and Money in Seychelles* (Berkeley, CA: University of California Press).

Bezboruah, Monoranjan (1977) *U.S. Strategy in the Indian Ocean: The International Response* (New York: Praeger Publishers).

Boolell, Satcam (1996) *Untold Stories (A Collection of Socio-Political Essays) 1950–1995* (Rose-Hill, Mauritius: Éditions de L'Océan Indien).

Bowman, Larry W. (1991) *Mauritius: Democracy and Development in the Indian Ocean* (Boulder, CO: Westview Press).

—— and Lefebvre, Jeffrey A. (1985) "The Indian Ocean and Strategic Perspectives," in William L. Dowdy and Russell B. Trood (eds.) *The Indian Ocean: Perspectives on a Strategic Arena* (Durham, NC: Duke University Press), pp. 413–435.

Collen, Lindsey (2002) "The Island of Diego Garcia, B52's and You and Me," in *Diego Garcia in Times of Globalization*, Lalit, ed. (Port Louis, Mauritius: Ledikasyon Pu Travayer). pp. 224–229.

—— and Kistnasamy, Ragini (2002) Lalit dimunn ordiner kont baz U.S. lor Chagos, pu reinifikasyon Repiblik Moris ek pu reparasyon, in Lalit (ed.) *Diego Garcia in Times of Globalization* (Port Louis, Mauritius: Ledikasyon Pu Travayer), pp. 109–122.

Cooley, Alexander (2005) "Base Politics," *Foreign Affairs*, Vol. 84, No. 6, pp. 79–92.

de l'Estrac, Jean-Claude (1983) "Report of the Select Committee on the Excision of the Chagos Archipelago," no. 2, Government of Mauritius, Port Louis, June.

Dræbel, Tania (1997) "Evaluation des besoins sociaux de la communauté déplacée de l'Archipel de Chagos, volet un: santé et education," report, Le Ministère de la Sécurité Sociale et de la Solidarité Nationale, Mauritius, December.

Foreign and Commonwealth Office (1999) *Partnership for Prosperity and Progress: Britain and the Overseas Territories* (London: Foreign and Commonwealth Office).

Foreign Relations of the United States (2000) *Foreign Relations of the United States, 1964–1968, Vol. XXI: Near East Region Arabian Peninsula*, ed. N. D. Howland, (Washington, D.C.: United States Government Printing Office).

Foster, James Bellamy (2006) "A Warning to Africa: The New U.S. Imperial Grand Strategy," *Monthly Review*, Vol. 58, No. 2.

Hayes, Peter, Lyuba Zarsky, and Walden Bello (1986) *American Lake: Nuclear Peril in the Pacific* (Victoria, Australia: Penguin Books).

Houbert, Jean (2000) "Colonization and Decolonization in Globalization: The Creole Islands of the Indian Ocean," in Sandra J. T. Evers and

Vinesh Y. Hookoomsing (eds.) *Globalisation and the South-West Indian Ocean* (Leiden, Netherlands: International Institute for Asian Studies), pp. 191–211.

Jeffery, Laura (2006) "Victims and Patrons: Strategic Alliances and the Anti-Politics of Victimhood among Displaced Chagossians and Their Supporters," *History and Anthropology*, Vol. 17, No. 4, pp. 297–312.

—— (2007) "Our Land Is Our Land: The Chagos Archipelago and Discourses on Rights to Land in the Indian Ocean," in S. Bunwaree and R. Kasenally (eds.) *Rights and Development in Mauritius: A Reader* (Reduit: OSSREA Mauritius Chapter/University of Mauritius), pp. 31–58.

Lalit (1986) Program LALIT lor Repiblik (Port Louis, Mauritius: Ledikasyon pu Travayer).

—— (1987) Program LALIT lor Internasyonalism ek Lalit Anti-Imperyalis (Port Louis, Mauritius: Ledikasyon Pu Travayer).

—— (2002) *Diego Garcia in Times of Globalization* (Port Louis, Mauritius: Ledikasyon pu Travayer).

Lallah, Rajni (2002) "AGOA: an instrument of the U.S. ruling class," in Lalit (ed.) *Diego Garcia in Times of Globalization* (Port Louis, Mauritius: Ledikasyon Pu Travayer).

Lassemillante, Hervé (2002) "R. v. Secretary of State Ex parte Bancoult," *University of Mauritius Law Society*, pp. 86–90.

Ly-Tio-Fane, H., and Rajabalee, S. (1986) "An Account of Diego Garcia and its People," *Journal of Mauritian Studies*, Vol. 1, No. 2, pp. 90–107.

Madeley, John (1985)[1982] "Diego Garcia: A Contrast to the Falklands," in *The Minority Rights Group Report 54* (London: Minority Rights Group).

Ramdas, J.-P. M. (2003) "Chagossian Desire For A Restoration and Resettlement Plan For Chagossian," unpublished report, Diego Garcia Island Council, Roche Bois, Mauritius.

Scott, Robert (1976)[1961] *Limuria: The Lesser Dependencies of Mauritius* (Westport, CT: Greenwood Press).

Seegobin, Ram, and Collen, Lindsey (1977) "Mauritius: Class Forces and Political Power," *Review of African Political Economy*, No. 8, pp. 109–118.

Selvon, Sydney (2001) *A Comprehensive History of Mauritius* (Mauritius: Mauritius Printing Specialists).

Subron, Ashok (2002) "Losean Indyin Zonn de Pe ubyin Zonn de Ger?" in Lalit (ed.) *Diego Garcia in Times of Globalization* (Port Louis, Mauritius: Ledikasyon Pu Travayer), pp. 85–107.

Teelock, Vijayalakshmi (2001) *Mauritian History: From Its Beginnings to Modern Times* (Moka, Mauritius: Mahatma Gandhi Institute).

United Nations (1960) "Declaration on the Granting of Independence to Colonial Countries and Peoples," Declaration 1514 (XV), Geneva, December 14.

—— (1965) "Question of Mauritius," Resolution 2066, Geneva, December 16.

U.S. Department of State (1965) "Memorandum of Conversation, Islands in the Indian Ocean, 15 April," LBJ, NSF, Country File, Box 207, U.K. Memos Vol. III 2/65–4/65, London, U.S. Embassy.

U.S. Embassy London (1964a) "Telegram to Secretary of State, 27 February," NHC, 00 Files, 1964, Box 20, 11000/1B.

—— (1964b) "Telegram to Secretary of State, 3 March," enclosure, U.S. Defense Interests in the Indian Ocean, NARA, RG 59/250/6/23/3–4, Subject–Numeric Files 1964–1966, Box 1638.

—— (1965) "Telegram to RUEHCR/Secretary of State, May 10, 1965," Lyndon B. Johnson Presidential Library, NSF, Country File, Box 207, U.K. Memos Vol. IV 5/65–6/65.

Vine, David (2003) "The Former Inhabitants of the Chagos Archipelago as an Indigenous People: Analyzing the Evidence," expert report for Washington College of Law, American University, Washington, D.C., July 9.

—— (2006) *Imperial Paradise: Expulsion and the U.S. Military Base on Diego Garcia*, Ph.D. dissertation, Graduate Center, City University of New York.

—— (2009) *Island of Shame: The Secret History of the U.S. Military Base on Diego Garcia* (Princeton, NJ: Princeton University Press)

—— Sokolowski, S. Wojciech, and Harvey, Philip (2005) "Dérasiné: The Expulsion and Impoverishment of the Chagossian People [Diego Garcia]," expert report prepared for American University Law School, Washington, D.C., and Sheridans Solicitors, London, April 11.

Walker, Iain B (1986) *Zaffer Pe Sanze: Ethnic Identity and Social Change among the Ilois in Mauritius* (Vacoas: Mauritius: KMLI).

—— (1993) "British Indian Ocean Territory," in *The Complete Guide to the Southwest Indian Ocean* (Argelès-sur-Mer, France: Cornelius Books), pp. 561–572.

7

ENVIRONMENTAL STRUGGLE AFTER THE COLD WAR: NEW FORMS OF RESISTANCE TO THE U.S. MILITARY IN VIEQUES, PUERTO RICO

Katherine T. McCaffrey

This chapter examines the case of Vieques, Puerto Rico, to consider shifting power relations between the U.S. military and civil society in the post-Cold War context. Vieques is a 51-square-mile island municipality of Puerto Rico, located six miles off the southeast coast of Puerto Rico. For 60 years, the U.S. Navy maintained a stranglehold on Vieques, wedging a residential civilian community between a live-bombing range and an ammunition facility. The navy recently shut down its live-fire range on the island after four years of mass mobilization and civil disobedience made continued training on Vieques impossible.

The chapter considers how the Vieques movement emerged from the changing political landscape created by the collapse of the Soviet Union. With the end of the Cold War, the central ideological justification for U.S. military domination – the fight against communism – evaporated. The loosening of this ideological grip created a new political space for the development of popular movements opposing military power.

By looking at Vieques, the chapter considers how environmental issues have become the new focus of struggle in long-standing conflicts between the military and civilian communities. Since the collapse of the Soviet Union, the U.S. military has contended with a wave of conflicts between bases and communities. Unlike some of the protests of the 1980s, when protestors burned American flags in the streets of Manila and Madrid, current grievances against the U.S. military are often expressed in terms of the environment, health, and human rights.

Before the early 1990s, Vieques residents never emphasized the health and environmental consequences of live-fire practices and bombing of the island. Though Vieques was bombed 180 days a year, discussions of the health effects and safety risks of living on a theater of war were not discussed. Rather, grievances were framed primarily in economic terms.

In my book (McCaffrey 2002), I examine the political reasons for this economic focus. In brief, Puerto Rico is deeply divided on the issue of political status. Islanders maintain a strong sense of Puerto Rican national identity, while supporting continued political and economic association within the United States. Competing visions of autonomy, statehood, and independence divide and often paralyze political debate.

Questions surrounding the role, influence, and activities of the U.S. military cut to the heart of Puerto Rico's relationship with the United States. The bombing of an island inhabited by 10,000 American civilians exposes Puerto Rico's lack of sovereignty and the second-class status of its residents within the U.S. polity. Given political divisions on the island, however, and Cold War tensions that long acted to squelch dissent in Puerto Rico (Acosta 1989), claims historically have been articulated not in political but in economic terms.[1] The focus on economic grievances avoided larger questions of sovereignty. Vieques residents have long been concerned that their battle against military incursions should not spiral into an unwinnable battle over colonialism.

In the post-Cold War context, however, we see the development of a new environmental framework for contesting military power. The chapter examines the way Vieques demonstrators built a successful popular mobilization premised on environmental and health claims. It considers how an environmental focus emerged in Vieques resulting from the power struggle between grassroots organizations and the military in the early 1990s over military entrenchment on the island. The Vieques movement eventually expanded beyond a discrete set of environmental claims into a mass coalition movement espousing themes of peace, human rights, and social justice. New actors mobilized in defense of Vieques: mainline Catholic and Protestant Churches, U.S.-based politicians, and Vieques' first women's organization. Rallying around a cry of *Ni una bomba más* (Not one more bomb) and *Paz para Vieques* (Peace for Vieques), this mass mobilization succeeded in shutting down one of the navy's key training grounds in the western hemisphere. The chapter concludes by considering how the environment continues to be a contested locus of struggle in Vieques as community groups and the navy battle over the cleanup process.

The Struggle for Power after the Cold War

For 60 years, Vieques languished as a Cold War hostage. Originally conceived as part of a Caribbean Pearl Harbor, Vieques developed into a naval training facility during the Cold War. During this period, the island suffered direct material harm as a consequence of U.S. military expansion and rivalry with the Soviet Union. The resulting power struggle between the U.S. Navy, which wanted the entire island of Vieques, and the Puerto Rican government, which resisted military imposition, created a surreal scenario in which a civilian population of approximately 10,000 American citizens lived on an international theater of war. The navy's control of three-quarters of the island's land, air, and water resources set up fundamental obstacles to a viable civilian community.

In opposition, a protest movement led by local fishermen erupted in the 1970s, aiming to evict the navy and reclaim island land. Increased Cold War tensions between the United States and the Soviet Union during this period, however, contributed to the movement's demise. To protest the military presence, to object to the intensification of weapons training and live bombing of an inhabited island, was deemed subversive and anti-American.

The collapse of the Soviet Union in 1991 fundamentally changed political dynamics in Vieques. The navy had long emphasized the centrality of Vieques in the war against communism as a bulwark against perceived encroachment in Latin America and the Caribbean. For example, after the Cuban revolution the military had argued for the importance of Vieques as a crucial staging ground for interventions in Latin America.[2] In addition, the military stressed the importance of Vieques as a missile training site, essential to maintaining a technological edge over the Soviet Union.[3] With the end of the Cold War, however, the primary justification for the military use of Vieques Island appeared to have vanished.

By the early 1990s, United States military priorities and commitments shifted and the military began a process of restructuring. The United States cut back operations at 275 overseas sites, including 14 major bases, and pulled thousands of troops out of Germany, the United Kingdom, South Korea, and Latin America (Goodno 1997). The closure of long-contested bases in the Philippines and Hawai'i signaled a shifting political climate and presented a new opening for Vieques residents to challenge the navy.

In response to this wave of closures, and in light of the loosening of the military's ideological grip, grassroots activists organized to lobby for the shutdown of the Vieques range. In the spring of 1993, activists launched a door-to-door campaign in Vieques, collecting signatures on a petition to the U.S. Secretary of Defense to close the military facilities in Vieques. They decided to take Vieques' case directly to the federal government, asking the Federal Base Realignment and Closure Committee to add Vieques' name to the list of facilities to be closed.

These moderate measures to oppose the naval presence gained popular support in Vieques. While residents were deeply divided after organized protest collapsed in the early 1980s, staying away from pickets and demonstrations, they supported petitions and lobbying efforts to close the base.

In light of rising discontent and agitation to close the base, Puerto Rican Resident Commissioner Carlos Romero Barceló introduced compromise legislation before U.S. Congress. The Vieques Land Transfer Act of 1994 proposed turning over roughly 8,000 acres of land in western Vieques to the municipality of

Vieques for public use. Although the navy used land in eastern Vieques for weapons testing and maneuvers, its land in the west was mostly vacant. There, 60 bunkers monopolized nearly one-third of Vieques Island. Romero's bill presented itself as a pressure valve, allowing the navy to keep its essential holdings while appeasing civilians by returning a significant amount of land with the closest transportation routes to Puerto Rico, a major advantage.

The military, however, firmly opposed the bill. In a world of "violent peace," the navy argued that Vieques served as a crucial training ground for U.S. forces deployed across the globe. Pilots patrolling the skies of Bosnia, troops on the streets of Haiti's Port-au-Prince, the U.S. forces in Kuwait, Libya, and Lebanon had all been trained in Vieques (U.S. House 1994:19). Furthermore, with overseas bases closing, particularly Panama bases, it was argued that the navy might need even more munitions storage facilities (U.S. House 1994:26).

Although the end of the Cold War suggested that Vieques' strategic significance would diminish, the navy emphasized the island's new importance in the war against drugs. The navy announced its intention to erect a $9 million "Relocatable-Over-The-Horizon-Radar" (ROTHR) installation in western Vieques. ROTHR was first developed by the Raytheon Company during the Cold War to monitor Soviet fleets in the Pacific Northwest. The sophisticated radar now had a new purpose: to scan the Caribbean and Latin America for aircraft carrying drugs to and from the United States. The installation would consist of three parts: a transmitter located in Vieques, a receiver in Lajas, Puerto Rico, and an Operation Control Center in Norfolk, Virginia. The menace of communism in Cuba and Nicaragua having passed, the defense of the Panama Canal was no longer crucial. With the ROTHR radar installation, Vieques would now play a central role in the war against international narcotics trafficking and arms smuggling.

The navy's refusal to compromise in the face of rising social discontent became a key factor in the development of a protest movement that eventually unseated the military from Vieques.

The navy's determination to erect the radar installation in Vieques and Lajas not only stimulated outrage, but gave its opponents a new focus on environmental and health claims that expanded support and coalesced into a mass mobilization.

No Al Radar! Organizing Environmental Claims

By the early 1990s growing consciousness of the potential health risks posed by the naval presence began to develop in Vieques. An article published in a Puerto Rican engineering journal (Cruz Pérez 1988) documented high concentrations of explosives in Vieques' drinking water. Because Vieques' water is piped in from Puerto Rico, it was hypothesized that contamination resulted from airborne explosives. Residents were becoming increasingly concerned about contamination from military explosives and reports of high levels of certain types of cancers in the community. The secretive nature of military activity and the community's lack of access to information intensified fear and suspicion.

Crosses for cancer victims exposed to toxins from bombing range, Vieques, Puerto Rico, 2005 (Catherine Lutz).

The navy's proposed ROTHR installation provided a focus to anxiety over environmental contamination. When news broke of the military's plan to erect 34 vertical towers ranging in height from 71 to 125 feet, anti-navy activists saw this as a new way for the military to ensure its continued presence on the island. They clearly recognized that it was only in the context of efforts to reclaim land that the navy suddenly found new use for land that had lain idle for decades. Activists were also concerned that electromagnetic radiation might expose the population to new risks of cancer. Though they originally organized to lobby for the closure of Vieques' range, activists then shifted their focus to resisting the imposition of the radar installation.

The struggle over ROTHR introduced an environmental and health focus to protest for the first time.[4] Activists decided to avoid direct confrontation with the navy and instead focus attention on the health dangers of the radar station. The threat of cancer, they felt, would be more effective in building popular opposition to the navy and its project. Ironically the navy itself catalyzed this new movement. In its resistance to returning land in western Vieques, the navy installed a radar installation that unified opposition and gave protest new energy.

Opposition to the ROTHR installation united people in Vieques as never before. The radar issue diverted attention away from status-oriented politics and focused attention instead on the environmental and health effects of the military presence. Concerns about the radar installation and its perceived "cancer causing rays" rattled even the most politically conservative islanders. Even North American seasonal residents, long stalwart supporters of the navy, opposed the ROTHR station.

Significantly, the navy's decision to erect the ROTHR receiver in Lajas inadvertently opened a second front in the resistance movement. In Lajas, a group calling itself the United Front to Defend the Valley of Lajas formed to oppose the radar project on the Puerto Rican mainland, bringing together a diverse group of local landowners, veteran independence advocates, and military veterans. The Lajas struggle took on a different character from the one in Vieques. Opposition to the radar installation in Lajas focused mainly on the perceived military expansion and takeover of agricultural land. The navy was seen as usurping the Puerto Rican agricultural heartland, which was at the center of national identity.

The Lajas front succeeded in significantly expanding the radar struggle. Vieques and Lajas activists formed a coalition and organized candlelight vigils and demonstrations on both fronts. The navy inflamed controversy with a poorly managed public relations campaign. A navy spokesperson declared that the military would unilaterally erect the installation with or without public consent because Puerto Rico was the property of the United States. The navy's comments outraged even the statehood party that had supported the radar installation in the context of war against drugs.[5]

In October 1995 opponents of the ROTHR installation organized one of the largest mass mobilizations in Puerto Rico since the Vietnam War. Tens of thousands converged on the streets of San Juan to voice their opposition. Delegations from Lajas and Vieques had effectively mobilized both cultural nationalist sentiment about the land and fear of electromagnetic radiation. Confrontation over military expansion and encroachment had been channeled away from divisive debates over sovereignty and into discussion about the environment and health. The coalition Vieques and Lajas activists forged was fundamental to understanding the broad-based anti-navy movement that erupted in Vieques in 1999.

Notwithstanding popular opposition, the navy erected its ROTHR towers in 1998. On the most obvious level, the navy had won the battle. But in the long run, the ROTHR eroded the military's hegemony. The erection of ROTHR in the face of widespread public opposition stirred a groundswell of resentment and confirmed suspicions that the navy was not only indifferent to islanders' health concerns, but was actually contributing to the perceived genocide of islanders.

The Rebirth of the Vieques Movement

Grassroots organizing around the issues of health, environmental contamination, and the danger of the military presence laid the foundation for a new social movement in Vieques. The catalyst to protest was the death of a civilian security guard. On April 19, 1999, 35-year-old David Sanes Rodríguez, was patrolling the Vieques live-impact range, when explosions rocked the navy firing range observation post (OP). Two F-18 jets, traveling at between 500 and 1300 miles per hour, missed their mark by one and a half miles. The jets dropped two 500-pound bombs not on the range, but on the barbed wire ringed complex where the navy surveyed the shelling. The navy's range-control officer and three security guards inside the OP were injured by fragments of shattered glass and concrete. Sanes, standing outside, was knocked unconscious by the explosion and bled to death from his injuries.

In the days after Sanes' death demonstrators entered the heart of the base, erecting tents on the live-impact range. They built settlements to fortify their claims to the land and to block bombing exercises. For more than a year demonstrators halted live-bombing exercises in Vieques with their bodies. Thousands were arrested for acts of civil disobedience. Hundreds of thousands marched in the streets of San Juan, New York, and Washington, D.C. demanding an end to the bombing and the naval presence on Vieques Island. Sanes' death galvanized a mass mobilization that eventually forced the navy off of Vieques.

Sanes' death gave Vieques a martyr, concrete proof of the navy's threat to the community. Vieques had long lived under the threat of a navy mishap. But popular outrage over accidental firings never crystallized into a sustained movement in Vieques, nor did protest in the late 1970s highlight this aspect of Vieques' woes. Charges that the navy was bombing an island that was simultaneously a civilian residential community took a back seat to other issues. It was not until David Sanes' death that Viequenses articulated the most dramatic element of their story – indeed, to the outsider, what often seems as the most salient and defining feature of the conflict: that the navy's weapons testing range is an island inhabited by people. That there can be no real buffer zone on a 21-mile-long island when planes travel between 500 and 1300 miles per hour. That there is no barrier to prevent dust and residues from explosives from traveling downwind, or contaminating the civilian water supply. Sanes' death focused the movement on the singular issue of the bombing, and gave rise to the movement's slogan: *Ni una bomba más*, "not one more bomb."

Activists' ability to effectively challenge the navy was the direct result of the ROTHR struggle. In the course of the four-year struggle against the radar, community organizers continually challenged the ROTHR installation as a health threat and tapped into fears surrounding cancer rates. Through countless marches, pickets, and candlelight prayer vigils, activists established moral authority. Community groups' non-partisan and diverse internal structure built and mobilized a strong coalition of supporters. In the 1970s, a narrow economic focus and emphasis on local claims and leadership impeded solidarity efforts. Grassroots organizing in the 1990s, however, cultivated a solidarity network that was crucial to the new movement's sustenance and expansion. Supporters from Lajas, for example, organized a benefit concert in solidarity with Vieques that raised over $10,000 to support civil disobedience encampments. Environmental organizations and scientists who forged links to Vieques during the radar struggle now collected data from the bombing range, for the first time analyzing contamination behind military fences and providing scientific evidence to bolster the community's claims.

The Vieques movement expanded beyond health and environmental issues into a mass mobilization that increasingly articulated itself in terms of human rights, social justice, and peace. Hundreds were arrested for acts of civil disobedience on the island, including prominent U.S. political figures such as Congressman Luis Gutiérrez, and environmental lawyer Robert Kennedy Jr. Vieques was the focus of solidarity efforts from Seoul, Korea, to Okinawa, Japan, to India and Europe. Nobel Peace Prize winners Rigoberta Menchú and the Dalai Lama spoke out on behalf of Vieques' cause. For the first time, mainline Catholic and Protestant churches and local women organized to protest the military presence. The religious sector's active participation and crucial leadership marked a significant shift.[6] In the 1970s, García Martínez (1978) described the overwhelming conservatism of both the Catholic and Protestant churches in Puerto Rico, and their lack of involvement in social struggles. This dynamic changed fundamentally in the 1990s. Mainstream religious institutions supported Vieques' cause as a struggle against militarism, war, and violence. They forged an unprecedented coalition of Protestant and Catholic denominations, including Pentecostal Protestantism, widely regarded as conservative and apolitical.

Religious groups provided sustenance and support to the movement on the grassroots level in a number of ways. Local ministers and priests attended conferences, pickets, marches, and prayer vigils. The Catholic Church celebrated mass in front of the gates to Navy Camp García, pushing church pews up against chain link fence. The churches sent dozens of clergy and laypeople to the bombing range to act as human shields against naval maneuvers.

The solid backing of the religious sector gave Vieques' struggle a new legitimacy and moral authority. Church involvement helped change the Cold War framework that depicted opposition to the naval installation in Vieques as anti-American or communist inspired. With priests and ministers in congregations throughout Vieques and Puerto Rico celebrating Vieques' work for peace, the movement expanded. Individuals who never felt comfortable participating in pickets or demonstrations joined in prayer vigils for peace. Catholic, evangelical Protestant, and Pentecostal denominations formed an ecumenical coalition and organized one of the largest mass demonstrations in Puerto Rican history for "Peace for Vieques."

In addition, women for the first time organized along gender lines to protest the Naval presence.[7] Rallying behind the banner of the Vieques Women's Alliance (*Alianza de Mujeres Viequenses*), women opposed live-bombing exercises on Vieques Island and the health and security threat that military forces and training practices posed to islanders. Alliance activists embraced an ideology that celebrated women's roles as housewives as they struggled for a

Vieques "clean" of the navy. Banging pots and pans, distributing white ribbons for peace, and demonstrating with megaphones at the gates to the base, Vieques women declared that they were acting in defense of their homes: "Vieques is our home, we want it clean, we want it neat, we want it in peace ... Navy get out!"

On the surface, the vision of women's identity embraced by the Vieques Women's Alliance seemed to emanate from conservative, even essentialist notions of women's roles and potential: the woman as housewife. Yet the decision to organize along gender lines was in part a strategy to assert the primacy of bread-and-butter issues and avoid more complicated debates over Puerto Rican sovereignty. Women's identification as homemakers created a space where they could contest military policy, without appearing politically subversive or embroiling themselves in controversies over Puerto Rican colonialism.

Women brought new energy and vision to the struggle and helped to mobilize new sectors to protest. "Feminine" rhetoric fused with fiery sentiment to establish women as a forceful presence in the limelight of Vieques' ongoing struggle. The Women's Alliance organized demonstrations and pickets and sent activists to speak in San Juan, New York, and Korea against the naval presence.

In sum, activists' focus on environmental and health claims and the mobilization of women and the church laid the foundation for a broad movement that galvanized international solidarity and ultimately made it impossible for the navy to continue its training exercises on Vieques Island.

Military Response to Protest: Encroaching Civilians and Sustainable Range Management

From the military's perspective, conflict in Vieques and the eventual loss of the base was more important in political than in strategic terms. Over the course of the anti-base mobilization, the value and the necessity of military facilities on Vieques Island were repeatedly called into question. The munitions depot, which the navy declared as essential to national defense in 1994, was shut down in 2001 in response to protest, and its land reverted to civilian use. Despite its insistence on the unique importance of the Vieques bombing range, the navy was clearly able to train its troops and prepare for combat elsewhere. For the one year that protestors occupied the target range, the navy relocated its live-fire exercises to North Carolina. The navy's ability to function in North Carolina despite its insistence on the unique importance of the Vieques range raised new questions about the centrality of Vieques to U.S. military strategy.[8] The battle of Vieques Island appeared to be not a struggle over national defense, but an example of military entrenchment.

The navy was ultimately more concerned with the political ramifications of ceding to pressure in Vieques than it was with the particular practices conducted on the island. Communities in Hawai'i, Okinawa, and Korea were closely watching Vieques and formulating their own strategies to resist military imposition. The navy was concerned about the ripple effect of conceding to the popular will in Vieques when its presence was increasingly disputed across the globe. In the words of a navy official, "Vieques is the first domino in a chain of dominoes" (Erwin 2001).

One of the main ways the U.S. military responded to the successful Vieques mobilization with its environmental focus was to shift its own discourse and strategy to address the environment. In response to new environmental forms of resistance, the military repositioned itself, emphasizing the significance of "civilian encroachment" on military training facilities and ranges as one of the most serious and complex problems facing the U.S. military.

In March 2001, at the height of the Vieques movement, leading military brass testified at the first ever hearings on "encroachment" issues before the military readiness subcommittee of the Senate Armed Service Committee. Military leaders described bases as threatened "national assets," like national parks or endangered species, which needed to be protected. According to the military, population and urbanization pressures on bases, stations, and ranges threatened their ability to train. "Encroaching civilians" complained about dust, noise, and the "expenditure of munitions." Furthermore, urban sprawl pushed endangered species to seek refuge on vast, undeveloped bases. The military argued that it was challenged by the dual burden of managing these species under existing regulations while carrying out training activities. In the face of these pressures, military leaders argued they needed to plan out a "sustainable range management program" that would balance the military's training requirements with the needs of the environment (U.S. Senate 2001).

The encroachment phenomena collapsed two distinct issues into one. First, real demographic pressures spawned by suburban growth after World War II brought civilian communities into increasingly uncomfortable proximity to military bases and created friction about the impact of training exercises. Within this encroachment rhetoric, however, was a second issue that had little to do with population pressure. Concerns with encroachment focused on the way long-standing struggles over military imposition at bases such as Vieques, the Massachusetts Military Reservation, and Makua Valley, Hawai'i were now being expressed in environmental terms. Grassroots organizations were strengthening resistance to the military by focusing on the environmental and health effects of military training exercises, and by leveraging environmental laws to constrain military activities. The effectiveness of building a movement around a set of environmental claims was demonstrated in Vieques and also by the shutdown of the firing range at the Massachusetts Military Reservation.[9] The Pentagon predicted that the encroachment issue would be the major impetus behind the next wave of base closures in 2005.

The military responded to the strength of these movements by turning environmentalism on its head, presenting itself as endangered by encroaching civilians and in need of governmental protection. Beneath the military's rhetoric of victimization, however, was a significant power play over maintaining bases and evading responsibility for cleanup. The wave of base closures in the 1990s revealed the toxic legacy of military activity. One of the key problems was unexploded ordnance, not only because of its potential to explode, but because it leaks toxins into soil and water. According to a study by the Government Accountability Office, more than 15 million acres of former military bases were contaminated by unexploded ordnance.[10] Starting in 2002 the

Department of Defense urged Congress to pass legislation that would exempt the military from certain environmental laws that it claimed would interfere with military readiness. In reality, this struggle focused on exempting the military from any responsibility for contamination of soil and groundwater, and sought to block state and federal government agencies from exerting authority over the military. The military presented itself as victim as it sought exemption from environmental laws that would restrict its training exercises and hold it responsible for cleanup on former bases. While the Pentagon had abandoned responsibility overseas for its bases in Panama and the Philippines, domestically it was more difficult to evade responsibility.[11] Beneath the encroachment rhetoric, the military sought exemptions from environmental laws at the same moment community groups were seeking cleanup necessary for full recovery of land.

In 2002 and 2003, the Pentagon succeeded in winning exemptions from Congress for parts of the Endangered Species Act and Marine Mammal Protection Act. In 2004, under the second term of George W. Bush, the military intensified these efforts. Defense officials argued that state and federal environmental agencies had too much power to force the military to carry out costly and intrusive cleanups on military land. The Pentagon sought exemptions for 20 million acres of military land from key aspects of the Clean Air Act and two federal laws governing hazardous waste disposal cleanup. Although this move was opposed by 39 governors in the states where the military had created 130 toxic "Superfund" sites, the initiative had the full support of the White House.

Responsibility for cleanup was a major expense for the Pentagon, which spent $2.1 billion annually to clean up sites, an amount that was reduced by 20 percent between 2001 and 2003 by the Bush administration. However, these toxic sites were not only a matter of economics, but a potential health threat to millions of citizens. According to a recent USA Today analysis, one in ten Americans – nearly 29 million – live within ten miles of a military site that is listed as a national priority for hazardous-waste cleanup under the federal Superfund program.[12]

Since 2001, the military's concern for "civilian encroachment" has stalled cleanup efforts as the military adopted an aggressive new stance to resist cleanup responsibility. With the U.S. military embroiled in combat in Afghanistan and Iraq, the Bush administration prioritized military spending for its declared "War Against Terrorism" rather than for the toxic mess created by U.S. troops. This shift has been reflected in a growing number of struggles between U.S. states and the military over the degree of cleanup necessary, the definition of a "true" public-health risk, and the validity of scientific studies indicating contamination. In some cases, the military has refused outright to comply with state orders to clean up sites.

The military's aggressive resistance to cleanup has been paired with a decrease in funding from Washington to the Pentagon's cleanup budget, and a reduction of the enforcement power of the Environment Protection Agency. The U.S. military was extremely concerned by the precedent set by the 1997 EPA order to halt live-fire practice at the Massachusetts Military Reservation. Under the Bush administration, the EPA was defanged: the government cut EPA inspections of military bases, enforcement actions, and fines.[13]

As Vieques demonstrates, cleanup is the next frontier of struggle as grassroots organizations seek to reclaim land and rebuild civilian communities after military occupation. Power struggles remain in the realm of the environment as community groups pressure the military to take responsibility for ecological destruction and clean up land so that it can safely revert to civilian control.

The Struggle Ahead

In May 2003, after hundreds of arrests, daily incursions onto the bombing range, mass marches, constant pickets, and thousands of people putting their bodies on the line for four years, the navy was forced off Vieques Island. The struggle Vieques faces now is in terms of two interconnected issues: access to and cleanup of land.

Land use designation becomes the crucial point of contestation. When the navy left Vieques, the majority of its landholdings, 18,000 acres, was transferred to the U.S. Department of Interior. This land was designated a wildlife refuge and put under control of the U.S. Department of Fish and Wildlife. Fish and Wildlife's stewardship of this vast expanse of former base land has created a paradoxical situation in which the same terrain that was bombed 180 days a year, that is littered with both spent shells and live bombs, that is pockmarked with bomb craters and toxic-waste sites, is now officially a "wildlife refuge." The most devastated terrain, the 980 acre live impact area, is officially designated as a "wilderness preserve" and blocked from public access.

The main problem with identifying the land for "conservation" purposes is not only that it continues to estrange islanders from the majority of the island, but it allows the military to evade any responsibility for decontamination of the land. Land designated for "conservation use" would require only a superficial cleanup since presumably no humans would inhabit the land (Márquez and Fernández 2000).

Residents bristle at the new national park that has been established with the navy's departure. They widely perceive Fish and Wildlife as the handmaiden to the navy, the gatekeeper to land for which they have fought for decades. Grassroots organizations have organized demonstrations against Fish and Wildlife and have replaced slogans that once demanded *"Fuera la Marina"* with *"Fuera* Fish and Wildlife." As community groups clash with Fish and Wildlife over access, they mobilize a deep sense of entitlement to the land fostered over 60 years of struggle with the navy. Wresting land from Fish and Wildlife is part of a broader struggle over the cleanup and development of the island.

Cleanup issues are different in the east and west of Vieques Island. Navy land in western Vieques was used principally for ammunition storage and was also the site of a small operational base. While land in the west has not suffered the severe ecological destruction of constant bombing, the navy used multiple sites in the west as dumping grounds for a variety of hazardous materials. In 2005, the navy was investigating 17 potentially contaminated

Vieques protestors at Statue of Liberty (WNYW).

sites in the west.[14] Nearly 2 million pounds of military and industrial waste – oil, solvents, lubricants, lead paint, acid, and 55-gallon drums – were disposed of in different sites in mangroves and sensitive wetland area. A portion of this waste contained extremely hazardous chemicals. The extent to which this waste has leached into the ground water and coastal water is unknown. Of particular concern is a site used for disposing leftover and defective munitions. Old munitions, bomb components, and flares were burned in an open pit. The site was closed in the 1970s when three youths accidentally detonated a bomb when they lit a bonfire. Unexploded ordnance may still exist in this pit (Márquez and Fernández 2000; UMET 2000).

The cleanup of the eastern side of Vieques is clearly much more dramatic in scope than that of the west. The eastern area has been used for naval bombing exercises and maneuvers since the 1940s. The cleanup of firing ranges has proven one of the most dangerous, expensive, and challenging tasks in the military base-conversion process (Sorenson 1998). According to the navy, Vieques was bombed an average of 180 days per year. In 1998, the last year before protest interrupted maneuvers, the navy dropped 23,000 bombs on the island, the majority of which contained live explosives (Fallon and Pace 1999). The focal point of the most intense destruction was the live-impact range, which constitutes 980 acres on the island's eastern tip, an area roughly the size of New York City's Central Park. In 2005, the EPA formally listed the Vieques bombing range (Atlantic Fleet Weapons Training Area) on the National Priority List of the most hazardous waste sites in the United States. All 14,000 acres and surrounding waters in eastern Vieques have been used for a variety of military purposes, such as shooting ranges, amphibious landing sites, and toxic-waste dumps since the 1940s. Coral reefs and sea-grass beds have sustained significant damage from bombing, sedimentation, and chemical contamination (Márquez and Fernández 2000; Rogers, Cintrón, and Goenaga 1978). The groundwater has been contaminated by nitrates and explosives (Márquez and Fernández 2000).

The cleanup of unexploded ordnance on land is a clear safety issue that concerns residents. Of particular concern are revelations that the navy has fired depleted uranium munitions on the range and the particular dangers and risks that poses for the civilian population.[15] Despite the existence of numerous bombs off the shores of Vieques, cleaning the water is outside the purview of military cleanup requirements.

The live-impact range is seriously contaminated by heavy metals, and studies have documented that those metals have entered the food chain (Massol Deya and Díaz 2000a, 2000b). An important question is the extent to which this severe contamination in the eastern tip has fanned outward and what immediate and long-term risks it poses for residents. One study already mentioned

(Cruz Pérez 1988) documented contamination of the civilian water supply with explosives as being at the same level as in lagoons in the impact zone. This study suggests serious contamination by airborne explosives at significant distances from the impact range. A more recent study by the Puerto Rican Health Department points to significant uranium contamination of sea-grass beds in the former eastern bombing range and all along the beaches on the southern coast of Vieques, including the public beach in Esperanza. These sea-grass beds feed not only turtle and manatees, but conch, lobster, and several varieties of fish consumed locally.[16]

The cleanup of the eastern land will be extremely expensive and time-consuming. Over time, live ordnance sinks beneath the surface of the land, requiring cleanup crews to remove both surface and subsurface soil. It is unclear how much depleted uranium was fired on the range, but cleaning up these munitions has its own unique problems. Depleted uranium, due to its mass and the size of the guns that fire it, can penetrate the earth to depths of hundreds of feet, requiring the removal of enormous amounts of soil to recover lost rounds (Sorenson 1998: 83, fn.174). In addition, cleaning groundwater is also extremely difficult and expensive. Subterranean water must first be located over thousands of acres of land, which in itself is a difficult process, then pumped to the surface, cleaned with scrubbing devices, and returned to the ground (Sorenson 1998:81).

As noted before, cleanup is currently constrained by land-use designation. While the navy has cleared surface ordnance in the west, Vieques' designation as a wildlife refuge – and the bombing range as a "wilderness zone," the most protected status – exempts the military from responsibility for a thorough cleanup. One possibility is that the government might decide that the live-impact range is too contaminated to clean and declare the 980 acre bombing area uninhabitable.[17] While the live impact range only constitutes a fraction of the total land mass currently controlled by the navy, it seems crucial to clean up this area to guarantee the health of the civilian population and its protection from continued contamination.

Conclusion

These issues of environmental contamination increasingly cut to the power of civilian authority over the military, which is at the heart of democratic society. After decades of secrecy surrounding its activities, the military is emerging as the single largest polluter in the United States, single-handedly producing 27,000 toxic-waste sites in this country.[18] The military, cloaked by the protective cover of national security interests, has not been held accountable for its toxic legacy.[19] It has acted well outside the purview of law, with seeming indifference to the will of civil society. Internationally, the struggle is even more profound.

In Vieques we see a connection between these struggles over cleanup and a much longer legacy of military indifference to civil society. In the 1960s, the navy sought to forcibly remove the civilian population from Vieques to clear the way for an expanded bombing range. Only a presidential order prevented them from carrying out this plan (Fernández 1996; Meléndez López 1989). In the 1970s, the navy defied congressional instructions to find an alternate training site to the Puerto Rico island of Culebra, and instead transferred live-bombing practices to Vieques (U.S. House 1994). Thus the navy's disregard for civil society, in a very concrete way, was at the core of the conflict that ultimately led to the base's closure.

Now as the military drags its heels on the cleanup process, it is continuing to challenge the rights of civil society to reclaim land. The navy always disputed any connection between its bombing exercises and contamination of the land with negative health effects in Vieques. It continues this posture as it questions the very existence of contamination within the bombing range.[20]

The environment thus remains the principle arena of struggle in post-Cold War struggles over the reach of military power. The Vieques mobilization demonstrated the strength of civil society in "refusing to accept" (Holloway 2002) injustices of state power.

While the Vieques activists have repeatedly pressed the Puerto Rican government to advocate their cause, and have inspired even U.S.-based politicians to fight for Vieques, grassroots mobilization remains crucial to advancing Vieques' interests. As the federal government weakens the enforcement power of key protective agencies such as the EPA, as the military wages bureaucratic wars of science, questioning the legitimacy of all community health and environmental claims, grassroots mobilization will continue to play a fundamental role in defending the rights of civil society.

Notes

1. See McCaffrey (2002:67–97).
2. When the Bay of Pigs invasion of Cuba failed in 1961, the surviving forces gathered in Vieques.
3. *El Imparcial*, May 1, 1964.
4. Throughout the 1980s, the navy emphasized its role as environmental protector in an attempt to diffuse conflict, even as it bombed Vieques 180 days per year (McCaffrey 2002:98–123).
5. *San Juan Star*, December 3, 1995.
6. While there were individual clergy who supported Vieques' struggle, major religious denominations were conspicuously absent.
7. This section draws on McCaffrey (2008). ·
8. Two retired navy admirals, John Shanahan and Eugene Carroll, have argued that the training the navy conducted in Vieques was neither unique nor necessary for contemporary amphibious warfare. Shanahan argued that the amphibious landings the navy rehearsed in Vieques were akin to the "Army's practicing cavalry charges" (Shanahan 2001: 3). "Proof that we are not capable of opposed amphibious assaults today," noted Carroll, "is that we had major amphibious forces in the Persian Gulf in 1991 and did not put one troop ashore because of the certainty of unacceptable casualties" (personal communication).
9. In 1997, the EPA ordered a halt to live artillery training at Camp Edward, Massachusetts Military Reservation, because chemicals from munitions were leaching towards the aquifer that provides clean water for approximately one-half million people on Cape Cod.
10. *USA Today*, December 14, 2004.
11. For other examples, see Lindsay-Poland (2003) and Satchell (2000).
12. This same report concluded that the Defense Department was responsible for more than 10 percent of all of the 1,240 sites identified for priority cleanup under the Superfund program, which aims to restore the nation's most polluted properties, both public and private (*USA Today*, December 14, 2004).

13. *USA Today*, December 13, 2004.
14. www.epa.gov/region02/vieques/sectors.htm#west.
15. A discussion of the depleted uranium controversy is available online at www.viequeslibre.addr.com/ and at the Military Toxics Project, www.miltoxproj.org. Date last accessed October 14, 2007.
16. *Vieques Times*, Summer 2004.
17. Sorenson (1998:82) notes that 55,000 acres of former base property were so contaminated by unexploded ordnance that they will remain controlled by the government in perpetuity.
18. *Environmental News Service*, June 26, 2001 and Sorenson (1998:78).
19. See Howard (1997).
20. For example, the navy's plan to evaluate soil contamination in the Vieques firing range proposed to investigate the background levels of inorganic compounds in Eastern Vieques by collecting control samples at locations that might also have been contaminated by the navy's activities.

References

Acosta, Ivonne (1989) *La Mordaza: Puerto Rico, 1948–1957* (Río Piedras, Puerto Rico: Editorial Edil).

Bhatia, Eduardo (2005) "Letter to Daniel Rodríguez, Vieques Remedial Project Manager, Enforcement and Superfund Branch, Environmental Protection Agency, Caribbean Environmental Protection Division," Puerto Rico Federal Affairs Administration, Commonwealth of Puerto Rico, June 8.

Cruz Pérez, Rafael (1988) "Contaminación Producida por Explosivos y Residuous de Explosivios en Vieques, Puerto Rico," *Dimensión*, Vol. 8, No. 2, pp. 37–42.

Erwin, Sandra (2001) "Training Commanders Tout Gulf Coast Ranges," *National Defense*, November.

Fallon, Vice Admiral William (Commander, U.S. Second Fleet) and Pace, Lieutenant General Peter (Commander, U.S. Marine Corps Forces, Atlantic) (1999) "The National Security Need for Vieques: a Study Prepared for the Secretary of the Navy," July 15.

Fernández, Ronald (1996) *The Disenchanted Island: Puerto Rico and the United States in the Twentieth Century* (New York: Praeger).

García Martínez, Neftalí (1978) "Puerto Rico Siglo XX: Lo Histórico y lo Natural en la Ideología Colonialista," *Pensamiento Crítico*, Vol. 1, No. 8, pp. 1–28.

Goodno, B. (1997) "Converting Subic Bay," *Technology Review*, Vol. 95, No. 2, pp. 18–19.

Holloway, John (2002) *Change the World Without Taking Power: The Meaning of Revolution Today* (London: Pluto Press).

Howard, Malcolm (1997) "Environmental Secrecy: A Lawsuit Alleges Environmental Crimes at the Country's Most Secret Military Base," *Amicus Journal*, No. 19, pp. 34–36.

Lindsay-Poland, John (2003) *Emperors in the Jungle: The Hidden History of the U.S. in Panama* (Durham: Duke University Press).

Márquez and Fernández (2000) "Environmental and Ecological Damage to the Island of Vieques Due to the Presence and Activities of the United States Navy," paper presented at the Special International Tribunal on the Situation of Puerto Rico and the Island Municipality of Vieques, Graduate Center, City University of New York, November 21.

Massol Deya, Arturo, and Díaz, Elba (2000a) "Biomagnificación de Metales Carcinógenos en el Tejido de Cangrejos de Vieques, Puerto Rico," Casa Pueblo de Adjuntas y Departamento de Biología del Recinto de Mayagüez, Universidad de Puerto Rico.

—— (2000b) "Metales Pesados en la Vegetación Dominante del Area de Impacto de Vieques, Puerto Rico," Casa Pueblo de Adjuntas y Departamento de Biología del Recinto de Mayagüez, Universidad de Puerto Rico.

McCaffrey, Katherine T. (2002) *Military Power and Popular Protest: The U.S. Navy in Vieques, Puerto Rico* (New Brunswick: Rutgers University Press).

—— (2008) "Because Vieques is Our Home: Defend It! Women Resisting Militarization in Vieques, Puerto Rico," in Bárbara Sutton, Sandra Morgen, and Julie Novkov (eds.) *Rethinking Security: Gender, Race and Militarization* (New Brunswick: Rutgers University Press).

Meléndez López, Arturo (1989) *La Batalla de Vieques* (Río Piedras, Puerto Rico: Editorial Edil).

Rogers, Caroline S., Cintrón, Gilberto, and Goenaga, Carlos (1978) "The Impact of Military Operations on the Coral Reefs of Vieques and Culebra," report submitted to the Department of Natural Resources, San Juan, Puerto Rico.

Satchell, Michael (2000) "What the Military Left Behind," *U.S. News and World Report*, Vol. 128, No. 3.

Shanahan, John J. (2001) Declaration of John J. Shanahan, Commonwealth of Puerto Rico v. Hon. Donald Rumsfeld et al., United States District Court for the District of Columbia.

Sorenson, David (1998) *Shutting Down the Cold War: The Politics of Military Base Closure* (New York: St. Martin's Press).

UMET (Universidad Metropolitana) (2000), "Resumen de Estudios y Datos Ambientales en Vieques," New Jersey Institute of Technology y el Centro de Acción Ambiental.

U.S. House (1981) Committee on Armed Services Report of the Panel to Review the Status of Navy Training Activities on the Island of Vieques, Puerto Rico, 96th Congress, 2nd session, No. 31.

U.S. House (1994) Subcommittee on Insular and International Affairs of the Committee on Natural Resources, Vieques Land Transfer Act of 1994, hearings on H.R. 3831, 103rd Congress, 2nd session.

U.S. Senate (2001) Committee on Armed Services, Subcommittee on Readiness and Management Support, 107th Congress, 1st session, March 20.

8

OKINAWA: WOMEN'S STRUGGLE FOR DEMILITARIZATION

Kozue Akibayashi and Suzuyo Takazato

On September 12, 2001, U.S. military bases on the island of Okinawa and other locations on mainland Japan went to "Delta," their highest alert level. While the attack on the United States was broadcast live in Japan and drew intense attention from the public, to the majority of the Japanese population, these incidents were "a fire on the other side of the globe." To the people in Okinawa, however, the threat was real. As many people in the United States who live near national landmarks feared the possibilities of another attack, people in Okinawa feared that the next target could be, say, Kadena Airbase of the U.S. Air Force, the largest in the Far East, or Futenma Air Station of the U.S. Marine Corps, located in the midst of a highly populated area of Ginowan City, or many of the other U.S. military facilities on their island. Fortunately, there was no attack on the U.S. bases in Okinawa; the island was instead pummeled by a week-long typhoon that prevented any flights, military and civilian, from entering or leaving Okinawa.

One of the 47 prefectures of Japan, Okinawa has since the end of the Asia Pacific War in 1945 "hosted" 75 percent of those facilities located in Japanese territory that are exclusively used by the U.S. military and has played a crucial role in the U.S. military operations as the "keystone of the Pacific." The reality of the lives of the people of Okinawa under long-term active foreign military occupation is often neglected within the realist paradigm of power politics. This chapter introduces the history of colonization of

Okinawa and the struggle of the people, particularly women, who have called for an end to military occupation and for demilitarization of the global security system.

Geopolitical Conditions of Okinawa in U.S. Military Strategies

Okinawa prefecture consists of a vast semi-tropical archipelago of 160 islands located in the East China Sea, 40 of which are inhabited. Its land area represents 0.6 percent of the Japanese total, and its population of roughly 1.3 million constitutes 1 percent of the entire population of Japan. Its semi-tropical climate, natural beauty, and attractions such as coral reefs, which do not exist in other parts of Japan, make tourism the key industry. In Okinawa, agriculture was devastated by the Asia Pacific War, and after the war, self-sustaining agriculture and industry hardly developed as entire aspects of people's lives were affected by the U.S. military bases; this was in strong contrast to the mainland of Japan, whose economy prospered during post-war reconstruction. Okinawa is known as one of the country's most economically depressed prefectures, with an unemployment rate of around 8 percent, compared to the national average of less than 5 percent,[1] and the lowest average per capita income in Japan.

The geopolitical importance of Okinawa has always been featured in discussions of military security in East Asia. Naha City, the capital of the prefecture, is located midway between Tokyo and Manila, and all the major cities in Asia are within a concentric circle of 2,000 kilometers. Even before the end of the Asia Pacific War, the U.S. military started to expropriate the Japanese Imperial Army bases and they expanded the bases during the post-war U.S. occupation of Japan that lasted until 1951 on the mainland and 1972 in Okinawa. These military bases were legitimated by the Treaty of Mutual Cooperation and Security between Japan and the United States of America, signed and put into effect in 1960 (hereafter the Security Treaty). Personnel of the U.S. Armed Forces and their dependants and families are stationed on the gated bases.

The U.S. military is stationed at 89 locations throughout Japan, occupying a total land area of 313 square kilometers. The exact number of personnel is difficult to determine, but according to military researcher Hiromichi Umebayashi (2002), the number is between 51,000 and 60,000, including the personnel of the Seventh Fleet home-ported in Yokosuka, Japan.

Map of U.S. bases on Okinawa (Okinawa Prefectural Government).

Okinawa is the largest home of U.S. military bases in Japan; 37 facilities, comprising 75 percent of all those exclusively used by the U.S. military, are located in Okinawa, occupying about 20 percent of the main island. The total number of U.S.-military-related personnel stationed in Okinawa is 45,354: 22,339 soldiers, 1,503 civilian employees, and 21,512 dependants.[2] One of the distinctive characteristics of the U.S. military stationed in Okinawa is the high proportion of the U.S. Marines Corps: about 17,700 of the 21,600 U.S. marines in Japan are stationed in Okinawa. The facilities in Okinawa include Kadena Air Base, Futenma Air Station for the Marine Corps, the Northern Training Area that caters to the need of jungle warfare training, and other training sites such as the live-ammunition drill sites. The U.S. military bases in Okinawa are said to fulfill a vast range of functions central to achieving the goals of U.S. military strategists in managing two wars simultaneously.

While U.S. occupation of Okinawan land is more visible, air and sea areas are also under control of the U.S. military for their training. When flying into the civilian Naha Airport, which handles heavy tourist traffic, aircraft fly in at a very low level. This is not to please passengers, however, with a clear view of the beautiful ocean, but is required by air control, which gives higher priority to military aircraft. Local fisheries are also affected by the water-training areas of the U.S. military: 29 areas are designated as training sites, thus limiting the local fisheries from entering, giving priority to military exercises such as bombing training.

In maintaining these U.S. bases in Japan, the Japanese government has provided a considerable amount of financial aid, known as Omoiyari Yosan (Sympathy Budget). Omoiyari Yosanin refers to a part of the host-nation support (HNS), a cost born by host nations to maintain the U.S. military. The entire HNS budget for the fiscal year 2006 is about $4.1 billion (Y473.2 billion), which covers such costs as rent of the land used by the U.S. military. Omoiyari Yosan for the same year is about $1.9 billion (Y215.1 billion) and is the part of the HNS[3] that was originally stipulated by a Status of Forces Agreement (SOFA). The name originates from the wording of Shin Kanemaru, then Minister of the Defense Agency, when he was urged in 1978 by his American counterpart to increase the financial support for the U.S. bases in Japan. As there was no legal rationale for the new budget, Kanemaru explained to the Japanese Diet (parliament) that it was *omoiyari* (sympathy) for the U.S. government. The Sympathy Budget covers salaries of Japanese workers on the bases, utilities, and construction of base housing and recreational facilities. In the more recent case of the U.S. military realignment plan, the Japanese government has agreed to bear $6.09 billion of the total $10.27 billion cost for relocation of the Marine Corps stationed in Okinawa to Guam.[4] Researcher Chalmers Johnson (2001) points out that this provision by the Japanese government is disproportionately high among the allies of the United States, and that without this financial support, the U.S. military in Japan, especially in Okinawa, could not possibly be sustained.

Modern History of Okinawa: History of Colonization by Japan and the United States

The military presence in Okinawa, a heavy burden recognized even in the recent joint statement on the U.S. forces' realignment initiatives issued in 2006, is a result of colonial policies imposed on Okinawa by Japan and the United States that go back to the nineteenth century. The establishment of Okinawa as a prefecture of Japan, when it was formally annexed by the central Japanese government in 1879, ended centuries of the independent Ryukyu kingdom. Located in the East China Sea, this kingdom was at the crossroads of trade among Japan, Taiwan, China, Korea, the Philippines, and other Southeast Asian nations. Due to its location, the Ryukyu kingdom mingled together those various cultures to create its own (Higa, Shimota, and Arasato 1963). At the same time, it had to contend with domination attempts by more powerful nations such as China and the local Japanese feudal Satsuma government in the sixteenth and seventeenth centuries. Finally, the kingdom surrendered its autonomy to become a part of Japan in the so-called Ryukyu Disposition of 1879, an outcome the central Japanese government achieved by force. The purpose of the annexation was the creation of both a military outpost to protect the Japanese mainland and a staging area for Japanese imperial ventures in Asia (Fujishima 1996b). Even then, the Japanese government was not the only one to consider the crucial role of Okinawa as a location for military bases. The basic research on which the post-World War II U.S. occupation and domination of Okinawa was based had already been conducted in 1853 by Commodore Matthew Perry, who Americans saw as "opening" feudal Japan to the world (Fujishima 1996a). In both cases, Okinawa was recognized as the "keystone" in their military operations in the Pacific, first by Japan, then later by the United States.

After the annexation, Japan's Meiji government's imperial policies in Okinawa reflected the growing nationalism of the mainland, and were promulgated with a rhetoric of "modernization" (Higa, Shimota, and Arasato 1963). The "victories" of Japan in the Sino-Japanese War (1894–1895) and the Russo-Japanese War (1904–1905) prompted the colonization of neighboring countries, including Korea in 1910. Okinawa was also the subject of these colonization policies, despite the fact that it was now a part of Japan. Assimilationist policies and denigration of Okinawan ethnicity were reflected in the imperial education system, which, for example, strictly forbade Okinawans from using their language in public, with the standardized Japanese language being required instead (Rabson 1999).

The Japanese government did not recognize the diversity of the nation and its ethnic minorities, including Okinawans, who faced severe discrimination both in daily life and national policies (Onga 1996). Imperial education, which continued to be implemented until the Asia Pacific War, resulted in some acculturation and assimilation to a "Japanese" national identity. The discriminatory attitude of the Japanese government towards Okinawa became even more obvious in the military tactics used from the Japanese invasion of China in the early 1930s onward.

The Battle of Okinawa in 1945

In order to halt the advance of the United States to the Japanese mainland, Okinawa was sacrificed by the Japanese government (Fujiwara 1991). The war experience of Okinawans vis-à-vis the Japanese Imperial Army made it clear that they were not considered equal to other Japanese nationals. In the fierce Battle of Okinawa in 1945, described as a "typhoon of steel," the Japanese Imperial Army was nothing less than desperate and arbitrary (Okinawaken Koukyouso Nanbushibu Heiwa Kyouiku Iinkai 1985). A quarter of Okinawan residents died in the battle. Some were killed by the Japanese soldiers who prioritized military strategies over protecting civilian Okinawan lives. Some were executed by Japanese soldiers after being accused of spying when they spoke their own local language. There were incidents of *shudan jiketsu* (mass suicide), in which Okinawan civilians, mainly children, women, and the elderly, killed each other to avoid surrendering to the enemy, which imperial education had strictly taught was a deep shame and a betrayal of the emperor (Miyagi 2000). In fact, the Imperial Japanese Army operations in the battle were not designed to protect the people of Okinawa, despite their being Japanese citizens entitled to protection (Fujiwara 1991), but had as their first priority saving the emperor in Tokyo by prolonging the battle as long as possible.

U.S. Military Occupation: 1945–1972

After the war, Okinawa was again dominated, this time by the United States. After its defeat in 1945, mainland Japan experienced occupation by the United States until 1952, a period during which U.S. economic policy was to rebuild the Japanese economy on the mainland in order to strengthen the alliance against communist regimes, while separately controlling and governing Okinawa as a base and outpost of U.S. military operations (Bello 1996; Fujii 1996). Colonization of Okinawa by Japan may have been officially terminated, but it was only replaced by the colonization by the United States.

U.S. occupation of the mainland was brought to an end in 1952 by the San Francisco Peace Treaty. A bilateral security treaty, the antecedent of the security treaty renewed in 1960, was signed and took effect simultaneously. Japan's official independence was acknowledged, but Okinawa remained under U.S. occupation as the U.S. bases became even more fortified to support the wars in

Korea during the 1950s and Vietnam during the 1960s. In this escalating Cold War context, in addition to its use of what had been Japanese Imperial Army bases, the U.S. military expropriated private lands during and after the Battle of Okinawa for use as U.S. bases, and also controlled the island's economy by differentiating its exchange rate from that of mainland Japan, thus preventing new Okinawan businesses from emerging in the postwar reconstruction. Okinawans had no choice but to become a virtual colony of the United States (Fujishiima 1996b). The purpose of U.S. occupation of Okinawa was largely military; for the Japanese government, it was a bargaining chip with the United States for its own "rearmament" with a "police reserve force," which later became the Self-Defense Forces (Nakano and Arasaki 1976). In the mid 1950s, an emerging reactionary nationalism in the Japanese government insisted on and planned for the nation's rearmament. The welfare of the people of Okinawa again suffered (Bello 1996).

In 1946, the United States drafted a new constitution for the defeated and occupied Japan. The constitution's Article 9 renounced war as a means of resolving international conflicts, and was generally welcomed. However, this document did not seem to apply to Okinawa (Nakano and Arasaki 1976); Okinawa was forced to be involved in wars waged by the United States. In order to maintain and expand its military power, the United States kept control of the island. It was clear to Okinawans and to the U.S. military there that the U.S. presence was neither for the benefit of the Japanese nor, even more obviously, for Okinawa's own protection (Sakugawa 1996).

While the consequences and influences of the security treaty were not highly visible to mainland Japanese, they represented a threat to Okinawans' everyday lives. It may not be a coincidence that the Okinawans' memories of the most intense crimes committed by U.S. soldiers overlap with the periods when the United States was engaged in fierce wars in Asia. For these soldiers, Okinawa was the last stop before actual deployment to the battlefields in Korea and Vietnam. A Vietnam veteran of the Marine Corps, Allen Nelson, recalled that his training became more realistic after he and his fellow marines arrived in Okinawa, where, for example, targets shaped like human figures were used in live ammunition training (Nelson 1999). He also recalled that the young soldiers' behavior towards locals indicated that they believed that Okinawan people were not equal human beings. This attitude may explain the fact that during this period of the U.S. occupation, felonies committed by U.S. military personnel were rampant, but perpetrators were often not even identified (Military Base Affairs Office 1995).

According to the 1956 Price Report of the Special Subcommittee of the U.S. House of Representatives' Armed Services Committee, the U.S. military had expropriated 45,000 acres (about 182 square kilometers) of land for its military installations in 1945 without paying the landowners, on the grounds that this was an act of war.[5] As it expanded its bases in the late 1940s and early 1950s, the United States intensified its expropriation of Okinawan land, reflecting U.S. foreign policy opposing the establishment of the People's Republic of China in 1949. Okinawans saw this forced expropriation of their land as confiscation "by bulldozers and bayonets" (Arasaki 1996).

The expropriation was a highly significant event in Okinawa's contemporary history as well as in its history of resistance. Some landowners kept fighting to reclaim their land, whereas others accepted its loss in return for rent under the terms of a lease. The resistance to the expropriation of one of the smaller islands, Ie-jima, led to an islands-wide movement in the 1950s for a return of sovereignty over the islands to the Japanese government (Ahagon 1989; Chibana 1997). Having experienced U.S. domination, the people of Okinawa aspired to this reversion, since this would bring Japan's new constitution, especially Article 9, into effect in Okinawa and therefore lead to Okinawa's demilitarization. This aspiration led to their strong opposition to America's precarious nuclear policy and the use of the bases in Okinawa during the Vietnam War. They also expected that if they returned to Japanese rule, the level of their living conditions would be adjusted to that of the mainland.

In 1972, according to the terms of the Okinawa Reversion Agreement of 1971, the United States gave Okinawa to Japan in exchange for compensation. The Japanese envoy to the meeting between the leaders of Japan and the United States has since revealed that the two governments also agreed on a secret pact to allow the entry of nuclear weapons into Okinawa, overriding the no-nuclear-weapons policy that Japan had already adopted (Wakaizumi 1994). While the Japanese government still denies the pact on the ground that no record was found in the Japanese government archives, research in the archives in the United States supports the account (Gabe 2000).

Despite the high hopes and expectations of the Okinawan people, there was no substantial change with regard to the U.S. bases. The security treaty was renewed in 1970 without much protest on the mainland, in contrast to the strong protest by the Japanese at its re-signing in 1960. This agreement stipulated detailed conditions of the status of U.S. bases and military personnel in Japan and codified an unequal relationship between the Japanese and U.S. governments. In the event of crimes committed by U.S. military personnel, for example, the U.S. authorities are, in accordance with SOFA, allowed to retain custody of the suspects until an indictment is filed by the Japanese authorities, thus giving U.S. military personnel legal protection.

During the 60-year post-war period, little has changed in Okinawa. The continued control of the island's local economy by Japan and the United States still prevents its sound growth, and has jeopardized any Okinawan attempt to become economically independent from the U.S. base-related industries (Maedomari 1996).

In addition, crimes and accidents involving U.S. soldiers and dependants have caused fatalities in Okinawa. There were 4,790 criminal charges brought against U.S. military personnel between 1972 and 1995. Among them are 12 cases of murder, 355 of robbery, and 111 of rape (Arasaki 2000). It needs to be noted that there were many more unreported cases, and there are no official statistics available before the reversion. During the period of U.S. occupation, local authority did not have the right to arrest or investigate. After the reversion, the U.S. military was given jurisdiction in cases where crimes were committed by U.S. military personnel; thus many who have committed crimes have not been brought to justice under the Japanese judicial system.

Resistance of the People Against Double Colonization

Even after reversion, the Okinawan people's struggles continued. Under the security treaty, the island remains under the double domination of Japan and the United States. While both governments have recently paid lip service to the idea of reducing the U.S. military "footprint" on Okinawa, neither government gives any consideration to the Okinawan hope for basic human rights, such as the right to land, safety, and to live in peace (Ota 1999). As a result, the resistance movement has continued. An anti-war landowners' group was organized in 1982 to resist the unreasonable, and even unlawful, use of land by the U.S. military. This group has been one of the major peace movement actors in Okinawa in organizing protest actions. The Japanese government, however, has at times arbitrarily enacted laws to enforce expropriation (Arasaki 1996).

In addition, people have physically but nonviolently resisted U.S. military operations. Residents of Onna village, where a live-ammunition drill site is located, mounted sit-ins on the only road to the site to protect the area, where, incidentally, they had hidden and survived during the Battle of Okinawa (Mercier 1996). Another manifestation of the people's protest was the human chain that surrounded Kadena Airbase on June 21, 1987, in which approximately 25,000 people gathered and completely ringed its 17.5-kilometer circumference. Moriteru Arasaki characterizes this event as a gathering of activists and citizens of various peace and human rights groups (Arasaki 2005).

It was within the political context of increased Japanese nationalism and revived loyalty to the emperor, as well as the long-standing Okinawan anger and frustration towards the Japanese government for its inaction regarding Okinawan suffering, that the rape of a 12-year-old girl by three U.S. military personnel occurred in September 1995. The event shocked the people of Okinawa even in the face of the experience of a history of crimes by U.S. military personnel against the civil population. Okinawans were further infuriated when the United States refused to surrender the three suspects to the Japanese authorities, invoking Article 17 of the SOFA on jurisdiction over U.S. military personnel accused of crimes committed in Okinawa.[6] A number of citizens' groups demonstrated their opposition and anger towards the U.S. and Japanese governments, and this protest spread to all the Japanese islands. Protestors demanded that the two governments revise or even discontinue the security treaty and the SOFA, the sources of their experiences of domination (Arasaki 1996). On September 28, 1995, propelled by this strong protest and by supporting public opinion on the mainland, the prefectural governor, Masahide Ota, a liberal in his second term, refused to sign the land lease of forced expropriation in proxy for the anti-war landowners who had refused to renew the leases on their lands. The Japanese government soon filed a lawsuit against the governor to force him to sign these leases.[7]

In order for the voice of the Okinawan people to be heard, there emerged a movement for a prefectural referendum on the U.S. base-reduction issue. Though non-binding, this was the first attempt at a prefectural referendum in Japan, and it introduced an innovative strategy to citizens' action, encouraging citizens to participate in the policy-making process. On September 8, 1996, the referendum was held and 53 percent of the 910,000 registered voters favored the base reduction and the revision of the SOFA (Ota 2000).[8] This referendum was scheduled in order to demonstrate, before the Supreme Court, the Okinawan people's will to render a decision on the land lease trial in which the prefectural government of Okinawa was the defendant. Governor Ota himself testified before the Supreme Court on July 10, 1996 (Ota 1999). The court decision was expected in October, 1996; however, the Japanese judicial system, hardly independent from executive government influence, disappointed and infuriated the people of Okinawa by upholding the order of the Japanese government on August 28, 1996, even before the referendum.[9]

The apparently strong and powerful protest began to fade again in the face of the power and the measures taken against Okinawa. Against the hope of many Okinawans, Governor Ota announced that he would sign the leases on September 13, 1996. The package offered by the U.S. government during the visit of President Bill Clinton to Japan earlier that year gave the false impression that there would be a downsizing or partial removal of the bases through the return of the Futenma Marine Corps Air Station, located in the highly populated central Okinawan city of Ginowan. In September 1996, however, a few days after Ota announced his intention to sign the leases, Prime Minister Ryutaro Hashimoto visited Okinawa. He spoke of a more specific plan for the return of Futenma Air Station which would involve building a new heliport off the shore of Camp Schwab, a Marine Corps base, in the less populated northern part of the prefecture.

The plan for the return of Futenma Air Station has been a major political-agenda item for Okinawan citizens since then. When the relocation plan with the specific site proposal was raised by Prime Minister Hashimoto, the citizens of Nago City, the northern city where Camp Schwab is located, suddenly became the visibly interested party. Camp Schwab is located in the Henoko section of Nago city, which, during the Vietnam War, was known in Okinawa as the location of clubs and bars which catered to U.S. bases, meaning that its economy was dependent on the U.S. soldiers' expenditure on R&R (rest and recreation.) With the disparity in economic power between Japan and the United States closing, however, Henoko's prosperity now belongs to the past. The population decreased because, compared to the mainland capitals, there is no industry except for some modest construction business to support the livelihood of local people.

The division of the community and its public opinion seemed a common tactic that the Japanese and U.S. governments had adopted, and the case of Nago was not an exception. Each time they have faced political decisions regarding U.S. bases, the citizens of Nago have split into two camps, one in favor of the presence of U.S. bases because they are directly connected to government subsidies to the local communities, and the other in opposition to militarization and ecological destruction, and in support of more democratic control of the area. Economic disparities exist between and within Okinawan cities and towns. Nago City is less developed than others, such as Naha, the prefectural capital, which is located in the southern part of the main island. Within Nago, the section of Henoko, which is less developed than central Nago, is called Higashi-Kaigan (the East coast). The population of central Nago are less affected by the presence of Camp Schwab in terms of noise and other effects, even at present, than are the people in Henoko and the neighboring sections of the base.

In 1997, the newly emerging anti-U.S.-bases movement led to another referendum in Nago City, held on December 21, 1997. Meanwhile, in April 1997, the Diet passed a bill to revise the U.S. bases land-lease law, permitting the government to sign in lieu of landowners who refused and increasing the pressure by the Japanese government on Okinawa to promote the relocation plan. Eighty percent of those eligible voted at the non-binding Nago referendum, 54 percent of them opposing the construction, yet the citizens' will expressed in the referendum did not count. The Japanese government persuaded Tetsuya Higa, then the mayor of Nago, to announce the acceptance of the relocation plan. He did so, and resigned.

In the past decade, three mayoral elections and three gubernatorial elections have been held in Nago. In each campaign, the issue of building a new military facility in Henoko was cleverly shifted away from the focal point of the elections. Instead, candidates supported by the ruling Liberal Democratic Party pushed matters concerning the local economy, including larger government subsidies, as the central issues, dividing the small communities in the locality and Okinawa as a whole by campaigning as if the only alternatives to economic depression were government subsidies provided to Okinawa in return for hosting U.S. bases.

To widespread surprise, Nago City was selected as the site of the G8 summit to be held in July, 2000. Since the city had no background in hosting conferences at the international level, this decision implied the promise of more construction business for the infrastructure, together with more development aid from the central government. At the summit, "exotic" culture and performing arts of Okinawa were praised, but the contradiction of the militarized security policies that have caused insecurity in the lives and livelihood of the people in Okinawa was never addressed.

Since 1997, some residents of Henoko have mounted protest actions against the plan to build a new U.S. military facility by organizing the group "Inochi-wo mamoru kai" (Association to protect lives). Mainly consisting of elderly members of the community who survived the Battle of Okinawa, the group has appealed to the public for better understanding of the situation in Henoko and policies over the issue, and has monitored the beach from the hatch built at the entrance of the bay to halt any construction initiative. In April 2004, the Japanese government attempted to survey the offshore construction site by building several scaffolds on the coral reef of the bay. This move induced nonviolent direct protest action by the group and its supporters from other parts of Okinawa and Japan. By paddling canoes and diving into the sea, the protestors literally blocked the construction boats from proceeding with the work, while others sat on the scaffolds days and nights as a new form of "sit-in" on the ocean. As a result, the Defense Facility Agency of Japan removed the scaffolds from the bay in September 2005, and the plan to build the new facility on the coral reef was withdrawn. The joy and relief of the local residents did not last long, however. In April 2006, the Japanese government and the city of Nago released a new plan showing that the new facility would be built in the bay with two V-shaped runways on a landfill, closer to Camp Schwab than the previous plan.

Within the history and political context of the steady and systematized denial of the democratic rights of Okinawan citizens, Okinawa Women Act Against Military Violence (OWAAMV), a women's peace, human rights, and demilitarization advocacy movement, emerged. Their activities are deeply affected by these events and history. Clearly, the people of Okinawa feel less secure in this ongoing situation of military occupation and political repression. Many challenge the authenticity of the "mutual security" that was to be assured by the presence of U.S. military bases, and OWAAMV's analysis and action offer a gender perspective to the discourse as well as to peace movements.

Women's Peace Movement: Whose "Security"?

Only recently has the women's peace movement gained public attention as a distinctive analysis of the militarized security system. Throughout the world, these movements are calling attention to the rise in military violence against women. Many are also challenging the military system itself, as well as the integral element of misogyny that infects military training. Some are raising crucial questions about the prevailing realist concept of security that rationalizes the present proliferation of U.S. military bases around the globe. Women in Okinawa were among the first and most active in posing the challenge and raising the questions.

In the past decade, women involved in the peace and human rights movements in Okinawa have gained increasing visibility by raising their distinctive voices. These women started another "island-wide" protest against the 1995 rape which coincided with the United Nations Fourth World Conference on Women held in Beijing, China, with 71 Okinawan women participating in an NGO Forum organized in conjunction with the intergovernmental conference. One of the workshops they offered, entitled "Military Structural Violence and Women," presented their analysis of the consequences of the long-term active foreign military presence in their lives. At this workshop, the group presented the history of sexual and gender violence committed by U.S. military personnel against women and children in Okinawa, and demonstrated that the military is a violence-producing institution to which sexual and gender violence are intrinsic. The workshop argued that because soldiers, especially marines, are prepared to engage in life and death combat, they are trained to maximize their capacity to attack and destroy an "enemy," a dehumanized other. Sexism that devalues the dignity and humanity of women is a primary process of dehumanizing others, and denigration of women is integral to much military training. Pent-up feelings of frustration, anger, and aggression that soldiers acquire from combat training and experiences are often vented against women in their base locality, a reflection of misogyny and racial discrimination. In demonstrating this analysis of the military, the group posed fundamental questions on the notion of militarized security. Whose security does the military provide? From their experience of living in close proximity to an active foreign military whose presence is intended to assure "security," people in Okinawa knew that the military has in fact been a source of insecurity to local people, especially women and children.

When the Okinawan delegation learned, upon its return from Beijing, of the rape by three U.S. soldiers, the committee members immediately took action to protest, responding to the young victim's courage in reporting the crime to the local police, which, media reports asserted, she said that she had done because she did not want the same crime to be repeated. The NGO Forum participants' public protests spearheaded island-wide protests against U.S. military bases, including the Citizen's Rally held in October 1995, which drew approximately 100,000 participants on the main island and other smaller islands.

As the focus of the protest movement began shifting from the human rights of women and children to the unfair bilateral security treaty upon which the conventional male-dominated peace movement had focused, women realized the necessity of consolidating and developing their newly emerged movement to continue the focus of action on military violence against women. The official establishment of OWAAMV was announced on November 8, 1995, and was followed by a 12-day sit-in demonstration at the Peace Square in Naha, in which dozens of women participated every day. Here, these women expressed their deep anger at another occurrence of sexual violence committed by U.S. military personnel, called for protection of the human rights of women and children in Okinawa, and called on the Japanese government to severely punish such sexual crimes and to revise the SOFA, gathering 511,963 signatures on a petition during the sit-in demonstration. On November 17, 1995, a delegation of 25 members visited the Japanese Foreign Ministry in Tokyo to hand over the petition and a statement addressed to then Foreign Minister Yohei Kono, protesting against the September 4 rape and demanding closure of U.S. military bases and withdrawal of the U.S. military from Okinawa.

Military Violence Against Women and Children

When OWAAMV women spoke out against the rape in 1995, one of the questions most commonly posed to them by the mainland Japanese media regarded the statistics of sexual crimes committed by U.S. soldiers in Okinawa. Although OWAAMV women often presented the official statistics released by the local authority, they also emphasized the difficulty in estimating the actual number. Furthermore, no official statistics were available about the crimes committed by U.S. soldiers during the period of U.S. occupation. Few women victimized by U.S. soldiers revealed their experiences, even after the occupation had ended. This reluctance resulted in part from the stigma imposed on victims by societies ridden with different levels and forms of patriarchy. In addition, in the Japanese legal system, rape victims are required to report the crime in order for the police to start an investigation. Needless to say, numerous women and girls chose to remain silent. The official statistics on sexual crimes by U.S. soldiers, therefore, reflect only the tip of the iceberg.

Having worked with many victims and survivors of sexual violence, OWAAMV women started to compile the cases which were brought to their attention or those which occurred in their own communities that were never reported to the police, including in the accounts and memoirs both documented cases and those recorded as oral histories. The most current, the seventh revision of the chronology, accounts for around 300 cases of different sorts of assaults against women and girls, including cases of gang rape, attempted rape, abduction, and murder. OWAAMV members' efforts to collect cases from various sources including oral histories illustrate the realities of military violence against women.

Women in Okinawa have been exposed to gender-based military violence for over 60 years. They have come to analyze their daily and historical experiences and have theorized that the violence against women committed by U.S. soldiers in Okinawa is an inevitable result of the state-based military security system. Cases listed in the chronology reveal the interplay between war preparation and the intensity of military violence. This chronology demonstrates that gender-based military violence in Okinawa began when the U.S. military landed on the island in 1945, during the last stage of World War II. Since then, women and children have been exposed to violence and have lived in fear. In the period between World War II and the Korean War, during which people in Okinawa lived on land that had been damaged by fierce battle, struggling for survival, women experienced rampant and indiscriminate military violence that can be characterized as follows:

1. A group of between two and six soldiers would abduct one woman at gun- or knifepoint.
2. After being gang-raped, the victim would often be given to other groups of soldiers for more gang rape.
3. Soldiers did not hesitate to kill or severely injure those who tried to help victims.
4. Assaults might take place anywhere, including in fields, on streets, around wells, by the water, or in front of families.
5. Assaults often demonstrated brutality. Women with infants on their backs were raped and killed, and victims' ages ranged from 9 months to the mid 60s.
6. Victims gave birth as a result of rapes. In the four years following World War II, 450 children were identified as having been fathered by U.S. soldiers.
7. Perpetrators were mostly not apprehended, and were often left unpunished.

During the Vietnam War in the 1960s and 1970s, violence was directed towards women working in the sex industry around the bases, often by soldiers returning from the front who brought the fear and anger of the battlefield to Okinawa. Rape cases were rampant. Three or four women were strangled to death each year. A survey conducted in 1969 found that approximately 7,400 women worked in the sex industry. These women earned dollars in the still economically depressed environment, and many were forced to sell sex because of large loans imposed on them in forced managed prostitution. Furthermore, many of these women were nearly strangled to death more than once, an experience that left them suffering from trauma. More recently, troops stationed in Okinawa were deployed to the Persian Gulf in the 1990s. During this period, military violence against women in various forms again increased in its intensity.

In current cases of sexual violence, date-rape types of military violence seem to be increasing, rendering such violence less visible and more difficult to prosecute. There are cases in which an off-duty soldier meets a woman at a night club outside the base, brings the woman back to the base – in violation of the military codes – and rapes or gang-rapes her. These crimes occur within the context of a higher percentage of the Marines Corps among troops in Okinawa and the declining relative economic power of the United States vis-à-vis Japan. Marines constitute 60 percent of the U.S. military personnel stationed in Okinawa – the largest number of marines stationed outside the United States; 80 percent of them are between the ages of 18 and 22 and they are stationed in Okinawa for only 6 months. These young soldiers, with less economic power, try to meet women for sex at night clubs instead of patronizing the sex industry. Okinawan or Japanese women with more money than soldiers do visit night clubs to meet American men. When these women are victimized, they are reluctant to report the crimes to the police because victims of date rape are often blamed for the crime in Okinawan and Japanese society.

Moreover, in some of the recent cases, perpetrators of assaults or attempted assaults tend to be increasingly confrontational at trials. In an assault case in June 2001, in which a soldier raped an Okinawan woman in the parking lot of a leisure area, the perpetrator, a special service unit soldier who had been stationed in Okinawa for four years, never withdrew his insistence that the incident had involved "consensual sex."[10] The Japanese court determined that the victim had been raped, yet the difficulty which she faced in this case implies the possibility of victims' reluctance or unwillingness to come forward based not only on fear of social stigma in the community but also fear of retaliation by the U.S. military.

OWAAMV established the first private rape crisis center in Okinawa in October 1995, culminating a long-time dream of those who had worked closely with survivors of sexual and gender-based violence in Okinawa. The center, Rape Emergency Intervention Counseling Center Okinawa, offers counseling to victims and supports them in their efforts to pursue lawsuits and to gain independence and autonomy. Through the activities of REICO, more and more cases of military violence, most of which had gone unreported to the police, were brought to the attention of OWAAMV women. The September 11 attacks, too, brought direct changes to the military violence against women in Okinawa. As training and base security intensified, there is a widespread sense that crimes committed by U.S. soldiers have increased or become more brutal, as the wars in Afghanistan and Iraq have clearly affected transfer plans and training. For example, in an August 2003 rape and assault case, the perpetrator might have returned to the United States had there been no war; however, his tour of duty was extended by 6 months, during which he committed the crime.

Children are also targets of military violence. In 2005, on a Sunday morning of the long July 4 weekend, a soldier who lived off base molested two girls aged 10 and 11. The perpetrator was arrested and is currently undergoing trial in the Japanese court, where his lawyers are pleading for lighter punishment, arguing, irrelevantly, that he has a good service record. (Cases tend to occur more frequently during U.S. national holidays observed on the bases. Such relaxation times for U.S. soldiers turn into times of increasing insecurity for women and children around the bases.)

These are only a few of the numerous cases of military violence committed by U.S. soldiers in Okinawa. To achieve the goal of stopping these crimes, a system that focuses on protection of the human rights of women and children must be established.

International Network

Among peace movements in Okinawa, OWAAMV's approach to violence committed by the U.S. military, to long-term military occupation, and to further demilitarization of global militarized security features intentional networking with citizens of other countries. As early as the 1980s, some of the members initiated solidarity networks with feminist peace activists in, for example, Buklod Center of the Philippines and Du Rae Bang of Korea, who have supported victims and survivors of military violence.

After the group's official establishment, OWAAMV members organized America Peace Caravan to meet with U.S. citizens for direct dialogue on the problems that the U.S. military have caused in host nations. In 1996, the caravan flew to the United States and visited several states to present on Okinawan history and the U.S. military presence, as well as their gender analysis of the military and militarized security system. Inspired by this caravan, an international solidarity network called East Asia–U.S.–Puerto Rico Women's Network Against Militarism was established by feminist peace activists in San Francisco to connect feminist peace activists who resisted violence by the U.S. military, as well as militarization and militarism, in their communities.

The East Asia–U.S.–Puerto Rico Women's Network Against Militarism, which is made up of women from Okinawa, mainland Japan, Korea, the Philippines, the United States, Puerto Rico, and Hawai'i, held its first international meeting in Naha, Okinawa in 1997. Participants identified common problems faced by the residents in the host communities of U.S. military from a gender perspective, including sexual and gender-based violence against women and children; environmental destruction caused by U.S. military training and operations; conversion of U.S. bases; unequal SOFA agreements between the U.S. government and the host nations; and conditions regarding Amerasian children in Asia fathered by U.S. soldiers. These interconnected issues illuminate the structural problems inherent in militarized security systems and militarism as analyzed by OWAAMV women: the military is a system that has subdued other nations and peoples through the legitimized display and use of power. The essence of military forces is their pervasive, deep-rooted contempt for women, which can be seen in military training that completely denies femininity and praises hegemonic masculinity.

Through actions, discussions, and other solidarity works with feminist peace activists in different parts of the world, the network members have devised an analytic framework of authentic security that should satisfy the following conditions: (1) the environment in which we live must be able to sustain human and natural life; (2) peoples' basic survival needs for food, clothing, shelter, health care, and education must be met; (3) respect for cultural identities and for people's fundamental human dignity must be honored; and (4) people and the natural environment must be protected from avoidable harm.[11] Women active in this international network are convinced that these conditions are necessary to achieve a humane demilitarized security system.

Towards Achievement of a Demilitarized Security System

In the OWAAMV movement, it is believed that closing the U.S. bases and troop withdrawal need to be implemented in the larger context of demilitarization of the entire security system. As the discussions of the movement's international networking reveal, closing or decreasing the capacity of one Asian base has often led to the reinforcement of other military bases in the region as a means of minimizing the negative effects of the closure on the U.S. military's global strategies. For instance, when the bases in the Philippines were closed in 1992, those troops previously assigned there were transferred to bases in Okinawa and Korea. More recently, "lessening the burden of people in Okinawa," a phrase in the Security Consultative Committee (2006) document, will be achieved by build-up on Guam.

From the perspectives of the international community and of the U.S. military, which limits access to such "highly classified" information on security policies to a handful of people, thereby creating a new hierarchy, this may be an obvious tactic. It has been very difficult for grassroots peace activists to make such analyses and predictions due largely to the lack of resources and information. In recent years, however, this type of observation of global strategies has been made possible through international solidarity and the exchange of information among areas. Through these networks, members of grassroots movements in Asia and in other parts of the world are now connected and are better equipped to cope with the dwarfing information giant of the U.S. military. People have to unite with each other. There is an increasing understanding among people in the struggle against the U.S. military empire that security of people can never be achieved without demilitarizing the security system.

Feminist international scholars have already argued that a gender perspective effectively reveals an unequal dichotomy between the protector and the protected on which the present security system has been built (Peterson 1992). The OWAAMV movement illustrates from a gender perspective that "the protected," who are structurally deprived of political power, are in fact not protected by the militarized security policies; rather their livelihoods are made *insecure* by these very policies. The movement has also illuminated the fact that "gated" bases do not confine military violence to within the bases. Those hundreds-of-miles-long fences around the bases are there only to assure the readiness of the military and military operations by excluding and even oppressing the people living outside the gated bases.

The practical aspect of analysis, connection, and solidarity among feminist activists worldwide has not been the only empowering experience for women in the struggle. As has happened so many times in the past, people in communities hosting U.S. bases have been divided over such issues as public economic support for the financially distressed localities, and thus have felt isolated and disempowered, unable to mount or maintain protest actions. OWAAMV women have also, at times, been lone voices against a patriarchy that is, they argue, the source of the militarized security system. Not only people in the local communities but also members of communities across borders share knowledge, analysis, and deep rage against injustice, as well as a vision of a demilitarized world with gender justice. Here, we see possibility and hope for transformation. Those who struggle for the achievement of a demilitarized security system may have a long way to go, but they never lose hope.

Notes

1. Nihon Ginko Naha Shiten, "Okinawa ken no kanzen shitsugyoritsu ni tsuite [On unemployment rate in Okinawa prefecture]," February 2, 2001, available online at http://www3.boj.or.jp/naha/tokubetu0012.htm. Date last accessed September 30, 2007.
2. Military Base Affairs Office, Okinawa Prefectural Government, 2004, available online at http://www3.pref.okinawa.jp/site/view/contview.jsp?cateid=14&id=1034&page=1. Date last accessed August 24, 2008.
3. Boei Shisetsucho [Defense Facility Agency], "Heisei 18 nendo bouei shisetsucho yosan sogaku hyo," 2006.
4. Security Consultative Committee Document, "United States–Japan Roadmap for Realignment Implementation," May 1, 2006; Security Consultative Committee Document, "U.S.–Japan Alliance: Transformation and Realignment for the Future," October 29, 2005.
5. "Okinawa mondai ni kannsuru 'praisu' houkokusho [Price Report on Okinawa]," *Jurist*, August 15, 1956. pp. 22–29.
6. *Okinawa Times*, September 9, 2005; *Ryukyu Shimpo*, September 8, 1995.
7. *New York Times*, October 5, 1995; *Japan Times*, August 26, 1996.
8. *New York Times*, September 9, 1996; *Daily Yomiuri*, September 9, 1996.
9. *Japan Times*, August 29, 1996.
10. *Okinawa Times*, July 3, 2001.
11. Final statement, International Women's Summit 2000, July 5, 2000, Naha, Japan.

References

Ahagon, S. (1989) *The Island Where People Live*, translated by H. Rickard (Hong Kong: Christian Conference of Asia).

Arasaki, M. (1996) *Okinawa gendaishi* [*The Modern History of Okinawa*] (Tokyo: Iwanami Shoten).

—— (2005) *Okinawa gendaishi shinban* [*The Modern History of Okinawa*], new edition (Tokyo: Iwanami Shoten).

—— (ed.) (2000) *Profile of Okinawa* (Naha, Okinawa: TECHNO).

Bello, W. (1996) "The Balance-of-Power Doomsday Machine: Resurgent U.S. unilateralism, regional realpolitik and the U.S.–Japan Security Treaty," *AMPO Japan-Asia Quarterly Review*, Vol. 27, No. 2, pp. 12–29.

Chibana. S. (1997) "Land and Life: The Okinawan struggle continues," *AMPO Japan–Asia Quarterly Review*, Vol. 28, No. 1, pp. 10–13.

Fujii, H. (1996) "Amerika gunjisenryaku ni okeru Okinawa no ichi [Okinawa's position in American military strategies]," *Jokyo*, April, pp. 51–66.

Fujishima, U. (1996a) "Okinawa sabetsu toiu genzai [The sin of discrimination against Okinawa]," *Gunshuku Mondai Shiryo [Disarmament]*, No.184, pp. 54–61.

—— (1996b) "Kokunai shokuminchi Okinawa to nihon seifu: Rekishi no kyoukun [Okinawa, a domestic colony, and the Japanese government: Lessons from history]," *Gunshuku Mondai Shiryo [Disarmament]*, No. 192, pp. 6–13.

Fujiwara, A. (1991) *Showa tennno no 15nen senso [The 15-year War of the Emperor Showa]* (Tokyo: Otsuki Shoten).

Gabe, M. (2000) *Okinawa henkann towa nandattanoka: Nichibei sengo koushoushi no nakade [The Meaning of the Reversion of Okinawa: Post WWII Japan–U.S. diplomacy history]* (Tokyo: NHK).

Higa, S., Shimota, M. and Arasato, K. (1963) *Okinawa* (Tokyo: Iwanami Shoten).

Maedomari, H. (1996) "Okinawa keizai no jiritsuteki hatten [Independent development of Okinawan economy]," *Gunshuku Mondai Shiryo [Disarmament]*, No. 192, pp. 14–19.

Mercier, R. (1996) "Lessons from Okinawa," *AMPO Japan–Asia Quarterly Reviews*, Vol. 27, No. 1, pp. 24–31.

Military Base Affairs Office, Okinawa Prefectural Government (1995) *Military Bases in Okinawa: The Current Situation and Problem* (Okinawa, Japan).

Miyagi, H (2000) *Haha no nokoshitamono: Okinawa, Zamamito "shudan jiketsu" no atarashi shogen [My Mother's Legacy: A New Testimony on "Mass Suicide" on Zamami Island, Okinawa]* (Tokyo: Kobunken).

Nakano, Y. and Arasaki, M. (1976) *Okinawa sengoshi [Post-WWII History of Okinawa]* (Tokyo: Iwanami Shoten).

Nelson, Allen (1999) *I Know War: Allen Nelson Cries Out for Peace* (Tokyo: Kamogawa Shuppan).

Okinawaken Koukyouso Nanbushibu Heiwa Kyouiku Iinkai (ed.) (1985) *Aruku, miru, kangaeru Okinawa [On Okinawa: Walk, Observe and Think]* (Naha, Japan: Okinawa Jiji Shuppan).

Onga, T. (1996) "Okinawa no rekishi wo yomu [Reading Okinawan history]," *Jokyo,* April, pp.109–143.

—— (1999) "Governor Ota at the Supreme Court of Japan," in C. Johnson (ed.) *Okinawa: Cold War Island* (Cardiff, CA: Japan Policy Research Institute).

—— (2000) *Okinawa no ketsudan [The Decision of Okinawa]* (Tokyo: Asahi Shimbun).

Peterson, V. S. (1992) "Security and Sovereign States: What is at stake in taking feminism seriously?" in V. S. Peterson (ed.) *Gendered States: Feminist (Re)visions of International Relations Theory* (Boulder, CO: Lynne Rienner Publishers), pp. 31–64.

Rabson, S. (1999) "Assimilation Policy in Okinawa: Promotion, Resistance, and 'Reconstruction,'" in C. Johnson (ed.) *Okinawa: Cold War Island* (Cardiff, CA: Japan Policy Research Institute), pp. 133–148.

Sakugawa, S. (1996) "Okinawa no genjo to heiwa kempo [The current situations in Okinawa and the Japanese Peace Constitution]," *Gunshuku Mondai Shiryo [Disarmament]*, No.184, pp. 8–17.

Security Consultative Committee (2006) "United States–Japan Roadmap for Realignment Implementation", May 1.

Umebayashi, H. (2002) *Zainichi beigun [U.S. Military in Japan]* (Tokyo: Iwanami).

Wakaizumi, K. (1994) *Tasaku nakarishi o shinzemu to hossu [I Wanted to Believe That There Was No Other Way]* (Tokyo: Bungei Shunju).

9

OPPOSITION TO THE U.S. MILITARY PRESENCE IN TURKEY IN THE CONTEXT OF THE IRAQ WAR[1]

Ayşe Gül Altınay and Amy Holmes

On March 1, 2003, the Turkish Grand National Assembly voted "no" to the deployment of both U.S. forces in Turkey and Turkish forces in Iraq. This decision marked a turning point in the war plans on Iraq and U.S.–Turkish relations, as well as the anti-war movement in Turkey. As a NATO member and "traditional ally" of the United States, Turkey had been expected to cooperate fully with the United States as it prepared for the invasion of Iraq. The price of non-cooperation was regarded as an impossible political and economic bargain for a country that relied heavily on IMF funding for its slow recovery from one of the worst economic crises in its history.

Existing analyses of this unexpected turn of events almost completely ignore the role of the anti-war movement in this process. This chapter addresses this gap and explores the dynamics of political resistance to U.S. war plans by incorporating sociological and anthropological insights about how micro-processes reverberate back to the macro-level of parliamentary decision making. Based on fieldwork and participant observation around the largest U.S. military base, Incirlik, and anti-war organizing in 2002 and 2003, as well as interviews with protesters and organizers in Istanbul, Ankara, and Izmir in 2005,[2] we analyze the forms of protest against the war and the U.S. military presence, the strong coalitions built for anti-war organizing before and during the invasion of Iraq, and the new forms of political action and lobbying undertaken in the nation's capital, Ankara, in the period leading up to the March 1 decision.

We first present a historical overview of the U.S. military presence in Turkey and resistance to it. Second, we outline U.S.–Turkish relations and negotiations between 2001 and 2003, and the nature of the anti-war and anti-base activism leading up to the critical vote on March 1. Third, we discuss the voting process and its aftermath for U.S.–Turkish relations, and then focus on anti-war and anti-base activism after 2003. Finally, we discuss how this period of intense activism has reshaped oppositional politics in Turkey and analyze its implications.

Establishing a U.S. Presence in Turkey: The Militarization of a Fig Orchard

Often the history of the U.S.–Turkish military partnership is subsumed under the larger story of the development of NATO, with 1952 usually cited as the year in which the bilateral security relationship began, marked by Turkey's entrance into NATO and participation in the Korean War. However, the foreign military presence in Turkey is essentially an American, not a European phenomenon. Some observers have even claimed that Turkey's NATO membership is "in many respects simply the external packaging of what is essentially a bilateral defense relationship with the U.S."[3]

The U.S. presence in Turkey begins a decade earlier than is usually acknowledged, in the midst of World War II in 1943 (Cossaboom and Leiser 1998). The first aid agreement between the two countries was signed in 1947 as part of the Marshall Plan, and two years later the Joint American Military Mission for Aid to Turkey (JAMMAT) was established (Criss 1993). In the spring of 1951, a large plot of land on the outskirts of Adana which had been cultivated as a fig orchard was leveled and the construction of the Incirlik Air Base was under way: while the United States Engineering Group constructed a 10,000 foot runway, the U.S. company Metcalfe, Hamilton, and Grove was responsible for building base facilities and infrastructure.[4] Between 1947 and 1951, JAMMAT – later renamed Joint United States Military Mission for Aid to Turkey (JUSMMAT) – had grown from a handful of people into one of the largest military advisory groups the United States maintained overseas, including 1,250 officers, enlisted soldiers, and civilians (Wolf 1969).[5]

Even after Turkey joined NATO in 1952, the bilateral relationship with the United States remained strong. In 1954 a secret treaty regulating the U.S. presence in Turkey, known as the Military Facilities Agreement, was signed. According to Mehmet Gonlubol, the treaty was to remain secret because it might otherwise have reminded the Turkish people of the capitulations granted to foreigners at the end of the Ottoman Empire: the agreement's colonial framework is evident in the fact that its concessions exceed those in SOFA agreements concluded with other NATO members. Secrecy could also hide the fact that the Turkish government gave the United States access to 32 million square meters of land, paid the expropriation costs of the land, and took responsibility for protecting the bases and maintaining environmental security – costs estimated at approximately $80 million annually in current U.S. dollars (Gonlubol 1975).[6]

Despite the fact that the most sensitive aspects of the treaty were not known to the public, there were already murmurs of popular discontent. In the 1958–1960 volume of the official State Department publication *Foreign Relations of the United States* (FRUS), the chapter on Turkey contained an admonishment about the growing number of "incidents" between Turkish civilians and U.S. personnel and emphasized the necessity of creating pro-U.S. sentiment in Turkey (U.S. Department of State 1993). The large number of Turkish casualties in the Korean War had also led some to question the alliance with the United States. During the years that followed, the phrase *Kore yolunda öldü* (He died on the way to Korea) came to mean "He died for nothing" in everyday usage.[7] However, these popular attitudes did not result in any large-scale organized anti-war activities; only a small group called "Barı severler Cemiyeti" (Association of Turkish

Peace Lovers) issued a flyer against the Korean War and were promptly imprisoned.[8]

Conventional wisdom says the end of World War II brought prestige to the United States while its allies felt more or less secure under the protective umbrella of NATO, and U.S.–Turkish relations were characterized by warmth and sympathy on both sides. However, as the above-mentioned warning in the FRUS document indicates, even in the absence of social movements, the American military authorities in Turkey were apparently already concerned about popular attitudes towards the United States a mere four years after the Incirlik base had opened, and long before the tribulations of the late 1960s and 1970s.

When explaining the shift from the amicable atmosphere of the 1950s to the increased tensions of the 1960s, scholars of U.S.–Turkish relations usually cite the 1960 U2 spy-plane incident, the 1962 Cuban missile crisis, the Johnson letter of 1964, and the recurring Cyprus crises. Due to the clandestine nature of security relations – 41 of the 54 bilateral agreements between the United States and Turkey signed between 1947 and 1965 were secret – these incidents were significant not only because they caused trouble within the foreign policy elite, but because they drew attention to the U.S. presence in Turkey.[9] Until Gary Powers was shot down it was not known that the United States had been carrying out such espionage activities from Turkish bases, and until the United States promised to remove the missiles stationed in Turkey in return for the Soviet Union withdrawing its missiles from Cuba, it was not known that the United States had kept missiles on Turkish territory.

As significant as these incidents were, the Johnson letter of 1964 caused the most significant shift in popular opinion; this letter signaled that the United States would not necessarily defend Turkey if the USSR attacked it over its actions in Cyprus. The betrayal felt by many Turks helped begin the shift of the image of "Uncle Sam" to that of "Imperialist America" (Candar 2000:140). By 1966, the Turkish government was requesting revisions in 20 of its 54 bilateral agreements.[10] Around the same time, these state-level tensions were upstaged by tensions emanating from below as social resistance to the U.S. military presence became increasingly organized. Protest of the U.S. presence ranged from opposition within the parliament to strikes by Turkish personnel on U.S. bases to the more spectacular student movements in Istanbul in which the U.S. sailors of the Sixth Fleet were greeted by students who threw them into the waters of the Bosphorus. In addition to these organized movements, throughout the decade there were occasional outbursts of unorganized violence which spanned the gamut from small-scale fist fights to large-scale rioting.

The U.S. response to the resistance of the 1960s was radical by most standards: with the 1969 Defense and Economic Cooperation Agreement (DECA), the number of American personnel in Turkey was reduced from 30,000 to approximately 7,000. When one considers that this took place at the height of the Vietnam War and long before anyone could imagine the end of the bloc confrontation, this is all the more remarkable. By simply eliminating the bulk of the U.S. presence, the defense planners in Washington apparently hoped that bilateral relations could continue more or less peacefully. Nevertheless, it was not long before this assumption was proven to be mistaken.

The defining event of the 1970s in terms of U.S.–Turkish relations was undoubtedly the 1974 Turkish invasion of Cyprus and the subsequent U.S. arms embargo. According to the Turkish government, if Washington was no longer providing arms and aid, then Turkey no longer had any reason to provide space for U.S. facilities, and, in June 1975, Ankara took the unprecedented step of ordering the suspension of all activities at U.S. bases. This meant that out of the 27 bases in the country, only one – Incirlik – remained in operation. Here it should be noted that bases in Turkey fell into two categories: those benefiting both Turkey and the United States or NATO in general, and those primarily serving U.S. interests. Examples of the latter included monitoring stations in Karamursel, Sinop, Diyarbakir, and Ankara. In fact, since the Soviet Union viewed the American bases in Turkey as a provocation due to their proximity, these facilities may even have increased the risk to Turkey of Soviet aggression, although they were enormously important to Washington because 25 percent of all intelligence concerning the USSR was gathered at Turkish sites. Hence the closure of these sites had a serious impact on U.S. monitoring activities and U.S.–Turkish relations.

By the late 1970s, social movements in Turkey had become radicalized, and the streets had turned into battlegrounds between "rightist" and "leftist" groups. In addition to street fighting and political executions, there were numerous attacks against American institutions and personnel. This chapter cannot provide an adequate account of the political dynamics during this time, nor can it adequately assess the impact on these movements of the 1980 coup. However, it is safe to say that during the 1960s and 1970s, anti-imperialism was perhaps what best united the various factions on the highly diverse left spectrum. With nationalism on the right and anti-imperialism on the left, the U.S. military presence came under attack from all sides. As the most visible symbol of U.S. power within Turkey, protest against the U.S. military presence was something which united many political factions that otherwise had very divergent agendas. Nevertheless, this type of social unrest did not outlive the 1970s. After the military coup of September 12, 1980, the left essentially found itself outlawed and social activism came to a standstill (Lipovsky 1992). Under these circumstances the U.S. and Turkish militaries were able to renew their cooperation, and Turkey's commitment to NATO was once again reinforced. The new Defense and Economic Cooperation Agreement already signed on March 29, 1980 solidified these changes, whose primary purpose was to maintain access to the facilities which the United States had temporarily "lost."

In the early 1990s, with the Cold War over, the "new world order" proclaimed by George Bush Sr. just beginning, and a good ten years after the 1980 coup and the erstwhile silencing of progressive activism, the unrest related to the U.S. military presence in Turkey was still a thorn in the establishment's side. According to former U.S. Ambassador Morton Abramowitz, the use of bases during the Gulf War was most likely the single most controversial issue in U.S.–Turkish relations at that time (Abramowitz 2000:155). Turkey's policy of allowing the coalition to use the air bases in Incirlik, Diyarbakir, Malatya, and Batman, closing off the Kerkuk–Yumurtalik pipeline, and ending all regular trade with Iraq was a compromise between President Turgut Özal's initial ambitions to fully support the Bush administration and reluctance within other branches of the government and public opinion (Sever 2002:27).

Beginning in April 1991, six weeks after the end of Operation Desert Storm, Incirlik was used to patrol the no-fly zone over Iraq, and hence the basing issue remained "the most important specific factor in U.S. policymaking toward Turkey for much of the past decade" (Abramowitz 2000:157). The use of Incirlik for the northern no-fly zone was not much less controversial, as it turned out, than its use during the bombing campaign. The fact that the Turkish population did not feel "comforted" by what the U.S. administration referred to as "Operation Provide Comfort" was apparent in how the no-fly zone was referred to in the Turkish media: "Operation Poised Hammer." Despite the unpopularity of the no-fly zone and the Gulf War, this widespread sentiment did not result in any significant anti-war movements in Turkey comparable to what was to happen in 2003.

It is difficult to overemphasize the importance of the Incirlik Air Base for U.S. power projection in the Middle East, particularly since the early 1990s; for more than a decade, the entire Iraq policy of the United States hinged on Incirlik. When one considers that Iraq was either at or near the top of the foreign-policy agenda for three subsequent administrations, one could argue that Incirlik was perhaps the single most important overseas base in the world. The Incirlik Air Base is undoubtedly one of the reasons that Turkey was elevated to the role of a "strategic partner" of the United States during former president Bill Clinton's visit to Turkey in November 1999 (Güney 2005). No longer merely an ally on NATO's southern flank, but a "strategic partner" of the United States, by 2003 the pressure on Turkey to cooperate with U.S. war plans was mounting; wracked by economic crises and dependent on U.S. aid and support for the European Union accession process, the stakes were high.

The Road to March 1

War Preparations

One of the key texts about U.S.–Turkish relations in the context of the Iraq war, journalist Murat Yetkin's 2004 book, *The Motion: The Real Story of the Iraq Crisis*,[11] introduces an unorthodox chronology of the Iraq war. The book opens with the story of President Süleyman Demirel's response to U.S. Secretary of Defense William Cohen on November 6, 1998: "War would be wrong and risky. But other means should be considered" (Yetkin 2004:13). According to Yetkin, Cohen conveyed, for the first official time, President Clinton's desire to cooperate with Turkey in a possible military operation aimed at regime change in Iraq and to deploy ground forces through Turkey (Yetkin 2004).

Turkey's cooperation with the U.S. bombing and occupation of Afghanistan in 2001 came relatively smoothly. On September 21, 2001, Turkey opened its airspace to U.S. military flights from the European bases to Afghanistan and granted permission for U.S. planes to land at all airports in Turkey. In Yetkin's (2004) view, this cooperation was the first step in Turkey's military involvement in post-September 11 developments in its region. The next major step was the November 1, 2001 parliamentary decision to send soldiers to Afghanistan, as part of the NATO forces.

By the early days of 2002, closed-door U.S.–Turkish discussions, as well as U.S. government public statements, had shifted towards Iraq. Intervention in Iraq was the major topic of discussion during Turkish Prime Minister Bülent Ecevit's visit to Washington, D.C. in January 2002 and U.S. Vice President Cheney's visit to Turkey two months later, which led to an unsuccessful letter diplomacy Prime Minister Ecevit tried to initiate with President Saddam Hussein (Yetkin 2004).

High-level visits from U.S. officials continued during the spring and summer of 2002. Paul Wolfowitz' mid-July trip would prove particularly important in increasing the pressure on Turkey to support the U.S. war effort. The official request for military cooperation against Iraq came in September, and included permission for full access to at least five military airports (in addition to the Incirlik base), eight additional airports for support operations, and five seaports for use as supply stations. It was expected that 80,000 U.S. soldiers[12] and 250 warplanes would be deployed in Turkey (Bila 2004). The channel used to convey this request (from U.S. military officials to Turkish military officials) was highly inappropriate, because the decision for such cooperation was a political matter, requiring the democratic process, governmental decision, and parliamentary support (Yetkin 2004).

The November 2002 elections in Turkey dramatically changed the parliamentary representation of parties. The coalition parties of the previous government lost all their seats in parliament to the ruling AK Party (Justice and Development Party) and the opposition party CHP (Republican People's Party). Many of the 365 AK Party representatives were new to the parliament. This would later be discussed as a factor in the "No" vote on March 1. The responsiveness of the new parliamentarians to their voters and to the growing anti-war stance throughout Turkey would be seen (by public commentators) as an outcome, at least partially, of their "lack of experience" in national politics.

U.S. pressures on the new AK Party government to secure permission to use Turkey for the deployment of troops to Northern Iraq grew daily. On December 3, Marc Grossman and Paul Wolfowitz were in Ankara to meet with the new Prime Minister Abdullah Gül and the leader of the party Tayyip Erdoğan. A week after this meeting, the AK Party was given full access to the White House, in anticipation of full cooperation with the United States in its campaign for war; Erdoğan would meet with President Bush and Secretary of State Powell in Washington, D.C. the following week.

The United States had broken down its expectations into the three steps of site inspection, site preparation, and physical use. The first step would require permission for U.S. personnel to inspect possible military sites in Turkey. In the second step, these sites would be "prepared" for use by the U.S. forces through necessary investment and improvement. The final step would be the physical use of these sites for the invasion of Iraq, with 60,000 U.S. and British soldiers to be deployed on Turkish soil, along with necessary vehicles, warplanes, helicopters, and weapons (Yetkin 2004). Site inspection would not require parliamentary approval if the personnel used for the inspections came predominantly from Incirlik.[13] This permission was given in December, with the provision that it did not guarantee subsequent permissions for site preparation and deployment.

In exchange for Turkish cooperation, Wolfowitz had promised that the unity of Iraq would not be jeopardized after the war, responding to the deep-seated fear among the Turkish leadership that the war would lead to the establishment of an independent Kurdish state in Northern Iraq (Yetkin 2004).[14] This prospect was treated by state officials as a major "threat" for Turkey's national integrity. The internal war between Kurdish insurgents and the Turkish state between 1984 and 1999 in Turkey's southeast (i.e. Iraq's neighboring provinces) had claimed more than 30,000 lives, and a sizeable group of armed insurgents remained in Turkey's mountains, as well as in Iraq.[15] An independent Kurdistan with access to Iraq's major oil resources or a federal Iraqi state with strong autonomy for the Kurds was the nightmare scenario of the Turkish political and military establishment. In fact, it can be argued that throughout 2002 and 2003, the most widely shared motivation to cooperate with the United States was the perceived need "to have a say in the future of Iraq."

Assurances regarding post-war Iraq were not the only "carrots" in the heated negotiation process (Güney 2005). There was also a substantial $26 billion aid and credit package to be allocated for Turkey. During the negotiations for the three memoranda of understanding (military, political, and economic), which would provide the basis for cooperation in Iraq, the United States even agreed to have its soldiers tried in Turkish courts if they violated Turkish law outside the bases (Yetkin 2004). That the Pentagon was willing to make such an unprecedented concession underlines once again Turkey's importance for the war planners.[16]

Site inspection had been ongoing since December. On February 6, 2003, the parliament passed a motion allowing the United States to invest $300 million to upgrade Turkish facilities (Yetkin 2004). The more difficult motion which would allow U.S. and British deployment in Turkey and which would give the government the authority to send Turkish soldiers to Iraq was handed from the cabinet over to the parliament after more than six hours of discussion on February 24. While this decision did not reflect a consensus in the cabinet, it was taken as a sign by observers that Turkey would give in to U.S. demands.

Because the February 28 statement of the National Security Council was one of the shortest in its history, with no recommendations or comments regarding the motion, the decision rested with individual members of the Grand National Assembly. The opposition party, CHP, had already declared its strong resistance to the motion. But it would be the 100 AK Party votes that made the unexpected difference that led to the ultimate rejection of the motion.

Anti-War Organizing

As the political, military, and diplomatic traffic between Ankara and Washington, D.C. increased, anti-war sentiments and protests in Turkey dramatically intensified across ideological and historical divides. In all major cities, anti-war platforms, coalitions, or coordination centers were established to orchestrate joint action against the U.S. war effort and against Turkey's participation in the war. The 250,000 member UCEAT (Union of Chambers of Turkish Engineers and Architects) was one of the most important components of the anti-war movement. It and other groups participated in the first large demonstration held on December 1 in Istanbul, the coalition later calling itself "No War on Iraq Coordination." Their call for action stated the main principles that had brought together more than 160 political groups and parties: "We demand that Turkey not take part in the war and not open its air space and the Incirlik Base for the death weapons of the USA." While the December rally was smaller than the organizers had wished (about 10,000 people participated), the diversity of the groups and individuals represented was promising. Moreover, the carnivalesque nature of the event was new to Turkish oppositional culture (İ. Aktan 2002). Dancing and drumming, shaking coin-filled soda cans, a group of colorfully dressed youth chanted: "We are anti-capitalists ... We won't kill, we won't die, we won't be anybody's soldiers."

Large rallies organized by anti-war coalitions in major cities were supplemented by press releases and small protests throughout Turkey. One of these demonstrations, organized by the Human Rights Association of Turkey, was held in front of the Incirlik military base as the final stop of their "Peace Train" (January 24, 2003). The group's press statement said: "Being aware of the fact that we cannot enjoy our rights and freedoms without peace, we oppose all wars on our own land or anywhere else in the world. We also oppose the use of Incirlik as a military base."[17]

The Peace Weekend of January 25 and 26, organized by the Peace Initiative of Turkey (*Barış Girişimi*), was a major international event. It included the Peace Assembly which brought together 100 representatives from 20 professional groups for a series of anti-war statements to be followed by a joint declaration for peace. A mass rally of 15,000 people gathered, despite the police announcement that they would not allow the rally to take place. Many families arrived with children, carrying home-made banners which said "children should not die." The famous actor Mehmet Ali Alabora described the lack of police resistance to the rally:

> I was at the very front lines of a group of about 2–3,000 people. We were walking towards the square when we realized that the road was blocked by hundreds of police. The police chief was at the front ... When we reached the police cordon, the police chief smiled, shook my hand and said "Welcome". He then signaled the police men and women to clear the road. In return, I pointed at the crowd behind me and told him "they are all with me!" And we passed.

Humor and the participation of unlikely groups and people, such as famous TV stars, in anti-war organizing were signs of the changing nature of political protest in Turkey.

The Peace Weekend also included a conference in Istanbul at which Turkish anti-war activists, including the renowned writer Orhan Pamuk, spoke alongside prominent intellectuals and activists from seven countries; the "gala" performance of the Peace Song written by the famous rock band *Mor ve Ötesi*; and visits to the Turkish Grand National Assembly in Ankara. Accompanied by news of numerous other protests across the country, including the arrival of the Peace Train in Incirlik, a reading by 10 conscientious objectors of their declarations against war, militarism, and military service, and the long "human chain" in Izmir, the motto of this long weekend was "Let Ankara be the capital of Peace."

The visit to the parliament on January 27 was of particular significance. Coordinated by the Peace Initiative, the commission met with political leaders to convey the consistent message: "The world is watching you. As you vote next week, please 'remember your humanity, and forget the rest' for the sake of the world."[18]

The major U.S. newspapers either ignored or trivialized protest to U.S. war plans in Turkey. For instance, *New York Times* reporter Dexter Filkins' article on February 5, a few days after the long Peace Weekend, argued that:

> opposition to the war has been mostly muted here. There have been relatively few public demonstrations, and even fewer that have drawn sizable crowds. Many Turks say they would like nothing more than to see Saddam Hussein ousted from Iraq, and in recent days, there was a growing chorus among Turkish journalists and business leaders that Turkey was running the risk of seriously damaging its half-century-old alliance with the United States.[19]

Filkins, among others, seems to have missed the significant point that the "growing chorus" in Turkey had been a chorus not of mainstream journalists and certain businessmen but of organized as well as individual opposition to the war.[20] A Turkey-wide survey held between January 11 and 20 would show that 90 percent opposed the war and 83 percent opposed Turkey's cooperating with the United States for this war.[21]

The growing anti-war sentiment was expressed in a variety of forms. Street rallies as well as individual acts of protest, such as the case of a group of people immersing themselves into the cold January sea waving "No to War" banners over their heads, were the most obvious and publicized. One form of protest was the daily act of turning lights on and off and creating noise at 8 p.m. "One Minute of Darkness for Peace" was introduced by the No War on Iraq Coordination on February 15, the global day of action against the war. "Darkness" was soon transformed into "blinking lights" through popular participation. In some venues, this protest took the form of walking outside with candles, in others, whole neighborhoods were spotted blinking their apartment lights while making noise with pots, pans, and whistles through opened windows. Some TV stations would transmit live broadcasts of this widespread protest against the war from a different place each night.

If blinking lights was a safe option for those who wanted to avoid visibility and attention, others started taking unprecedented steps to establish direct contact with parliamentarians in Ankara. There were widespread letter- and e-mail-writing campaigns, which soon took the form of sending short messages over mobile phones to individual parliamentarians. The AK Party members of parliament we interviewed in 2005 mentioned mobile messages as a major form of pressure. In Faruk Ünsal's words, "the power of the street was crucial in the formation of the democratic will. The mobile messages were very effective. They would come at any time, day and night. Very many came."[22] Some parliamentarians would write messages in response or call the activists sending the messages, sometimes to ask them to stop, other times to inquire about their motivations and views. This form of direct contact between citizens and politicians, the implications of which we discuss below, was unheard of prior to 2003.

The Groundbreaking "No" and Its Aftermath

On the eve of March 1, the months of intense political and diplomatic traffic in Ankara and of anti-war activism had reached their peak. More than 100,000 people gathered a few miles from the Turkish Grand National Assembly in one of Ankara's largest squares. Although familiar to those who lived through the 1970s, such big rallies had become history after the coup d'état of 1980. The March 1 rally was a turning point for post-coup political practice, not only because it was one of the largest rallies in recent history, but also because an estimated quarter of the crowd were individual protesters who did not belong to any particular political group or party.[23] The fragmented nature of rally space through party flags and other markers in conventional rallies had been replaced by movement, mixture, and individual protest. Among the crowd were high-school students in groups of two or three, easily visible by their uniforms, families with children, headscarved women walking meters behind gay and lesbian groups, and leftist trade unionists standing next to Islamist human rights groups under similar banners, chanting joint slogans: "I want to live!" "We won't kill and we won't die, we won't be anybody's soldiers!" "Don't be silent, make a noise against the war!" "If the Parliament votes yes to war, the Parliamentarians should go and fight!" "War kills," "Don't Ask Bush, Ask the People," "Humans or People Before Profit," and "A World Without War is Possible."

Meanwhile, the atmosphere in the Grand National Assembly was heating up. The Speaker of the Assembly had made the critical decision to allow TV broadcast of the final speeches of party representatives before the vote, which significantly increased the pressure on AK Party parliamentarians, now conscious that they were voting against voters' wishes. In addition, a group of parliamentarians had compiled a rich collection of cartoons published in international newspapers, ridiculing Turkey's position vis-à-vis the United States. One such cartoon showed Turkey as a belly dancer asking the United States for a tip. Minutes before the voting took place, the parliamentarians found copies of these cartoons in front of them. As one parliamentarian said to us: "Those cartoons touched everyone's honor." Not all such critical cartoons portrayed Turkey as a woman, but the overall message of Turkey "selling itself out" to the United States had obviously touched the strings of masculinized honor among the parliamentarians.

Of parliament's 550 members 533 were present for the voting, with 264 accepting the motion and 250 rejecting it. The motion asked the parliamentarians to give authority to the government to "deploy Turkish Armed Forces to foreign countries" and to allow the deployment of a maximum of 62,000 foreign military personnel, 255 planes and 65 helicopters in areas determined by the government (Yetkin 2004; Bila 2004). What appeared to be an approval at first sight was quickly announced as a rejection because of the 19 abstentions. Due to parliament procedures, the approval required a majority *of those who were present.* The 19 abstentions would thus amount to a "no" vote in effect. Significantly, almost a third of governing party members voted against the motion.

In the meantime, the Turkish people were jubilant. For Yıldız Önen of the No War on Iraq Coordination of Istanbul, the March rejection of the motion had multiple meanings:

> It showed, that we could do it. It was a brilliant result. People were walking like drunken people for one month, not just for one day. We were smiling, kissing each other. Because in Turkey after the 1980 coup, there was no big success for everyone. There may have been a success for students or for women or for workers, but this was a big success for *everyone*. Everyone said "I did it!"

March 1 was not only one of the major successes of the anti-war movement worldwide, but this whole period marked a turning point in the post-1980 (i.e. post-coup) political culture of Turkey.

The reaction to this result was one of shock in Turkey and elsewhere. The next day, a prominent columnist, Oktay Ekşi wrote: "We experienced great shock. There are serious risks involved in this result. Will Turkey be able to overcome the heavy consequences of this decision?"[24] There were fears that Turkey would lose its strong political ties to the United States and become isolated, and could also experience an economic crisis.

Prior to the voting, many prominent journalists (many of whom would call themselves liberal) had argued for the motion, presenting this as the "rational" choice, or indeed an "inevitability." These arguments were based on the assumption that "realistic foreign policy" required Turkey's participation in the U.S.-led coalition.

The "idealists" of the anti-war movement were warned about the grave responsibility they shouldered, forcing Turkey into political isolation. For instance, columnist Taha Akyol suggested that Turkey must decide between "moral ideals and 'realpolitik'" and that it would suffer more by remaining out of the war.[25] According to Hasan Cemal it was the time to be "rational" and realize that both Turkey's interests and "realpolitik" required Turkey to say yes.[26] Mehmet Barlas reminded the politicians that falling outside of the global alignments could result in "chaos, political and economic crisis, coups and even civil war."[27] The editor-in-chief of Turkey's most popular daily *Hürriyet,* Ertuğrul Özkök, warned that by staying out of this war, Turkey would have to pay a heavy price for 50 years to come and that it would be the "romantics who said 'no to war'" that would ultimately push Turkey into a war.[28] The debate over whether the motion should pass was at the same time about what constituted realism and idealism in the contemporary political scene. The science of economics and the realpolitik of international relations were the main reference points of arguments made in favor of "reason" and "realism." According to the popular economist–journalist Ege Cansen, "[economic] calculations showed that acting alongside the USA would certainly be in the benefit of Turkey in regard to the wealth of its population."[29]

While almost all statements made in the days immediately after the vote by politicians and anti-war groups alike focused on its possible economic consequences, none of the pessimistic expectations were realized. Instead, the Turkish economy continued its upward trend throughout 2003. According to journalist Mustafa Karaalioğlu, "the Turkish economy was not destabilized because the motion failed, but it could have been destabilized if it had passed."[30]

The other feared outcome – political retaliation by the United States – did not materialize either. Despite the serious setback this decision meant for U.S. war efforts, the initial statements by U.S. officials were very cautious. By March 20, the United States had moved to "Plan B," attacking Iraq without Turkey's support. On the night of March 19, Colin Powell called the minister of foreign affairs, Abdullah Gül, to tell him that the agreement was off the table and that they were only asking for the use of Turkish air space, which was granted (Yetkin 2004).

The following months were marked by a series of events that created a range of problems for U.S.–Turkish relations, from uneasiness to direct conflict. The Turkish military and politicians were growing increasingly concerned about the strong support that the Kurdish groups in northern Iraq were receiving from the United States. The overall anxiety was that by being left out of the war, Turkey would not be able to control political and military developments in northern Iraq. Most parliamentarians, including members of the opposition party, seemed to agree that Turkish soldiers should be deployed to northern Iraq (Yetkin 2004). This caused a strong reaction by Kurdish groups in Iraq and concern on the part of the U.S. administration. In early April, President Bush would sign a financial aid package[31] of U.S.$1 billion to Turkey on the condition that the Turkish military not go unilaterally into Iraq (Yetkin 2004).

U.S. Bases and Anti-Base Resistance since 2003

Although the debate over Turkey's participation in the coalition forces seemed to come to an end with U.S. Defense Secretary Rumsfeld's statement on November 6 that Turkish forces would not be needed in Iraq (Yetkin 2004), the negotiations over the Incirlik base remained on the political and military agenda. Much less is publicly known about these negotiations and the ultimate agreements reached. Three secret cabinet decrees, on June 23, 2003, a year later on June 22, 2004, and finally on April 18, 2005, granted permission for the use of Turkish bases, including Incirlik, by the U.S. and coalition forces, based on the United Nations Security Council Resolution 1483 of May 22, 2003, which had lifted the sanctions on Iraq and opened the door for the resumption of "humanitarian" assistance.[32] Each permission was for one year. The government claimed that they did not need parliamentary approval because these permissions were being given for U.N.-sanctioned transfers for the restructuring of Iraq.[33]

In 2005, the agreement allowed for the Incirlik base to be used as a "logistics hub,"[34] and it was emphasized that this permission excluded the transfer of "lethal weapons and supplies."[35] A month after this third secret decree, Minister of Defense Vecdi Gönül said in an interview that it was a mistake not to have passed the March 1 decree, but that the government could not override the decision of the parliament. He added that the overflight permission (granted on March 20, 2003) had allowed for 4,300 planes from bases in Europe to fly over Turkey during the Iraq war,[36] but insisted that the Incirlik decree was mainly for the transfer of humanitarian aid, goods, and services for the restructuring of Iraq, not for weapons.

There was heated debate in 2005 when the secret decrees on Incirlik first appeared in the news. According to CNN-TÜRK,[37] the United States was planning to invest $20 million at Incirlik, which "showed the significance of Incirlik for the U.S." This had come soon after Rumsfeld's statement in February 2005 that Turkey was responsible for the chaos in Iraq and Robert Pollock's piece in the *Wall Street Journal* which called Turkey the "sick man of Europe"; the latter is perhaps the most prominent example of anti-Turkish sentiment within the American press at the time.

It is significant that the decision to renew permission for the use of Turkish bases for another year was granted in April of 2005, despite the fact that the change would take effect on June 23. Why had the cabinet issued this decree two months in advance? One interpretation, shared by a wide range of analysts, was the connection between the granting of this use and a critical date for Turkish foreign policy, April 24.[38] Each year, April would be a busy month for the Armenian and Turkish lobbies in Washington. The Armenian lobby would urge the U.S. president to refer to the deportation and massacre of Ottoman Armenians by the Ottoman State in 1915 as genocide and the Turkish side would argue against it. 2005 was a special year because it marked the ninetieth anniversary of 1915. Several days after the renewal of the permission for Incirlik to be used as a "logistics hub," the newspapers this time reported that "once again," Bush had not used the term "genocide."[39]

Anti-War Resistance after March 1

Anti-war protests did not stop after March 1, in part because there were signs that the government might consider a second motion along the same lines. A number of protests in March were held in Iskenderun and Incirlik. Iskenderun was the main port on the Mediterranean that the United States would be using to transfer soldiers and supplies, and there were reports that the supply transfer was taking place, regardless of the rejection of the motion. In protest, Greenpeace activists chained themselves on a truck with a sign that said "No to War, USA Go Home!"[40] On March 9, the left-wing ÖDP (Freedom and Solidarity Party) organized a march from Mersin to Incirlik with such slogans as "The USA out of Turkey and the Middle East!" and "We don't want this land to be a U.S. military base!"[41] After the war began and it became clear that Turkey would not be taking part in the war, the protests died down. In 2004, anti-war organizing took the form of anti-NATO organizing, prompted by the fact that NATO's 17th Summit was held in Istanbul that year. From cycling against NATO[42] to asking people leaving the NATO site whether they had any "weapons of mass destruction, nuclear missiles and the like" on them as a form of "security check," there were more than 150 protests against NATO in six months.[43]

Turn Incirlik Into ...

In 2005, besides a few anti-war/anti-occupation rallies, the focus of protests shifted to the Incirlik base, given the April cabinet decree that renewed the use of the base by the United States as a "logistics hub." A group of feminists preparing for the May 1 (International Labor Day) rally in Ankara decided to problematize Incirlik in the context of gendered violence. According to feminist activist Gülsen Ülker, who carried the sign "Destroy Incirlik, Turn It Into a Women's Shelter" on May 1, "this was probably the first time that feminists were taking an issue with Incirlik in a mass rally."[44]

Two weeks later, on International Conscientious Objectors' Day, a group of anti-militarists from Istanbul, Ankara, and Izmir organized the second annual "Militourism Festival" in Izmir. More than 100 activists visited a number of "militarist" sites in the city, including the NATO Base in Şirinyer where the demand was made to turn it into something more "meaningful and useful," such as a park or a women's shelter.[45] The Militourism Festival was one of the rare events at which feminist and gay-rights politics were at the center of the analysis of militarism and war. Several women that day had declared their conscientious objection, which they interpreted as the refusal to take part in militarism at large. Moreover, the main focus of the event was to raise awareness and show solidarity with the gay conscientious objector Mehmet Tarhan, imprisoned for over a month, awaiting trial for "insubordination."[46]

Since 2003, almost all rallies have included slogans about turning the Incirlik base into a football field, a park, a fairground, or a women's shelter. For some groups, like the conscientious objectors, it was not only Incirlik (i.e. American bases) but all military sites that needed to be demilitarized. For the majority of activists across the political spectrum, this proposition was too radical. Their consensus was limited to the demand to close down Incirlik, increasingly seen as the main symbol of American "imperialism."

Between May 16 and June 10, 2005, Greenpeace organized a "Peace Embassy" directly outside the Incirlik Air Base in southern Turkey, which was supported by a number of unions and one socialist party. It coincided with the Base Realignment and Closure report being discussed by the U.S. Congress, which was considering stationing additional nuclear weapons in Turkey. Greenpeace demanded that the weapons be sent back to the United States and dismantled.

With the end of the Cold War many people assumed that the threat of nuclear weapons had disappeared along with the Berlin Wall. However, more than 15 years later the United States still stores 480 nuclear weapons in Europe, 90 of which are said to be in Turkey (Kristensen 2005). Despite the secrecy which surrounds the issue for both public and parliament, recent years have witnessed a growing awareness about the issue. A 2004 survey showed that 45 percent of the respondents believed there were nuclear weapons stationed in Turkey, 30 percent did not believe so, and 26 percent did not want to answer the question. However, of those who knew that nuclear weapons existed in Turkey, only 11 percent knew that they were under NATO control, whereas 50 percent believed they were under Turkish control (Tümer 2006).

Campaigns such as that of Greenpeace have undoubtedly increased the "public-ness" of knowledge about nuclear weapons. The largest and most publicized campaign against Incirlik as a military base (and not just against the weapons stationed there) was initiated by the Global Peace and Justice Coalition (Küresel BAK), in conjunction with a number of other initiatives and parties which ranged from the leftist Freedom and Solidarity Party (ÖDP) to the Islamist, conservative Saadet (Happiness) Party. More than 1,000 people traveled to Incirlik in buses to ask for the secret decree to be made public and for Incirlik to be "closed down" and turned into a "park for children." When we met Tayfun Mater, one of the key organizers, a week later, he said that according to him "Incirlik [was] Turkey's most important problem at the moment."[47] Like Kaya Güvenç, Mater was among those who had been protesting Incirlik for nearly a lifetime. In January 2006, the Global Peace and Justice Coalition announced another campaign, which they called "Close Down Incirlik, USA Go Home!"[48] According to Yıldız Önen, protesting existing bases in peacetime is particularly important: "If you have a base, at one point you will use it."

The Changing Face of Oppositional Politics

Although there is a long history of activism against American bases in Turkey, the post-1980 period was a time of little debate and action against the presence of U.S. forces and against war in general. To the contrary, after the beginning of the armed conflict between PKK and the state in 1984, there was a sharp polarization between those who supported the "war on PKK terror" and those who supported the "war for Kurdish freedom." In that sense, the anti-war movement of the post-2002 period marks a new beginning. In the words of Tayfun Mater, "this is a brand new movement." We would like to conclude by first discussing the challenges and internal tensions of this "brand new movement."

One of the major limitations of the movement has been the visible lack of Kurdish participation. Although the Kurdish opposition outside of the parliament makes up one of the most organized and populous oppositional sectors, their representation in the anti-war movement has been extremely limited. Although they were present in the anti-war platforms of 2002 and 2003, Kurdish parties did not participate in anti-base campaigns, and their participation in mass rallies was always limited to a few hundred activists. Yıldız Önen sees two main reasons for this. First, the Kurds in Turkey wanted to be in solidarity with Iraqi Kurds, who were the United States' major ally in the invasion and the occupation. So Kurdish writer Ümit Fırat remarked in 2002 that Kurds had two views on the Iraq war, one official and the other personal. Officially, they are against the war, but personally, they support it because of "their deep-seated hatred of the Saddam regime" (H. Aktan 2002). The second reason for the lack of Kurdish participation in the anti-war movement, according to Önen, was the "accusation" that the anti-war movement has not sufficiently addressed the Kurdish issue: "they are blaming us and saying that we don't see the Kurdish problem in Turkey. But the same accusation can be made for other issues: addressing the military intervention of September 12, 1980 or addressing environmental problems." This second point was raised by others as well. The women's group Amargi, for instance, organized simultaneous events against the Kurdish war in Turkey and the possible invasion of Iraq to draw attention to the discrepancy between attitudes towards external and internal wars. In return, activists in the anti-war movement highlighted the discrepancy between the calls for peace in Turkey and the pro-Iraq-war stance adopted by Kurdish parties.

If lack of Kurdish participation in the anti-war movement was one source of tension, the opposing attitudes of different groups towards the military was another. As Kaya Güvenç remarked in his interview with us, there were some leftist groups, as well as rightist nationalist groups, who believed the military was key to maintaining Turkey's sovereignty. For them, the main issue is not the military, but U.S. aggression and imperialism. According to Önen, this is a challenge in the anti-war movement, because it limits their room for action against militarism as a general phenomenon. In fact, "militarism" is hardly present in the political vocabulary of either the left or the right. Tayfun Mater, one of the leaders of GPJC, is not pessimistic. He believes that "people are slowly realizing that it is militarism that we need to oppose."

Differential attitudes towards the military are not the only factor that has limited the course of action in the anti-war movement. If coalition politics has been a major strength of the movement, it has also been its major challenge. The need to reach a consensus makes meaningful political action rather difficult. This was most evident in the campaign around the NATO summit in 2004. Not all members of the coalition were against NATO or Turkey's participation in NATO. The campaign slogan (*Gelme Bush* – Do not come, Bush) ended up being limited to a reaction against the U.S. president George W. Bush. One major political axis that made consensus politics difficult was the tension between the Kemalist wing of the left (who supported an authoritarian form of laicism) and radical Islamists (who insisted on their right to the Islamic way of life and dress). Although these groups ended up walking side by side in the rallies, it was a serious challenge to keep this dormant conflict under control (Özgül 2003).

Another source of tension in the movement, if rarely vocalized, has been the conflict between the patriarchal structures of political parties and organizations and the growing feminist consciousness of young activists, both male and female. Most anti-war events were marked by patriarchal hierarchies: even when women were the main organizers of certain events, men would end up reading the final declarations or making speeches on stage, and there would be no reference to sexism or patriarchy as an aspect of war and militarism. The Militourism Festivals of 2004 and 2005, the declarations of women conscientious objectors, the activism of the women's group Amargi, and the organization of the World Tribunal on Iraq in Istanbul were notable exceptions that gave voice to women and feminist perspectives. The activists who organized these events agreed with Cynthia Cockburn that "a theory of war is flawed if it lacks a gender analysis" (Cockburn 2007:257). As such, they challenged the "mainstream" anti-war movement by simultaneously introducing sexism and patriarchy as key aspects of war and emphasizing the need to address militarism and militarization, in addition to war.

Despite the limitations posed by these internal tensions, anti-war organizing has changed the face of political activism in Turkey in the past years. The first important outcome has been the demarginalization of street activism. The anti-war rallies of late 2002 and early 2003 were not only the most crowded political events of the past decades, but were marked by an increasing number of independent activists and "ordinary people." The second key change was in the forms and mood of activism. Whereas mass demonstrations before 2002 were marked by angry slogans, disciplined groupings, and a very "serious" mood, the new demonstrations had more color, discord, and individual action. It can be argued that the changing public perception was partly a result of this new tone. Third, the urgency to unite in the face of war has enabled the formation of new alliances which would have been considered impossible before. Fourth, this period marked the growing visibility of "anti-militarism." Whereas problematizing militarism as an ideology and militarization as a process was a marginal position in both the right and the left of the political spectrum before, slogans such as "we won't kill, we won't die, we won't be anybody's soldiers" had become surprisingly popular during mass rallies and anti-militarist initiatives were growing in size.

A final significant outcome of this process was the (re)internationalization of oppositional politics. Feeling empowered by the "global street," activists broadened their political imagination beyond borders. This involved both direct participation in international events such as the World Social Forum, the European Social Forum, anti-war and anti-summit protests across Europe, and a new language of global situatedness. Significantly, the anti-war movement became institutionalized through the formation of the Global Peace and Justice Coalition, which had originated with the Global Peace and Justice Declaration coming out of the United States. This was yet another sign that opposition to the U.S. government's policies was not being translated into crude expressions of anti-Americanism.

In short, the reaction to the U.S. military presence in Turkey in recent years is often based on a nuanced critique of U.S. global militarism. One of the main reasons that anti-war sentiment in Turkey did not translate into a crude form of anti-Americanism has been the presence of a strong anti-war movement in the United States. Although the re-election of George W. Bush represented a major disappointment, many anti-war activists still maintain a fine balance between their reactions to the American government and their relationship to the American people in general. If one of the challenges for the future of the movement is to maintain this balance, another is to take up the critique posed by feminists and anti-militarists to expand the analysis of war and militarism to include not just U.S. militarism, but the webs of gendered political, economic, and cultural militarism in Turkey as well.

Notes

1. We would like to thank our interviewees, who spared hours of their precious time to share their ideas and experiences. We learned tremendously from them. Special thanks to Osman Alper Aydemir, Aslı Erdem, and Nazan Maksudyan for their valuable research assistance.
2. We conducted in-depth interviews with more than 20 people, among them parliamentarians, journalists, academics, and activists.
3. *Financial Times*, May 14, 1984.
4. Available online at www.globalsecurity.org/military/facility/incirlik-history.htm. Date last accessed October 14, 2007. Incirlik in Turkish literally means "place of the fig orchard."
5. During this time there were more U.S. troops in Germany and Japan, but these were occupying forces and not advisory groups.

6. It is often assumed that only wealthy countries pay towards base infrastructure costs, but this case illustrates that this outsourcing occurs in less developed countries as well.
7. Interview with Faruk Bildirici, December 24, 2005.
8. *Hürriyet*, July 29, 1950.
9. *Daily News*, October 17, 1966.
10. *Daily News*, October 17, 1966.
11. See also Bila (2004).
12. This number ranges from 60,000 to 80,000 in different documents related to the negotiation process.
13. The military team who undertook the site inspections was in fact not from Incirlik, but flown in from the United States, and included logisticians, engineers, and communications experts. *Wall Street Journal*, December 12, 2002.
14. For an analysis of this fear and its consequences for Turkey's domestic politics and regional foreign policy, see Somer (2005). Güney (2005, 348) cites fear of an independent Kurdish state as one factor in Turkey's reluctance about the war on Iraq.
15. See Mater 2005 for an account of this war through the perspectives of the soldiers who fought during 1984 and 1998.
16. *Newsweek*, January 20, 2003.
17. "Savaş Karşıtları İncirlik'teydi," January 24, 2003, available online at www.bianet.org. Date last accessed October 14, 2007.
18. *Istanbul Indymedia*, February 5, 2003, available online at http://istanbul.indymedia.org/news/2003/02/131.php. Date last accessed October 14, 2007.
19. *New York Times*, February 5, 2003.
20. Dexter Filkins later admitted that one neglected aspect of the situation was the "raucously democratic process"; *New York Times*, March 5, 2003.
21. *Radikal,* February 16, 2003.
22. Interview, June 9, 2003.
23. Interview with Kaya Güvenç, July 1, 2005.
24. *Hürriyet*, March 2, 2003.
25. *Milliyet*, February 25, 2003.
26. *Milliyet*, February 27, 2003.
27. *Akşam,* February 8, 2003.
28. *Hürriyet*, February 27, 2003, and March 5, 2003.
29. *Hürriyet*, March 1, 2003.
30. Interview, July 1, 2005.
31. This package could be used as financial aid of U.S.$1 billion (with no repayment requirement) or as credit of $8.5 billion (Yetkin 2004:201).

32. *Cumhuriyet,* May 7, 2005.
33. *Hürriyet,* June 24, 2003.
34. Referring to Incirlik Air Base as a "logistics hub" rather than a "military base" can be considered a cautious response to popular anti-war sentiment.
35. *Hürriyet,* April 21, 2005.
36. A few weeks later, Deputy Chief of Staff İlker Başbuğ mentioned 5,000 overflights (*Hürriyet,* June 6, 2005).
37. Kemal Türkeri, March 22, 2005, available online at www.cnnturk.com/HABER/haber_detay.asp?PID=318&HID=1&haberID=81814. Date last accessed October 14, 2007.
38. *Hürriyet,* April 21, 2005.
39. He had instead defined the events of 1915 as "human tragedy." *Hürriyet,* April 25, 2005.
40. *Radikal,* March 15, 2003.
41. "ÖDP'den Mersin-İncirlik Protesto Yürüyüşü," March 7, 2003, available online at www.bianet.org.
42. *Milliyet,* May 24, 2004.
43. Available online at www.sesonline.net. Date last accessed June 30, 2004.
44. Interview, June 9, 2005.
45. *Militurizm Festivaline Davet,* leaflet distributed on May 15, 2005. *Radikal,* May 16, 2005.
46. See Altınay (2004) for a discussion of the conscientious objection movement in Turkey and Mehmet Tarhan's contributions to it.
47. Interview, June 8, 2005.
48. *Radikal 2,* January 26, 2006.

References

Abramowitz, Morton (2000) *Turkey's Transformation and American Policy* (New York: The Century Foundation Press).

Aktan, İrfan (2002) "'Sen İç Cola, Coni Yağdırsın Bomba,'" www.bianet.org, December 23. Date last accessed August 22, 2008.

Aktan, Hamza (2002) "'Kürtler Savaşa "Resmen" Karşı,'" www.bianet.org, December 23. Date last accessed August 22, 2008.

Altınay, Ayşe Gül (2004) *The Myth of the Military-Nation: Militarism, Gender, and Education in Turkey* (New York: Palgrave Macmillan).

Bila, Fikret (2004) [2003] *Sivil Darbe Girişimi ve Ankara'da Irak Savaşları* (Ankara: Ümit Yayıncılık).

Candar, Cengiz (2000) "Some Turkish Perspectives on the United States and American Policy toward Turkey," in Morton Abramowitz (ed.)

Turkey's Transformation and American Policy (New York: The Century Foundation Press).

Cockburn, Cynthia (2007) *From Where We Stand: War, Women's Activism and Feminist Analysis* (London: Zed Books).

Cossaboom, Robert and Leiser, Gary (1998) "Adana Station 1943–45: Prelude to the Post-War American Military Presence in Turkey," *Middle Eastern Studies*, Vol. 34, No. 1, pp. 73–86.

Criss, Nur Bilge (1993) "U.S. Forces in Turkey," in Simon W. Duke and Wolfgang Krieger (eds.) *U.S. Military Forces in Europe: The Early Years, 1945–1970* (Boulder, CO: Westview Press).

Gonlubol, Mehmet (1975) "NATO and Turkey," in Kemal Karpat (ed.) *Turkey's Foreign Policy in Transition 1950–1974* (Leiden: E. J. Brill).

Güney, Aylin (2005) "An Anatomy of the Transformation of the U.S.–Turkish Alliance: From 'Cold War' to 'War on Iraq,'" *Turkish Studies*, Vol. 6, No. 3, pp. 341–359.

Kristensen, Hans M. (2005) "U.S. Nuclear Weapons in Europe: A Review of Post-Cold War Policy, Force Levels, and War Planning," February, Natural Resource Defense Council, Washington, D.C. Available online at www.nrdc.org/nuclear/euro/contents.asp. Date last accessed October 14, 2007.

Lipovsky, I. P. (1992) *The Socialist Movement in Turkey, 1960–1980* (Leiden: E. J. Brill).

Mater, Nadire (2005) *Voices from the Front: Turkish Soldiers on the War with the Kurdish Guerillas*, translated by Ayşe Gül Altınay (New York: Palgrave Macmillan).

Özgül, Ipek (2003) "A Coalition of Outsiders: The Alliance of Islamists and Leftists in Anti-War Activism in Turkey," unpublished cultural studies senior project, Sabancı University, Istanbul.

Sever, Ayşegül (2002) "Turkey and U.S. On Iraq Since the Gulf War," *Turkish Review of Middle East Studies*, Foundation for Middle East and Balkan Studies, Annual Report, No. 13, pp. 25–39.

Somer, Murat (2005) "Failures of the Discourse of Ethnicity: Turkey, Kurds, and the Emerging Iraq," *Security Dialogue*, Vol. 36, No. 1, pp. 109–128.

Tümer, Aslıhan (2006) "Die nukleare Teilhabe der NATO und Incirlik," *Wissenschaft und Frieden*, March.

Wolf, C. (1969) *Garrison Community: A Study of an Overseas American Military Colony* (Westport, CT: Greenwood).

Yetkin, Murat (2004) *Tezkere: Irak Krizinin Gerçek Öyküsü* (Istanbul: Remzi Kitabevi).

10

RESISTING MILITARIZATION IN HAWAI'I

Kyle Kajihiro

The more militarization transforms an individual or a society, the more that individual or society comes to imagine military needs and militaristic presumptions to be not only valuable but also normal. Militarization ... involves cultural as well as institutional, ideological, and economic transformations. (Enloe 2000:3)

E iho ana 'o luna	That which is above shall be brought down
E pi'i ana 'o lalo	That which is below shall be lifted up
E hui ana na moku	The islands shall be united
E ku ana ka paia!	The walls shall stand upright!

Pule Wanana A Kapihe, an ancient Hawai'ian prophesy that has become a contemporary Hawai'ian chant of unity and resistance

In Hawai'i, the U.S. military is an inescapable fact of life. Its iron embrace is achieved through hundreds of military installations that occupy and transform vast swaths of land, sea, and sky, including nearly a quarter of the most populated island of O'ahu. Military troops, their dependants, and veterans have nearly overtaken the population of Hawai'i's indigenous people and changed the political map of Hawai'i. But barbed wire and checkpoints do not mark the boundary of the military's influence; it has penetrated the economy, social fabric, and very culture of these islands. And people derive vastly different meanings from this overwhelming military presence, depending on their social position and history in Hawai'i.

For some, the military represents a paternalistic and benevolent protector of the Hawai'ian Islands and a source of security, status, and pride. This is the establishment narrative that portrays the military "as 'natural,' therefore as desirable, and constructive, therefore welcome" (Ferguson and Turnbull 1998:xiii). For others, the military is tolerated, or perhaps even solicited as a big-spending, but obnoxious patron that pays the bills and puts food on the table. And then there are those for whom the U.S. military represents an invading and oppressive force, "the muscle" of U.S. empire, which destroys the land and displaces the native people as it invades and wages war on other nations. In all cases, the contemporary roles and meanings of the U.S. military in Hawai'i are linked to its historical role in the invasion and occupation of the islands and to the building of American empire in the Pacific.

This chapter reviews the history and current status of the U.S. military in Hawai'i; analyzes current trends of militarization there in light of U.S. global plans; and discusses contemporary grassroots resistance to militarization. In the process, I will build on several assumptions and arguments. First, Hawai'i has been both a victim of and an accomplice to U.S. empire. Second, the militarization of Hawai'i involved collaboration by different sets of local elites as well as U.S. decision makers. Third, militarism evolved from maintaining social control through crude applications of force to more subtle and pervasive forms of hegemony through the education system and other social institutions, federal spending, and broad cultural transformations. Fourth, historically, Kanaka Maoli (Native Hawai'ian) cultural and political resistance to U.S. colonialism was the strongest source of opposition to militarization. Fifth, resistance strategies that failed to confront the larger forces at play, namely imperialism and militarism, or failed to allow the movement to widen its support beyond a narrow constituency, have been susceptible to co-optation and neutralization.

Invasion

On January 16, 1893, United States Foreign Minister John L. Stevens and U.S. Navy leaders conspired with the haole (white foreigners) elite in Hawai'i and "caused armed naval forces of the United States to invade the sovereign Hawai'ian nation" (U.S. Senate 1993b). Marines from the USS Boston landed at Honolulu Harbor and took up positions with their guns aimed at the 'Iolani Palace. They provided the necessary force for a small group of haole settlers to depose Queen Lili'uokalani the next day. Thus began a prolonged U.S. occupation of Hawai'i that is an enduring source of conflict between the military and Kanaka Maoli.

In 2007, the Gatling guns of 1893 have morphed and multiplied into the mighty warships, aircraft, weapons, and troops of the Pacific Command (PACOM). Hawai'i has become one of the most highly militarized places on the planet, a linchpin of U.S. empire in the Asia Pacific region. According to Kanaka Maoli activist Kaleikoa Kaeo, the U.S. military in Hawai'i can be symbolized by a monstrous *he'e* (octopus). Its head is represented by the Pacific Command headquarters, its eyes the mountaintop telescopes and radar facilities, and its brain and nervous system the supercomputers and fiber optic networks that crisscross the islands. The PACOM area of responsibility, the tentacles of the *he'e*, stretches over more than 50 percent of the earth's surface from the west coast of North America to the east coast of Africa, from Alaska to Antarctica, encompassing 43 countries, 20 territories and possessions and ten U.S. territories, 60 percent of the world's population, the world's six largest armed forces, and five of the seven worldwide U.S. mutual defense treaties.[1]

According to the U.S. Department of Defense, the combined services in 2004 had 161 military installations in Hawai'i (four large, four medium, and 153 small installations), covering 6 percent of its total land area. On O'ahu, the most densely populated island, the military controls fully 22 percent of the island. The military also controls vast stretches of ocean, including 210,000 square miles of ocean military operating areas and 58,599 square miles of special use airspace around the Hawai'ian archipelago.[2]

In 2003 there were over 44,000 active duty military personnel and 57,000 military dependants living in Hawai'i, representing 8 percent of its population.[3] Combined with the 116,000 military retirees, the military-connected population amounted to 17 percent of Hawai'i's total population, the largest percentage among the states.[4] Since 9/11, military spending in Hawai'i has risen considerably. In 2003, military expenditure grew by 13 percent over the previous year, reaching $4.5 billion, putting Hawai'i second in the United States behind Virginia in per-capita military spending.[5]

Militarizing the 'Aina

Hawai'ian studies professor Haunani-Kay Trask once commented, "Whenever the U.S. goes to war, the military takes more of our land."[6] During World War II, the military seized vast tracts of land for its operations, which resulted in the alienation of Kanaka Maoli from their ancestral lands, the loss of subsistence and cultural resources, and the contamination of the air, land, and water with toxic waste, unexploded ordnance, and radiation. The conflict over 'aina (land) is much deeper, however, arising from a fundamental contradiction between Kanaka Maoli and Western world views. In the Kanaka Maoli cosmology, the 'aina is the physical manifestation of the union between Papahanaumoku (Papa who gives birth to islands), the earth-mother, and Wakea, the sky-father. As an ancestor of humans, the 'aina could not be owned, sold or defiled. Lilikala Kame'eleihiwa writes "the 'modern' concepts of aloha 'Aina, or love of the Land, and Malama 'Aina, or serving and caring for the Land, stem from the traditional model established at the time of Wakea" (Kame'eleihiwa 1992:25).

Militarization greatly accelerated the dispossession of Hawai'ian lands. In 1898, the United States seized nearly 1.8 million acres of former national and crown lands of the Kingdom of Hawai'i. Existing in a kind of legal limbo, these so-called "ceded lands" are held in a quasi-trust status by the federal government and the state. In 1959, when Hawai'i was admitted as a U.S. state, the military retained control of approximately 180,000 acres of "ceded lands," while the rest reverted to the state as trustee (Miyahira 1981–82). Approximately 30,000 acres returned to the state were simultaneously leased back to the military for 65 years (Rohrer 1987). In most cases, the rent paid by the military was one dollar for the term of the lease. Today, "ceded land" makes up approximately 54 percent of military-controlled land.[7]

The military also illegally seized land from the Hawai'ian Home Lands trust. In 1983, a Federal–State Task Force concluded that 13,580 acres of Hawai'ian Home Lands were improperly withdrawn from the trust through presidential executive orders during World War II (U.S. Senate 1993a: 193–199). In 1999, the state and federal governments agreed to a land swap to settle the improper transfer. The Department of Hawai'ian Home Lands received 580 acres at the former Barber's Point Naval Air Station in exchange for land at Lualualei.

Environmental Assault

The U.S. military is arguably the largest industrial polluter in Hawai'i. The 2004 Defense Environmental Restoration Program report to Congress listed 798 military contamination sites at 108 installations in Hawai'i, 96 of which were contaminated with unexploded ordnance. Seven of the military contamination sites were considered "Superfund" sites.[8] According to the navy, the Pearl Harbor Naval Complex alone contains approximately 749 contaminated sites.[9] These numbers are low, since they do not include contaminated sites that have not yet been listed for cleanup responses. Military installations made up five of the top ten polluters in Hawai'i responsible for releasing persistent, bio-accumulative, and toxic (PBT) chemicals, which include lead, dioxins, mercury, and polycyclic aromatic compounds.[10]

Military-training activities are extremely destructive to the fragile and endangered Hawai'ian ecosystem, which due to its evolutionary isolation produced a diverse and unique community of native species, 82 percent of which are found nowhere else on earth. The uniqueness of Hawai'i's native species also made them vulnerable to external threats. The Bishop Museum lists 267 extinctions and more than 328 endangered native Hawai'ian species. Live-fire and maneuver training have caused habitat destruction, erosion, fires, and the introduction of alien species. In the oceans, powerful sonar tests have harmed marine mammals.

Military contamination hazards include unexploded ordnance; various types of fuels and petroleum products; organic solvents such as perchloroethylene and trichloroethylene; dioxins and PCB; explosives and propellants such as RDX, TNT, HMX, and perchlorate; heavy metals such as lead and mercury; and napalm, chemical weapons, and radioactive waste from nuclear powered ships. Cobalt-60, a radioactive waste product from nuclear-powered ships, has been found in sediment at Pearl Harbor. Between 1964 and 1978, 4.8 million gallons of low-level radioactive waste were discharged into Pearl Harbor. Several thousand steel drums containing radioactive waste were dumped 55 miles from Hawai'i. Recently, the military disclosed that more than 8,000 tons of chemical weapons were dumped in the sea off O'ahu. In January 2006, community groups leaked an internal army memo revealing that depleted uranium (DU) was unearthed at the Schofield range, after years of military denials that the restricted material was ever used in Hawai'i. In August of 2007, the army disclosed that DU was also found at Pohakuloa.

Military contamination poses the greatest threat to Kanaka Maoli, immigrant Asian and Pacific Islanders, and other low-income communities who tend to live nearest to contaminated sites. Many Asians and Pacific Islanders subsist on fish and shellfish from Pearl Harbor's contaminated waters. The Wai'anae district, where a third of the land is occupied by military installations, has the largest concentration of Kanaka Maoli and some of the worst health, economic, and social statistics in Hawai'i. In the late 1980s, powerful navy radio transmitters in Lualualei valley were suspected to be the cause of a childhood leukemia cluster in the nearby Hawai'ian Homestead. Unfortunately, Hawai'i's health authorities have failed to aggressively investigate the possible health effects of military environmental contamination. Activist groups are trying to push for environmental health studies, stricter environmental protection laws, and better enforcement to protect public health and safety.

Forced Assimilation and Cultural Disintegration

The displacement of Kanaka Maoli from their traditional lands and their forced cultural assimilation have contributed to a disastrous process of cultural disintegration. By severing the genealogical ties between Kanaka Maoli and their land and by disrupting their ability to practice and transmit their culture to future generations, the military continues to have profound impacts on the cultural survival of Kanaka Maoli. Researchers have described how the cumulative impacts of colonization have resulted in "cultural trauma," which contributes to the dismal health status of Kanaka Maoli (Cook, Withy, and Tarallo-Jensen 2003): Kanaka Maoli have the highest rates of homelessness, poverty, disease, and crime and the lowest educational achievement and life expectancy.[11] Kanaka Maoli make up 37 percent of persons incarcerated on felony charges (Office of Hawai'ian Affairs 2000: Table 7.13).

By generating population transfer of U.S. nationals to Hawai'i, the military has also had a profound impact on Hawai'i's culture and political demographics. Between 1900 and 1950, almost 300,000 people immigrated from the continental United States (Sai 2004:63). The current military-connected population of 17 percent has nearly eclipsed the Kanaka Maoli population, which stands at 19 percent of the total (State of Hawai'i 2000: Tables 10.4, 10.21, 1.03, 1.29). In the century since the U.S. occupation began, the flood of settlers has made Kanaka Maoli into a minority in their own homeland and stripped them of their ability to exercise self-determination. The process and consequences of this population transfer echoes patterns found in other occupied nations, such as Tibet, East Timor, and Palestine. A combination of economic, cultural, and political pressures has pushed nearly a third of Kanaka Maoli into diaspora.

Imperial Desires

The United States' obsession with Hawai'i began long before the invasion and coup d'état of 1893 and was driven by U.S. desire to expand trade with Asia and extend its influence across the

Pacific. Hawai'i in the nineteenth century was a vital refueling and provisioning stop for nearly all transpacific commerce, and as such, it was highly coveted by budding U.S. imperialists. In 1873, General John M. Schofield and Lieutenant Colonel Burton S. Alexander masqueraded as tourists and paid a visit to Hawai'i. Their secret mission was to identify a suitable natural harbor for a naval port. Upon spying Waimomi (literally "Pearl Water," now called Pearl Harbor), Schofield concluded: "It is the key to the Central Pacific Ocean, it is the gem of these islands" (Linn 1997:6).

Hawai'i's haole elite, the descendents of missionaries and business owners, leveraged the United States' desire for a naval base in Hawai'i to their advantage. In 1876, they pressured King Kalakaua to sign the misnamed Treaty of Reciprocity with the United States: it granted military and commercial privileges to the United States in exchange for lowering the tariff on Hawai'i-grown sugar. However, by 1887, Hawai'i's haole elite grew concerned that Hawai'i might lose favorable terms of trade for its sugar exports. Forming a clandestine group named the Hawai'ian League, they built a vigilante militia, seized control of King Kalakaua's cabinet, and forced him to sign what became known as the "Bayonet Constitution." The Bayonet Constitution shifted power from the head of state to the haole minority-controlled cabinet and dramatically disenfranchised most of the non-white population. Despite opposition by Hawai'ian nationals, the new cabinet moved quickly to renew the Treaty of Reciprocity (1887), which now contained new provisions granting the United States exclusive use of Waimomi.

King Kalakaua's successor, Queen Lili'uokalani, attempted to restore executive powers and civil rights through a new constitution, which prompted the conspiracy to land American troops and depose the queen.[12] Although U.S. president Grover Cleveland condemned the U.S. military intervention and called for the restoration of the Hawai'ian Kingdom as the legitimate government, Hawai'i's sovereignty was never restored.

Despite successful efforts by Hawai'ian nationalists to fend off two treaties of annexation, the outbreak of the Spanish–American

War triggered the full-scale military occupation of Hawai'i (Silva 2004; Sai 2004). On July 6, 1898, Congress passed a simple joint resolution that claimed to annex Hawai'i. Virtually overnight, Hawai'i became the hub of the United States' vast military enterprise in the Pacific and a launching pad for its imperial thrust into Asia.

Collaboration and Conflict

U.S. occupation ushered in a period of unbridled military expansion in Hawai'i. Construction of a naval base at Pearl Harbor began in 1900, destroying 36 traditional Hawai'ian fishponds and transforming what was once the food basket of central O'ahu into a vast naval station. This was soon to be followed by the construction of seven other military installations. General Macomb wrote "Oahu is to be encircled with a ring of steel" (Lind 1984–85:25).

In the territorial period leading up to World War II, Hawai'i's haole oligarchy collaborated with the military establishment to promote industrialization and to maintain haole rule in Hawai'i. The oligarchy reaped economic benefits from the military-driven development, such as the massive dredging and construction projects. On a deeper level, the haole oligarchy and the military shared a fear of Hawai'i's ethnically diverse population, especially the large Japanese community, which formed a basis for their collaboration (Lind 1984–85:30).

However, conflicts over land and political control between the military and the ruling elite of Hawai'i also emerged from time to time. The territorial government often complained about the military's voracious appetite for land, while military commanders grew impatient with the inefficiencies of civilian government in controlling the majority non-white population. On different occasions the military clamored for military government in Hawai'i, such as the turbulent times following the rape of Thalia Massey, a wife of a navy officer, and the retaliatory lynching of one of the accused Native Hawai'ian men (Lind 1984–85:34).

"Remember Pearl Harbor": Racism and Martial Law

The bombing of Pearl Harbor on December 7, 1941, provided the justification and opportunity for the military to finally bring Hawai'i completely under military discipline (Anthony 1955). Plans for concentration camps and martial law, which had been in the works for years, were implemented. Large tracts of land were also seized through presidential executive orders, swelling military land holdings to its peak of 600,000 acres in 1944 (Lind 1984–85:36–37). Under martial law, the entire archipelago was turned into a sort of concentration camp. Japanese community leaders with suspected ties to Japan were arrested and put in detention centers or shipped off to concentration camps in the United States. As Gary Okihiro explains, anti-Japanese racism drove the Japanese in Hawai'i to "superpatriotism" (Okihiro 1991:201). Many young Japanese men enlisted in the U.S. military to prove their loyalty to the United States. After the war, these Japanese American veterans returned home with heightened expectations of social and economic advancement. Many were educated on the GI Bill and entered business and government.

Ironically, even as the war unleashed intense racism against Hawai'i's Japanese community, it hastened the demise of the old plantation power structure and the transition from an agricultural to an industrial economy as it created new opportunities for economic and social advancement for Asians in Hawai'i (Fuchs 1961:299). World War II ushered in a period of military-driven economic, social, and political transformation, what Lind called a "military–industrial revolution" (Lind 1984–85:36–37). As the cohort of second-generation Japanese in Hawai'i came of voting age, they became a formidable political bloc that challenged and eventually overtook haole Republican dominance in island politics and contributed to a push for political equality and statehood. It is a tragic irony that this Americanization of Hawai'i's Japanese resulted in their increased collusion in the political and economic processes that have dispossessed and devastated Kanaka Maoli.

The Cold War Boom

The transition from World War II to the Cold War brought major changes in Hawai'i's military role. World War II transformed Hawai'i into the main hub from which the United States projected its power outward across the Pacific. It became an integral site in the nuclear arms race, with as many as 3,100 nuclear weapons stored on the islands. With so much U.S. military might amassed in one location, Hawai'i was a prime target in the event of a Soviet nuclear attack (Albertini et al. 1980:1).

The Cold War brought massive military expenditure in Hawai'i, which, combined with the expansion of corporate tourism, ushered in a period of unparalleled economic growth. In their rise to power, the Democratic leadership in Hawai'i forged a new partnership with the military. Looking to modernize Hawai'i's economy but lacking the capital to do so, the Democrats "embraced defense spending as a welcome alternative" to the plantation economy (Lind 1984–85:17). By the 1940s, military spending in the form of payroll expenditure and construction and service contracts had overtaken sugar and pineapples to become the largest sources of revenue for the islands. Democrats maneuvered themselves into key Congressional posts in which they could control military appropriations.

"New World Order"

The end of the Cold War brought limited reductions in military forces, infrastructure, and weaponry in Hawai'i, including the closure of Nike missile sites, and the transfer of a number of smaller installations to civilian agencies. In addition, the island of Kaho'olawe was returned after extended protest at the use of the island as a bombing range. While the amount of land controlled by the military remained otherwise the same, the number of military personnel based in Hawai'i dropped from 61,019 to 35,813 between 1980 and 2000. While the military will neither confirm nor deny the presence of nuclear weapons, their actual number in Hawai'i at any given time fluctuates as nuclear-armed ships and airplanes transit through Hawai'i. These reductions occurred as technological advances in transportation and communications had diminished some of the strategic advantage of Hawai'i's location.

In the mid 1970s the economic dominance of the military in Hawai'i was eclipsed by the rise of tourism, and by 2004, Hawai'i earned $10.9 billion from tourism versus $4.8 billion from the military (State of Hawai'i 2000: Table 13.01). Competition for developable land grew more intense during the post-statehood period. On several occasions after World War II, government officials pressed for the return of excess military land, forcing the military to evaluate its land-use requirements. At the same time, a growing Hawai'ian sovereignty movement began to demand the return of "stolen Hawai'ian lands."

Sites of Resistance

While overt political resistance to the military was suppressed during the territorial era, Kanaka Maoli and locals maintained a culture of resistance to the abuses of the military and the haole oligarchy. Occasionally resistance took the form of spontaneous violent confrontations between local youth and military personnel (Linn 1997). It was not until the 1970s that organized political resistance to militarization emerged. As urbanization spread to rural communities, a wave of land struggles followed. Rural communities in Hawai'i had long withstood the forces of capitalism and imperialism, what Davianna Pomaika'i McGregor has called cultural *kipuka* – oases of traditional cultural knowledge and practices that were sources of cultural regeneration.

The struggles that emerged in defense of these traditional communities were also a kind of *kipuka* for the formation of social movements. Communities fought back, aided by young local activists who took inspiration from the civil rights, anti-war, and national liberation movements of the period between the 1950s and the 1970s. Native American occupations of Alcatraz Island and Wounded Knee also influenced Kanaka Maoli activism. The land struggles that emerged in the 1970s, like those for Kalama

Valley and Waiahole-Waikane, inspired and honed the skills of a new generation of leaders, and prepared the ground for future struggles to take root and grow.

These energies converged on Kaho'olawe, a sacred island to Kanaka Maoli, which had been occupied and bombed by the U.S. Navy since World War II. Considered to be an embodiment of Kanaloa, god of the sea, Kaho'olawe contains one of the richest concentrations of cultural sites in Hawai'i. Originally part of the crown and government lands of the Hawai'ian Kingdom prior to the overthrow of 1893, Kaho'olawe was leased to ranchers and used to graze goats and sheep until World War II.

On December 8, 1941, the navy seized the entire island for target practice. More than 200 residents of the island were removed, and the island was closed to the public. From 1941 to 1967, the island and its surrounding waters were used as a target range. In 1952, an executive order by President Eisenhower gave the navy formal jurisdiction over Kaho'olawe, but it also stipulated that the navy was to rehabilitate the island and return it to the public in "reasonably safe" condition when it was no longer needed by the military.

Opposition to navy bombing began to emerge in 1969, when a 500-pound bomb landed seven miles across the channel on Maui, on a parcel leased by then Maui Mayor Elmer Carvalho. In 1971, Carvalho and the environmental group Life of the Land sued to stop the bombing and to seek an Environmental Impact Statement (EIS) for the navy's use of the island. In 1972, the navy released a hastily prepared EIS, and the lawsuit was dismissed.

Young Kanaka Maoli activists, many of whom gained experience in other land struggles, felt that direct action was needed to reclaim Kaho'olawe. On January 4, 1976, the Protect Kaho'olawe Association (later renamed the Protect Kaho'olawe 'Ohana, or PKO) staged the first in a series of bold land occupations of Kaho'olawe during scheduled naval exercises. While the navy and coast guard apprehended most of the 35 protesters who attempted to make the seven-mile crossing from Maui, nine managed to land on the island, and of the nine, two eluded capture for two days before turning themselves in (Morales 1984).

According to activists involved at the beginning of the movement, the initial actions to rescue Kahoʻolawe were almost spontaneous, driven by an impulse to save the island.[13] Guided by traditional *kupuna* (elders) such as Emma DeFries, Sam Lono, and Harry Mitchell, the PKO asserted traditional Hawaiʻian religious and cultural practices as the basis for their actions. The PKO planned to complete five landings symbolizing the five fingers of *limahana* (the working hand). The completion of the five landings symbolized the completion of the tasks and *laulima* (many hands working together) (Ritte and Sawyer 1978:3). The landings on Kahoʻolawe energized a cultural and spiritual reawakening and strengthened the resolve of the activists. The phrase "Aloha ʻAina" (love of the land) became the unofficial slogan of the movement. It was an expression that had been used by Hawaiʻian nationals a century earlier to identify their resistance movement against the U.S. takeover.

As the movement grew and matured, organization and political strategy sharpened, but ideological and cultural fissures also emerged. One branch of the movement drew heavily from the rural communities and saw the struggle as a Kanaka Maoli cultural issue first and foremost. Their primary goals were the restoration of traditional Kanaka Maoli religious and cultural practices, and they looked to the elders as the primary source of knowledge and guidance.

Another branch of the PKO consisted of young university-educated organizers, some with Maoist leanings, who defined the issue as resisting imperialism. They brought political discipline, an internationalist perspective, a keen political analysis of class, race, and imperialism, and organizing skills from earlier struggles. But they were denounced by more conservative members of the PKO as "communists" and accused of alienating the more "country Hawaiʻians" with political dogmatism. Other tensions developed over questions of reform versus revolution, lawsuits versus protest. Eventually, most left-wing members of the PKO were driven out.

Despite the internal struggles, Kahoʻolawe became a lens that brought into focus the conditions and dynamics of U.S. empire in Hawai'i. For some, Kaho'olawe helped to integrate Kanaka Maoli politics and culture with anti-imperialist ideology. During the 1977 occupation, George Helm, a PKO leader, wrote in his diary: "The occupation of the military reservation is not so much a defiance as it is a responsibility to express our legitimate concern for the land of the Hawai'ian [. . .] We are against warfare but more so against imperialism" (Morales 1984:72).

In 1976, the same year that protests had begun, the PKO filed a lawsuit against the navy, alleging violations of environmental, Native Hawai'ian religious-freedom, and historic preservation laws. The PKO won a legal victory when the federal judge ruled that the navy violated both the National Environmental Policy Act and an executive order that required the preservation of historic sites. The navy was ordered to revise its 1972 Environmental Impact Statement, but was allowed to continue training.

As the movement spread, local and international solidarity became an important element of the campaign to stop the bombing. Hawai'ian organizations, unions, religious organizations, and even the state government adopted resolutions calling for an end to the bombing. The Nuclear Free and Independent Pacific movement played a key role in pressuring foreign governments to withdraw from joint military exercises on Kaho'olawe. In 1984, Japan withdrew from RIMPAC[14] exercises. Delegates from the PKO also visited Culebra and Vieques in Puerto Rico to express solidarity with and to learn from those struggles.[15]

In 1977, two PKO leaders – George Helm, the charismatic president of the PKO and a well-known musician, and Kimo Mitchell, son of revered Kupuna Harry Kunihi Mitchell – disappeared while crossing the channel between Kaho'olawe and Maui. This blow may have exacerbated internal factionalism, but ultimately the two came to be seen as martyrs whose sacrifice generated wider public sympathy.

In 1980, the PKO and the U.S. Department of Defense signed a consent decree that partially settled the lawsuit. The document limited navy training on the island, mandated surface cleanup of unexploded ordnance on at least 10,000 acres, and recognized the right of the PKO to have regular access and to act as stewards of the island. Archaeologists, who were allowed scientific access to the island under the consent decree, discovered a wealth of prehistoric sites that confirmed for the government the cultural and spiritual significance of the island. As a result the entire island was listed on the National Register of Historic Places in January 1981.

The consent decree was controversial within the PKO movement, and some activists broke from the group as a result. Supporters of the consent decree believed that compromise with the navy was necessary so that Kanaka Maoli and researchers could have access to the island in order to document and restore cultural sites and practices. But many opposed the consent decree because it allowed training to continue and effectively provided consent to desecration.

Under the consent decree, the PKO organized cultural access to the island at least six times a year and continued to advocate closing the range. Although the navy maintained that the island was essential to national security, the constraints placed on their training on Kahoʻolawe forced them to seek other places to train.

In a surprise move that was widely conjectured to be an attempt to boost the sagging election campaign of Pat Saiki, a Hawaiʻi Republican candidate for the U.S. Senate, President George H.W. Bush issued an executive order on October 22, 1990, discontinuing the bombing of Kahoʻolawe. Saiki lost the election, but the bombs finally stopped. Congress transferred Kahoʻolawe to the state and appropriated $400 million to clean up and restore the island. The navy and state signed a memorandum of understanding (MOU) in 1994 to guide the title transfer, cleanup, and future uses of Kahoʻolawe. Under the agreement, the navy transferred title of Kahoʻolawe to the State of Hawaiʻi, but retained control of access until November 11, 2003, or until cleanup was complete, whichever came first. The navy agreed to the "removal or clearance of all unexploded ordnance from the surface of the island." The navy was also to clear another 25 percent of the island to a depth that would allow "reasonably safe use."[16] As a condition of transferring land to the state, the navy insisted that there be no future commercial use of the island, which permitted it to clean up the island to levels that were not as stringent as for residential or industrial uses.

Cleanup operations began in 1998 after the contract was awarded to Parsons UXB, a private military contractor that many felt had submitted an inferior bid. By 2000, the navy was already complaining that it would not be able to meet its goals. The navy's remedy was to lower its goals for clean up, and the Kaho'olawe Island Reserve Commission (KIRC), which was virtually powerless to enforce the MOU, sheepishly went along. Because bureaucratic processes and political compromises had already blunted the activist edge of the PKO, there were no protests to challenge the navy and demand full cleanup. Puerto Rican activist and scholar Deborah Berman Santana wrote that one PKO leader "did not endorse any public activism against either the navy or the State; any such activity would probably come from organizations besides the PKO."[17]

Although the navy declared that it had fulfilled its commitment to clean up the island and closed out its unexploded ordnance (UXO) cleanup project on Kaho'olawe on March 12, 2004, it had only cleared 71 percent of the surface and 9 percent at the subsurface level. On November 12, 2004, in an elaborate ceremony full of pomp and circumstance, the navy transferred control of Kaho'olawe to the State of Hawai'i. But some Kanaka Maoli activists who were angered by the failed cleanup and broken promises interrupted the speeches and challenged the participation in cultural protocols of politicians responsible for furthering the militarization of Hawai'i.

Saving Kaho'olawe was an important victory, but it may have come at a price for the movement as a whole. The movement to protect Kaho'olawe offers a number of indispensable lessons for demilitarization activism today. The Protect Kaho'olawe 'Ohana employed a variety of strategies and tactics, including direct action and legal, political, and cultural strategies, to finally stop the bombing and win a partial cleanup and the return of the island. The leaders of the PKO built their movement around Kanaka Maoli cultural values and indigenous rights. This was a deep source of spiritual energy for the movement and provided powerful and unequivocal claims to ancient rights and genealogical legitimacy from which to challenge the military's control of the island. Kahoʻolawe provided an opportunity for the keepers of traditional knowledge to assert long-suppressed and closely guarded practices, which gave rise to the Kanaka Maoli cultural renaissance and the modern Hawaiʻian sovereignty movement. Nonviolent direct action and civil resistance were essential to the growth and power of the movement, crucially disrupting the ability of the navy to conduct its exercises and galvanizing opposition to the military.

But Kahoʻolawe is also a cautionary tale about the dangers of co-optation by the state and of reactionary politics fracturing movements. Action-oriented activists expressed frustration that an overreliance on U.S. laws and legal remedies straitjacketed the movement and put lawyers too much in the driver's seat. Anti-communist reaction resulted in the loss of key leadership with valuable strategic and tactical knowledge.

After the cessation of bombing and the subsidence of protests, the PKO focused on environmental and cultural restoration efforts. Their energies were somewhat dampened by political compromises or consumed by the demands of managing the restoration and transfer of the island. A number of PKO leaders were absorbed by the newly created bureaucracy of the KIRC. Although the KIRC was stacked with PKO activists, its role in the cleanup was purely advisory, and it lacked the power and expertise to set and enforce policies and practices governing the navy's cleanup activities. Beholden to politicians holding the purse strings of congressional appropriations and consumed with the unmanageable task of overseeing the complex, costly, and ultimately unsuccessful navy cleanup effort, the PKO lost much of its activist vigor, to the detriment of the larger movement.

The PKO struggled and ultimately failed to balance tensions between two of its pillars, its Kanaka Maoli cultural roots and its anti-imperialist activism. A reformist (or perhaps pragmatic) line prevailed over more militant politics. After the ouster of its more radical members, the PKO withdrew from the forefront of struggles against militarization. This created a gap between the wealth of knowledge, seasoned leadership, and organization of the Kaho'olawe movement and the newly emerging anti-militarization struggles that it helped to inspire.

Sites of Resistance: Makua

The Kaho'olawe movement spurred resistance to militarization at Makua, an O'ahu valley with many cultural sites, including temple sites and burials that have been damaged by military exercises. Makua also contains critical habitat for more than 40 endangered native species, and the waters offshore are some of O'ahu's richest fishing grounds. Makua, which means "parents" in Hawai'ian, is believed by some Kanaka Maoli to be the place where Wakea (father sky) and Papahanaumoku (mother earth) came together to create life on earth. Kanaka Maoli consider Makua to be part of a large sacred area where there is a rock from which souls of the dead are believed to leap into the spirit realm. A Hawai'ian epic concerning Makua tells of Hi'iaka-i-ka-poli-o-Pele, sister of the volcano goddess Pele, who overcame adversity and performed miraculous deeds in her extensive travels. In what could be read as an allegory for the present struggle in Makua, Hi'iaka rescued and restored the life of a Makua girl who was killed by an evil, invading *kupua* (supernatural spirit). Hi'iaka fought and defeated the intruder, who had killed the girl because she refused his advances. Hi'iaka then taught the girl's parents to use medicinal forest plants of Makua to heal their daughter.

The military first began using Makua Valley for a gun emplacement in 1929, and took control of the entire western tip of O'ahu, including Makua, during World War II. By June 1942, the last private citizens were ordered to leave and their lands condemned. In May 1943, the territorial government issued the army a revocable permit for the "duration of the present war and six months thereafter," which required the army to restore the valley to "satisfactory" condition at the permit's expiration.[18]

The evictions and destruction of the community traumatized its residents. Homes and even the community church were used as practice targets by the military. Makua native Walter Kamana recalled:

> I was small, used to run when the plane come in. The plane had no respect for people living in the valley. Only had one small church. You ever seen your church get bombed one Sunday? I seen that, small boy. I seen my church get taken away by a bomb.[19]

After World War II, the army requested that 6,608 acres of land between Makua and Ka'ena be set aside as a permanent military reservation, which was opposed by the territorial government.[20] The army and the territory negotiated an agreement that would have opened up Makua for recreational use, but that still allowed the army to occasionally close the range for military maneuvers. However, the agreement was never implemented due to the army's unwillingness to clean up the unexploded ordnance as was required by the prior permit.

With the arrival of a new army commander in 1949, the army escalated its training and bombardment of Makua. In 1955, the army again asked that Makua be permanently set aside for military training, since it would never be able to fully remove all unexploded ordnance. In 1964, President Johnson designated 3,236 acres of the valley as a training facility. The state leased an additional 1,515 acres to the army for 65 years for a dollar.

Despite periodic harassment by the police and state authorities, Kanaka Maoli continued to use and live on Makua Beach. In 1965, when the Mirisch Corporation filmed the motion picture *Hawai'i* in Makua valley, the state issued an order to evict "squatters" from the beach.[21] Before long, Kanaka Maoli had resettled the beach and used the abandoned movie set to build their shelters.

In its training exercises, the military bombed and strafed the valley from the air, bombarded it from battleships, invaded it with amphibious assault teams, pounded it with mortars, howitzers, and rockets, and burned it with napalm. This has rendered most of the valley hazardous and off limits due to unexploded ordnance and toxic contamination. In the 1960s, a man was killed scavenging for scrap metal. The explosions, uncontrolled dumping of waste, and leakage from unexploded ordnance have released tons of toxic chemicals that contaminated the soil and groundwater.

Over the years, more than 270 fires from military activities have inflicted serious harm to endangered species and human settlements. In 1970, a blaze burned 1,525 acres and "converted the entire valley floor from dryland forest to a dense stand of highly flammable grass."[22] In 1995, another fire scorched more than half of the valley's 4,700 acres and burned the shelters of families living across the highway, and in 2003, shifting winds turned a controlled burn into a raging wildfire that consumed over 2,000 acres and destroyed several populations of endangered species.

Meanwhile, the beach community at Makua had grown to nearly 200 people. Makua had become a *pu'uhonua* (sanctuary) for families who had fallen through the cracks of the Western system and who returned to the *'aina* for healing. In 1996, beach residents organized the Makua Council to fight yet another eviction. Despite numerous rallies and growing community support, on Father's Day hundreds of police invaded Makua, cutting off media access to the scene and evicting the last residents from the beach. Sixteen persons were arrested and eleven later convicted for "trespassing." The Makua eviction highlighted the contradiction between military occupation of Hawai'ian lands and landless Kanaka Maoli.[23]

Although the occupation of Makua beach ended, confrontations over training continued. On Easter morning 1997, the Hawai'i Ecumenical Coalition and Malama Makua led a sunrise service on the shore, blocking a Marine Corps amphibious landing scheduled for that day. In September of that same year, the marines again announced plans to conduct amphibious training, and religious structures were defiantly built in the path of the proposed exercises. As calls for civil disobedience went out in the community, the marines backed down and moved their amphibious landing to another site, where their convoy was also greeted with protests.

The attacks on the World Trade Center and Pentagon on September 11, 2001, changed the political landscape for the Makua struggle. Evoking "national security" concerns, the army threatened to petition the court for an immediate return to training. Knowing that the jingoistic political climate immediately following 9/11 would work against their movement, Malama Makua reluctantly decided to settle the NEPA lawsuit in order to secure their gains. Under the settlement, the army agreed to complete a comprehensive EIS within three years, remove UXO from approximately a third of the valley surface, and allow cultural access to the valley at least twice a month. The settlement prescribed the number of days, types, and locations of military training that would be allowed in Makua. The agreement, like the Kahoʻolawe consent decree, was controversial.

The settlement has allowed the community to reestablish cultural ceremonies in the valley, such as the annual Makahiki ceremony.[24] Although access to the valley has been severely limited by the presence of UXO, hundreds of visitors have been able to walk in Makua and witness both its beauty and its tragedy. As of September 2008, the army has not finished its EIS and as a result, has been enjoined from conducting live-fire training in Makua by the courts.

The Makua activists helped to introduce environmental justice issues into the wider demilitarization struggle in Hawaiʻi. Whereas the Kahoʻolawe movement focused almost exclusively on unexploded ordnance, cultural resources, and endangered species, Makua activists raised awareness and organized the community to confront military contamination and its possible and unequal health effects, a set of issues that reached new constituencies.

New Resistance to Militarization

The resurgence of protests against the navy in Vieques in 1999 was influential to demilitarization organizing in Hawaiʻi. Within months of the bombing accident that killed civilian navy employee David Sanes and sparked massive civil disobedience, activists from Hawaiʻi traveled to Vieques on solidarity delegations. They returned invigorated with valuable observations about Vieques: (1) the struggle for peace in Vieques came from a from a long history of resistance to U.S. colonialism that helped to create the right conditions for recent protests; (2) the issues raised by

Vieques were of global concern, and at the same time spoke directly to local concerns; (3) the movement was strengthened by its ability to unite a wide range of ideological positions; (4) nonviolent direct action was an essential element in developing new and deeply committed leaders, widening support for their cause, and transforming social and political conditions in Puerto Rico; and (5) the struggle had the beneficial overflow effect of energizing civic participation that led to other positive changes in the community.

Other international anti-militarization movements have also been important influences and allies. There have been numerous exchanges and solidarity actions between Hawai'i activists and groups in Okinawa, Korea, Guam, the Marshall Islands, and the Philippines. The U.S. environmental justice movement was another important resource for Hawai'ian demilitarization efforts. Groups such as the Military Toxics Project and ARC Ecology provided valuable technical assistance and networking opportunities. Another important influence was the East Asia–U.S.–Puerto Rico Women's Network Against Militarism, which brought feminist and anti-imperialist perspectives to demilitarization activism. This network questioned the very concept of militarized security and promoted a different paradigm of human security based on human needs, cultural survival, and environmental sustainability.

In 2000, the Rethinking Militarism in Hawai'i conference brought together grassroots activists from a number of communities affected by militarization in Hawai'i, as well as activists from the United States, the Philippines, and Puerto Rico. This led to the formation in 2002 of the DMZ-Hawai'i/Aloha 'Aina network, consisting of groups and individuals working to address the impacts of the military in Hawai'i and united around four demands: (1) no military expansion; (2) cleanup, restoration, and return of military-occupied land; (3) promotion of peaceful, sustainable community-based alternatives to Hawai'i's dependency on military spending; and (4) just compensation by the military for its use of lands and its harm to the land and people.

Whereas the Kaho'olawe and Makua struggles focused on single locations, changes in the character and acceleration of military expansion in Hawai'i following 9/11 required new approaches. One change was the shift to a more flexible strategy that treated simultaneous multiple sites of resistance as parts of the same struggle. This allowed groups to conduct autonomous actions in support of local campaigns, while the network provided support and coordination around overall strategy.

Factors Contributing to Recent Military Expansion in Hawai'i

Several factors contributed to the expansion and acceleration of militarization in Hawai'i following the 9/11 attacks. First, U.S. strategy and military posture has increasingly concentrated on Asia and the Pacific, with special emphases on China as a strategic rival and the so-called "global war on terrorism" targeting radical Islamist groups in the southern Philippines and Indonesia. In a recent stopover in Hawai'i, Under Secretary of Defense for Policy Douglas J. Feith said,

> Hawai'i plays an important role ... It's strategically located. We have important facilities here and it's a secure location. The idea that we can have an important piece of American territory deep into the Asia Pacific region is something that figures in our thinking, of course.[25]

Second, the global restructuring of U.S. military bases will dramatically transform the Pacific region. The new Pentagon concept of "global sourcing and surge" would make U.S. forces more decentralized, modular, agile, and flexible, with supplies and staging areas situated around the world for easy access in case of any deployment. Additionally, resistance to U.S. bases in South Korea and Okinawa, as well as concerns that large forces massed along the border with North Korea make for easier targets, have caused the United States to propose reductions in its military footprint in both places. This will result in a significant realignment of forces to Guam and Hawai'i.

Third, the dramatic increase of military and homeland-security funding in the wake of 9/11 has created a "gold rush" mentality among local elites, and many have lined up to exploit this boom.

Finally, the power of Senator Inouye over military appropriations has influenced military plans in the Pacific to favor the maintenance or expansion of forces in Hawai'i.

Stryker Brigade Combat Team (SBCT)

In 1999, the army announced that it would transform its Cold War force into a leaner and quicker futuristic force, more suited to meet twenty-first-century challenges. A centerpiece of this army transformation effort was the creation of six Stryker Brigade Combat Teams, one of which was to be stationed in Hawai'i. Strykers are 20-ton, 8-wheeled, armored vehicles that are equipped with high-tech weapons systems. In theory, they are supposed to combine the "mobility and flexibility of traditional Army light forces" with the "lethality and survivability of traditional Army heavy forces."[26] However, many soldiers and military analysts have campaigned against the Strykers for what they see as fatal flaws – too thin-skinned to protect troops, major limitations as combat vehicles, and too large and heavy to meet their own rapid-deployment requirements. Government watchdog groups have also slammed the Stryker program as a boondoggle, fraught with accusations of conflicts of interest and fraud.

The proposed SBCT in Hawai'i would bring 328 Stryker vehicles, 800 additional soldiers plus their dependants, and 28 construction projects to upgrade training, maintenance, and housing facilities. One reporter called it "the biggest Army construction project in Hawai'i since World War II."[27] To meet training requirements for the SBCT, the army seized an additional 25,000 acres of land on O'ahu and Hawai'i Island. The extent of the Strykers' impacts would stretch across O'ahu and Hawai'i Island. The army's environmental study disclosed that the SBCT would result in a 25 percent increase in munitions released and a proportionate increase in the amount of toxic chemicals and unexploded ordnance released.[28] Other impacts of the SBCT include erosion and sediment runoff, fires bringing harm to endangered species, destruction of Kanaka Maoli religious and cultural sites, and strains on the social infrastructure due to the increased population.

In 2002, DMZ-Hawai'i/Aloha 'Aina began to raise awareness about the Stryker threat. By the time the army held a 2003 series of public hearings, there was significant opposition to the Strykers. Despite this public outcry and its own conclusion that the SBCT would cause significant impacts in Hawai'i, the army announced in 2004 that it would proceed with the expansion. Angry protests followed, including pickets of a traveling Stryker public-relations display. DMZ-Hawai'i/Aloha 'Aina delivered a dissenting peoples' report on the SBCT impacts to the army and elected officials.[29]

Demilitarization activists knew that framing public discourse about the Strykers would be crucial though difficult. The army argued that the SBCT was needed for national security and to provide troops with the best technology available. Politicians and business leaders, including the major local news media, cheered on the Stryker Brigade because of its promised $1.5 billion in military spending over the next decade. Activists were able to paint the SBCT as a land grab and a threat to the environment, Hawai'ian culture, and community health and safety. They pointed out the sheer hypocrisy of the military returning the 28,000-acre Kaho'olawe, contaminated with UXO, while taking and contaminating another 25,000 acres. While politicians and the military tried to distance Kaho'olawe from the Strykers, the DMZ-Hawai'i/Aloha 'Aina activists made it clear that the opposition to the Stryker Brigade was a continuation of the struggle for Kaho'olawe.

In January 2004, three Kanaka Maoli organizations sued the army for alleged violations of the National Environmental Policy Act (NEPA). They argued that the army's EIS was flawed because it failed to consider other alternative sites, and that the outcomes of the NEPA process were predetermined, rendering the process invalid. In court proceedings that were heavily colored by patriotic appeals, the federal judge ruled against the plaintiffs (Ferguson and Turnbull 2005). But the Ninth Circuit Court of Appeals overturned the lower-court ruling, halted most of the expansion projects, and ordered a supplemental environmental-impact statement.

Meanwhile, construction of some Stryker infrastructure had begun in Lihu'e, an area sacred to O'ahu's traditional chiefs that is used by the army for live-fire training. The army's own cultural monitors blew the whistle on the destruction of cultural sites and alleged violations of cultural-site preservation laws and agreements and have called for a halt to all ground-disturbing activities. Cultural-preservation staff for the Office of Hawai'ian Affairs have threatened legal action to halt the army's activities until adequate site surveys and protective measures are implemented.[30]

"Star Wars," UARC and Other Military High-tech Programs

"Star Wars" missile defense programs have grown in Hawai'i since the early 1990s, and their radar, tracking, and computing facilities have only increased the islands' importance to the military. Other advanced military research, development, and testing have become a lucrative source of military spending in Hawai'i. A recent proposal to establish a University Affiliated Research Center (UARC) at the University of Hawai'i (UH) sparked widespread protest among students, faculty, and community supporters.

Since 2001 the UH administration and the Office of Naval Research quietly conspired to establish a navy UARC to conduct basic and applied research to "improve system performance of DoD weapons systems."[31] Proponents of the UARC say that this program would only be a contracting vehicle that could bring in up to $50 million over five years. While many UH programs have received Department of Defense funding over the years, the UARC represents a qualitative as well as quantitative shift, a consolidation and entrenchment of military research at UH. When the proposal to establish the UARC quietly came before the UH Board of Regents in 2004, the Save UH/Stop UARC Coalition was formed to fight it. A 2005 takeover by students, faculty, and supporters of the UH president's office to demand he cancel the UARC generated international media coverage and tremendous support in Hawai'i. Protests in opposition to the plan are ongoing, and have delayed the UARC project by more than two years.

The Save UH/Stop UARC campaign helped demilitarization organizing in Hawai'i by bringing together diverse and new constituencies, including students, Hawai'ian independence activists, environmentalists, radical artists, and scientists. In addition, it has helped illuminate the hidden workings of military research. The occupation of the UH president's office energized new activists against militarism and provided an opportunity to model an alternative democratic space and grassroots leadership in action.

Conclusion

The U.S. military established itself in Hawai'i through sheer force. But its power and stature are maintained with the help of politicians, military elites, business groups, and some labor unions and civic organizations. Some have fully surrendered to worshipping at the altar of militarism. Others have decided that it is more profitable to collaborate than to resist, as with some Native Hawai'ian groups who have been seduced by lucrative military contracts and grants. The institutions and socialization processes that reproduce and reinforce militarism are constantly at work, as Kathy Ferguson and Phyllis Turnbull, two scholars of militarization in Hawai'i, observe:

> The notion of "homeland security" is a great enabler of both the growth of military presence in Hawai'i and the occlusion of effective resistance. "Homeland security" names an amorphous threat and simultaneously unleashes fantasies about assault and vulnerability. Within its terms, opposition is rendered unintelligible; to oppose the security of the homeland is unthinkable. As U.S. militarism intensifies, Hawai'i pays a high price. (Ferguson and Turnbull 2005)

While the U.S. military in Hawai'i today may seem unassailable, militarism has its contradictions and weaknesses, what Ian Lind calls "structural sources of tension" (Lind 1984–85:27). Lind suggests that "despite surface appearances, militarism is inherently unstable." These contradictions present openings for intervention, resistance, and social change. Furthermore, the contradictions of militarism in Hawai'i will inevitably ignite conflicts – flashpoints – that present teachable moments and opportunities for building resistance.

The attacks on September 11, 2001, spawned a new phase of American empire, but they also exposed the fallacy in the presumption that an ever greater degree of militarization can guarantee peace and security. Continuing revelations of government lies that led the United States into war and the worsening conditions in Iraq have finally begun to sour U.S. public opinion about the war and stimulate questioning about U.S. military power and what constitutes real security. Under pretext of the "global war on terrorism," the United States has made an unprecedented bid for what military planners call "full spectrum dominance," from the heavens above to the depths of the sea, from outer space to cyberspace. But this condition, variously described as "imperial overreach," "the empire of bases," and the "new American militarism," may prove to be America's ultimate ruin.[32]

When the BRAC Commission recently announced that it was considering Pearl Harbor Shipyard for possible closure or realignment, Senator Inouye's op-ed response was symptomatic, beginning by tapping public fear and vulnerability: "Last week's terrorist attack in London should say to us all that we need to remain vigilant and alert," he said, and went on to liken the BRAC Commission's announcement to "a bomb scare." Then he recited the centuries-old imperial mantra: "Pearl Harbor is of critical importance to our nation's security, ensuring that the Pacific Fleet is able to respond rapidly to crises in the Asia–Pacific region."[33] But as conservative scholar and veteran Andrew Bacevich warns, "There can be no recovery without first acknowledging the disease [of militarism]. As with any addiction, denial merely postpones the inevitable day of reckoning" (2005:226).

The global peace and justice movement is proclaiming a radical alternative to global empire, a world in which genuine security is based on human needs, human dignity, cultural integrity, environmental preservation, and global solidarity. In June 2000, the International Women's Summit to Redefine Security concluded that

> military security is a contradiction in terms. The present militarized international security system is maintained at the expense of the natural environment, the economic and social needs of many people, and fundamental human rights. This is a price we refuse to pay.[34]

It is a price Hawai'i cannot afford.

Notes

1. Available online at www.pacom.mil/about/pacom.shtml. Date last accessed October 14, 2007.
2. U.S. Department of Defense, Under Secretary of Defense (Personnel and Readiness), "Report to Congress: Implementation of the Department of Defense Training Range Comprehensive Plan," February 2004.
3. State of Hawai'i, Department of Business, Economic Development and Tourism, *State of Hawai'i Data Book 2003*, Table 1.03: Resident Population by Military Status, 1990 to 2003. In 2003, the Department of Defense listed 54,036 active duty military personnel in Hawai'i. U.S. Department of Defense, "Department of Defense Base Structure Report Fiscal Year 2003 Baseline."
4. *Honolulu Advertiser*, August 25, 2003.
5. *Hawai'i Business*, February 2005, pp. 24–30.
6. Haunani-Kay Trask, personal interview, June 2002.
7. Commander in Chief, U.S. Pacific Command, "Hawai'i Military Land Use Master Plan," 1995. The figure of 54 percent may be low since it does not include "ceded land" that was returned to the state after 1959 and then leased by the military.
8. U.S. Department of Defense, Defense Environmental Restoration Program, "Annual Report to Congress, Fiscal Year 2004."
9. Navy Environmental Public Affairs Office, Commander Navy Region Hawai'i, "Site Summary Evaluation Pearl Harbor Naval Complex, Hawai'i," fact sheet, June 6, 2002.
10. U.S. Environmental Protection Agency, "Hawai'i Report: 2003 Toxics Release Inventory," May 2005.
11. Forty percent of the homeless and 27 percent of welfare recipients are Kanaka Maoli; 31 percent of Kanaka Maoli receive annual incomes less than $4000; 32 percent drop out of high school; and only 5 percent have college degrees (Office of Hawai'ian Affairs 2000: Table

5:4). Kanaka Maoli have the highest mortality rate, the lowest life expectancy (4 years less than all other groups in Hawai'i), and the highest rates of suicide, cancer, stroke, diabetes, and infant mortality (Blaisdell 1993:2).

12. In order to prevent bloodshed, avoid a war with the United States, and maintain Hawai'i's neutrality, Queen Lili'uokalani yielded her authority to the superior force of the United States until such time that the United States restored Hawai'i's sovereignty.

13. Walter Ritte, interview with the author, May 2005.

14. Rim of the Pacific (RIMPAC) exercises are the largest multinational naval training exercises in the world. Kaho'olawe was once a regular RIMPAC target.

15. *Aloha 'Aina*, August–September 1978, published by the Protect Kaho'olawe Fund.

16. "Memorandum of Understanding Between the United States Department of the Navy and the State of Hawai'i Concerning the Island of Kaho'olawe," Hawai'i, 1994, p. 13.

17. Deborah Berman Santana, "Kaho'olawe Island: Lessons for Vieques," unpublished article, April 2002.

18. *Ka Huliau*, May–June 1983.

19. "Makua Valley Public Meeting," transcribed by Ralph Rosenburg Court Reporters, January 27, 2001, p. 59.

20. *Ka Huliau*, May–June 1983.

21. Marion Kelly and Sidney Michael Quintal, *Cultural History Report of Makua Military Reservation and Vicinity, Makua Valley, Oahu, Hawai'i* (Honolulu: Bernice P. Bishop Museum, 1977), 48–49.

22. Kikukawa, in Pam Smith, "Makua: Valley of the Duds," *Hawai'i Observer*, June 16, 1977, p.20.

23. *Makua: To Heal a Nation*, video, produced by Na Maka o ka 'Aina, 1996.

24. Makahiki is the season of the god Lono, and is marked by offerings, feasting, cultural activities, and a prohibition on war.

25. *Honolulu Advertiser*, November 13, 2004.

26. Department of the Army, "Final Environmental Impact Statement Transformation of the 2nd Brigade, 25th Infantry Division (Light) to a Stryker Brigade Combat Team in Hawai'i," Tetra Tech, Inc., Honolulu, May 2004, ES-3.

27. *Honolulu Advertiser*, April 22, 2002.

28. Department of the Army, "Final Environmental Impact Statement," Appendix M-1.

29. DMZ-Hawai'i/Aloha 'Aina, "Community Impact Statement on the Stryker Brigade Combat Team," July 6, 2004, available online at http://dmzHawai'i.org. Date last accessed October 14, 2007.

30. Relevant documents available online at www.dmzHawai'i.org. Date last accessed October 14, 2007.
31. More information available online at www.stopuarc.info. Date last accessed October 14, 2007.
32. See Bello (2005); Johnson (2004); Bacevich (2005).
33. *Honolulu Advertiser*, July 10, 2005.
34. "Final Statement," issued by East Asia–U.S. Women's Network Against Militarism, International Women's Summit to Redefine Security, June 22–25, 2000.

References

Albertini, James, Foster, Nelson, Inglis, Wallis, and Roeder, Gil (1980) *The Dark Side of Paradise: Hawai'i in a Nuclear World* (Honolulu: Catholic Action of Hawai'i/Peace Education Project).

Anthony, J. Garner (1955) *Hawai'i Under Army Rule* (Honolulu: University of Hawai'i Press).

Bacevich, Andrew J. (2005) *The New American Militarism: How Americans Are Seduced by War* (Oxford: Oxford University Press).

Bello, Walden (2005) *Dilemmas of Domination: The Unmaking of the American Empire* (New York: Metropolitan Books).

Blaisdell, Kekuni (1993) "The Health Status of the Kanaka Maoli," *Asian American and Pacific Islander Journal of Health*, No. 1, Autumn.

Cook, Bud Pomaika'i, Withy, Kelley, and Tarallo-Jensen, Lucia (2003) "Cultural Trauma, Hawai'ian Spirituality and Contemporary Health Status," *Californian Journal of Health Promotion 2003*, Vol. 1, pp. 10–24.

Docena, Herbert (2007) *"At the Door of All the East": The Philippines in United States Military Strategy* (Quezon City: Focus on the Global South).

Enloe, Cynthia (2000) *Maneuvers: The International Politics of Militarizing Women's Lives* (Berkeley: University of California Press).

Ferguson, Kathy E. and Turnbull, Phyllis (1998) *Oh, Say, Can You See? The Semiotics of the Military in Hawai'i* (Minneapolis: University of Minnesota Press).

—— (2005) "The Securitization of Hawai'i," paper presented at the annual meeting of the International Studies Association, Hilton Hawai'ian Village, Honolulu, Hawai'i, March 2005.

Fuchs, Lawrence (1961) *Hawai'i Pono: An Ethnic and Political History* (Honolulu: Bess Press).

Johnson, Chalmers (2004) *The Sorrows of Empire: Militarism, Secrecy and the End of the Republic* (New York: Metropolitan Books).

Kame'eleihiwa, Lilikala (1992) *Native Land and Foreign Desires: Pehea La E Pono Ai?* (Honolulu: Bishop Museum Press).

Lind, Ian (1984–85) "Ring of Steel: Notes on the Militarization of Hawai'i," *Social Process in Hawai'i*, Vol. 31.

Linn, Brian McAllister (1997) *Guardians of Empire: The U.S. Army and the Pacific, 1902–1940* (Chapel Hill: University of North Carolina Press).

Miyahira, Sheryl (1981–82) "Hawai'i's Ceded Lands," *UH Law Review* 3–4, pp. 101–148.

Morales, Rodney (1984) *Ho'iho'i Hou: A Tribute to George Helm and Kimo Mitchell* (Honolulu: Bamboo Ridge Press).

Office of Hawai'ian Affairs, State of Hawai'i (2000) *Native Hawai'ian Data Book* (Honolulu: Office of Hawai'ian Affairs).

Okihiro, Gary (1991) *Cane Fires: The Anti-Japanese Movement in Hawai'i, 1865–1945* (Philadelphia: Temple University Press).

Ritte Jr., Walter and Sawyer, Richard (1978) *Na Mana'o Aloha o Kaho'olawe* (Honolulu: Aloha Aina O Na Kupuna).

Rohrer, Judy Lee (1987) "Hawai'i and the Military: The Conflict Over Land," unpublished report (Honolulu: American Friends Service Committee Hawai'i Area Program).

Sai, David Keanu (2004) "American Occupation of the Hawai'ian State: A Century Unchecked," *Hawai'ian Journal of Law and Politics*, Vol. 1.

Scheer, Robert (2008) *The Pornography of Power* (New York: Little, Brown).

Silva, Noenoe (2004) *Aloha Betrayed, Native Hawai'ian Resistance to American Colonialism* (Durham: Duke University Press).

State of Hawai'i (2000) *State of Hawai'i Data Book* (Honolulu: State of Hawai'i).

US Senate (1993a) "Hearings Before a Subcommittee of the Committee on Appropriations United States Senate, One Hundred Third Congress, First Session" (Washington, D.C.: U.S. Government Printing Office).

—— (1993b) Committee on Indian Affairs, Senate Rep. 103–126. August 6, 1993. Reprinted in Richard J. Scudder (ed.) (1994) *The Apology to Native Hawai'ians* (Kapolei, HI: Ka'imi Pono Press).

AFTERWORD
DOWN HERE

Julian Aguon

These stories of ordinary people fighting extraordinary battles against military colonialism are to be cherished as much for their pure wealth of information as for their subtle announcements of the presence of beauty where it has survived brutality.

I've been thinking about beauty so much lately. About folks being robbed of it, folks fading for want of it, folks rushing to embrace only ghosts of it. This is the point: Empire is eating Everybody. All of us. The whole wide array of ancient narratives of what it means to be human on this planet – snack. Chomp, chomp.

Our world today is desperate – for us to get out into it. Throw our arms around it. *See it*. See Other People. Places and ruins and rocks and landscapes. Horses and the sun. Rising in different lands, over different people, with different – and the same – dreams. We need to get back to the dirt. We could use some fresh air. Those who don't know first hand what kinds of cancer come with the presence of U.S. military bases, or how it feels to always be coming back from burying the dead, need to travel to see – not take from – the world. So that awe may repair their eyes. So that the word "solidarity" would mean something. Something more. People cannot rush to the rescue of a world whose magic they haven't seen. They don't even know what the bombs are falling on. They don't know the people, haven't heard us tell our own stories. Haven't stood in our rivers or danced with us to our music. Moved for a while to our groove. Those at the top of the world cannot read about this magic.

At the time of this writing my own people, the indigenous Chamoru of Guahan (Guam), have both our hands up, and are holding the line as best we can. Fighting a war that no one thinks we can win. Facing down death. Mostly losing. U.S. military realignment in the Asia Pacific region, particularly the pending explosion of the U.S. military personnel population now set at 35,000, is rushing an endangered folk, colonized by Spain, Japan, and the United States since the 1500s, toward full-blown extinction. The boys and the bombers are coming. So are the nukes, the subs, the brand new bowling alleys and movie theaters and gas stations for the soldiers on now-expanding bases. Ruby Tuesday also. Home Depot. Walmart. All of it crammed onto the 30-mile island of which the United States already occupies a third. Of course none of this is unfamiliar to the activists who have penned these essays. Activists know too well that Empire comes with a bang. Back home, that banging by now is so loud that folks can't hear each other, are getting so tired shouting over the noise to reach each other, simultaneously so outraged and so sad, that many of our finest warriors have simply gone home and shut the door. To cry. Cook. Be with their children.

As Gerson notes in his chapter, they say now that "all Pentagon road maps lead to Guam." What a nightmarish truth for Chamorus, who have struggled faithfully for self-determination within the U.N. framework (as a non-self-governing territory) since 1946. Who have survived both the spite of the U.S. mili-political design for its colony in perpetuity and the fury of our own family members who have bought the lie that U.S. military bases embody our salvation. That they will save us, economically and from the "terrorists." That freedom doesn't come without a cost. But because we are seeing that that price is our children – Chamoru kids are currently serving and dying in the U.S. Armed Forces at the highest rate in the entire U.S. alongside their Micronesian and American Samoan brothers and sisters – we are getting hip to the truth. We don't matter all that much.

Nobody doubts that the way forward is solidarity. But how bruised has the word become? Or, bigger, what weight do our words carry in these topsy-turvy times where war is, you know, peace. U.S. National Defense, the Global Commitment. Folks on the ground, for the most part, are wonderfully gifted in this regard. In this Age of Flippery, they remain the untricked ones. The ones who know best that the United States is not the Democracy Bringer.

So what do we do? Where do we look? And if our arms are heavy already, where should we, really, cast our net of hope? My own small suggestion is that we do some serious inversion. If we're living in times of Bigger is Better (e.g. the rationale of Empire, global capitalism, and spreading militarization) – and we all agree these are dark days – then we do well to take notice of small things. Draw in our gaze. Forsake the horizon, at least for a while, for the hue. Yes, Empire is big. Obviously bad. And the struggle is long and hard and so often lonely. But there are moments in the struggle, as anyone on the ground knows, wherein we are so *remarkably* alive. Where we, as part, disappear into the whole for love of it. Down here, we are rescued in moments. Down here, a connection happens. I've seen it. I've been sustained by it. In Guam. In Hawai'i. And I know from other friends that the same thing happens elsewhere. In the other hot spots. We who fight daily for our homelands, our cousins, our loved ones' imaginations, our right to die from something other than cancer, are fighting for each other. We fight so that the sky doesn't fall down on our sister. That is love. In the time of cholera and everything else.

When we think of the manic U.S. military build-up of Guam, for example, we could conjure up more than China. More than the Big Relations. We could see Guam and the other islands that make up her natural archipelago – Saipan, Tinian, Luta, and the other northern islands. We could think of the Marshall Islands, the Federated States of Micronesia, the beautiful Belau (Palau). If the outside world would look carefully, it would see something as scary as it is heartbreaking: an entire region of the planet desperately trying to find its face in a foreign mirror. U.S. import culture is eating the people of Micronesia. Thankfully, it has not managed to smash our 3,000 to 4,000-year-old matrilineal civilizations to make them fit into cans of Spam and Western

Economic Theories of Development. We are folks whose survival will depend on an ability to recognize a quiet fact: we are heirs to civilizations born up to 2,000 years before Jesus. We've survived this long for a reason. And despite what they say, we don't have to do what we're told, and die.

War Talk is tiring.

That's why this book is hard to get through.

It conveys the gravity of what activists on the ground are up against when we "confront" Empire. And so I cannot help but reserve a last word for my sisters and brothers in the struggle. No one ever need tell us to keep on keeping on. That's our M.O.

One activist to another, I lay flowers at your feet. I can only think how tired they must be.

LIST OF CONTRIBUTORS

Writer–activist **Julian Aguon** is the author of three books that confront U.S. military colonialism in Guam: *Just Left of the Setting Sun*; *The Fire This Time: Essays on Life Under U.S. Occupation*; and *What We Bury at Night*. A son of Guam, he is a much respected speaker in the Asia Pacific region on issues of indigenous rights, self-determination, cultural preservation, and international law, and has been Guam's recent representative to the United Nations Sessions on the Decolonization of Non-Self-Governing Territories.

Kozue Akibayashi is a researcher at the Institute for Gender Studies, Ochanomizu University, and **Suzuyo Takazato** is co-chair of Okinawa Women Act Against Military Violence and one of the foremost Japanese peace activists and feminists who critically examines U.S. bases on Okinawa.

Ayşe Gül Altınay has a Ph.D. in cultural anthropology from Duke University and teaches anthropology, cultural studies, and gender studies at Sabanci University, Turkey. Her book *The Myth of the Military-Nation: Militarism, Gender, and Education in Turkey* examines how the myth that the military is central to Turkey's national identity was created, perpetuated, and acts to shape politics.

Tom Engelhardt is the editor of *TomDispatch.com*, co-founder of the *American Empire Project* and author of *The End of Victory Culture*.

Cynthia Enloe is professor of international development and women's studies at Clark University. Among her books are:

The Morning After: Sexual Politics at the End of the Cold War; *Bananas, Beaches and Bases: Making Feminist Sense of International Politics*; *Maneuvers: The International Politics of Militarizing Women's Lives*; and *The Curious Feminist: Searching for Women in a New Age of Empire*. Her feminist teaching and research includes focus on how women's emotional and physical labor has been used to support war-waging policies – and how many women have tried to resist both of those efforts.

Joseph Gerson is the director of programs of the American Friends Service Committee in New England. He is deeply involved in the U.S. peace and anti-war movement and participated in the founding conferences of United for Peace and Justice, The Asia Peace Assembly, and the European Network for Peace and Human Rights. His books include: *The Sun Never Sets: Confronting the Network of Foreign U.S. Military Bases*; *With Hiroshima Eyes: Atomic War, Nuclear Extortion and Moral Imagination*; and *The Deadly Connection: Nuclear War and U.S. Intervention*.

David Heller works with For Mother Earth (a member group of Friends of the Earth International) in Belgium. He has been actively involved in anti-nuclear and anti-militarist campaigns in Britain, Belgium, and other European countries since the early 1990s. His interest in the impact of (foreign) military bases was stimulated during the time he spent living at Faslane Peace Camp, outside Faslane naval base in Scotland.

Amy Holmes is a Ph.D. candidate in sociology at the Johns Hopkins University and co-editor of *Imperial Djihad: On Fundamentalism, Rogue States, and New Wars*, published in German. She is also a member of the Hopkins Anti-War Coalition.

Laura Jeffery holds a Leverhulme Early Career Fellowship in social anthropology at the University of Edinburgh, having been awarded a Ph.D. in social anthropology from the University of Cambridge in 2006. She carried out ethnographic fieldwork amongst displaced Chagossians in Mauritius in 2002–2004, and amongst migrant Chagossians in the U.K. in 2006–2007.

Kyle Kajihiro is program director of the American Friends Service Committee Hawai'i. Since 1996 he has been involved in community efforts to demilitarize military-controlled lands in Hawai'i and to build solidarity with the Hawai'ian sovereignty movement. He has written articles and produced cable television programs for local media and will have an article on the militarization of Hawai'i in a forthcoming book on settler colonialism in Hawai'i.

Hans Lammerant works with Vredesactie, the Belgian branch of War Resisters International, and since 1997 has been active on the Bombspotting Campaign.

John Lindsay-Poland has coordinated the FOR Task Force on Latin America and the Caribbean since 1989. He served on human rights observer teams in Guatemala and El Salvador with Peace Brigades International in the 1980s. He has worked extensively on struggles for the closure and environmental cleanup of U.S. military bases in Panama and Puerto Rico, and is the author of *Emperors in the Jungle: The Hidden History of the U.S. in Panama*. In 2004 he edited and co-wrote *Building from the Inside Out: Peace Initiatives in War-Torn Colombia*.

Catherine Lutz is professor of anthropology at Brown University and the Watson Institute for International Studies. She is the author of *Homefront: A Military City and the American Twentieth Century*, a historical and ethnographic study of the effects of Fort Bragg on Fayetteville, North Carolina in the United States as well as *Local Democracy Under Siege: Activism, Public Interests and Private Politics* (with Dorothy Holland and others). She has written extensively about militarization and empire.

Katherine T. McCaffrey is assistant professor of anthropology at Montclair State University and author of *Military Power and*

Popular Protest: The U.S. Navy in Vieques, Puerto Rico. Her fieldwork has focused on the conflict between the U.S. Navy and residents of Vieques. Since the navy left in May 2003, she has been evaluating the significance of the social movement and tracking the rapid social and economic transformation of the islands and the subsequent growing network of social movement responses.

Roland Simbulan holds the Centennial Professorial Chair in development studies and public management at the University of the Philippines. He is a former Faculty Regent of the U.P. Board of Regents, and former vice chancellor for planning, finance and development at U.P. He is the author of *The Bases of Our Insecurity, A Guide to Nuclear Philippines* and *The Continuing Struggle for an Independent Philippine Foreign Policy*, among other works. Professor Simbulan has been regularly invited as an expert resource person before the Philippine Congress for his views on defense and security issues, treaties, and international agreements of that country. He helped design strategies and tactics for the historic Senate rejection of the bases treaty in 1991 as well as the post-bases alternative development and bases conversion program of the Philippine government.

David Vine is assistant professor in the Department of Anthropology at American University in Washington, D.C. He is the author of *Island of Shame: The Secret History of the U.S. Military Base on Diego Garcia.* David's work has been published in, among others, the *Washington Post*, the *New York Times*, *Human Rights Brief*, and *International Migration.*

INDEX

Compiled by Sue Carlton

CPSIA information can be obtained at www.ICGtesting.com
Printed in the USA
BVOW01s1649310816

460749BV00008B/297/P

9 780814 752449